SURVIVE—and THRIVE!

Here's a bulletin from Randy W. Kirk, operator of fourteen different small businesses and president of AC International, boasting $7 million in annual sales: Only half of all start-up businesses will be around to celebrate their third birthday! What's the secret of success for a small business? It's attitude!

- Do you expect success?
- Are you prepared for failure?
- Can you conquer your fears?

If your answers are yes, you're ready. **RUNNING A 21st-CENTURY SMALL BUSINESS** is the Real Life 101 of small business advice guides.

"Must reading for any person going into—or contemplating going into—his or her own business . . . one of the few books that guides you through the maze."
—Daniel M. Gold, president, Diaper Dan's Delivery

"Right on target with nuts-and-bolts explanations . . . a well-researched, easy-to-understand guide written in plain English . . . [I] wish Kirk had written the book fifteen years ago!"   **—Susan Meadow, publisher, Meadow Publications, Inc.**

"A comprehensive guide to launching your business . . . offers pages and pages of useful advice."   **—Your Company**

"A hands-on, step-by-step guide to cover all the pitfalls! This book appears to have it all . . . a real winner."
—Neal P. Workman, CEO, Seafax

RUNNING A 21st-CENTURY SMALL BUSINESS

The Owner's Guide to Starting and Growing Your Company

RANDY W. KIRK

WARNER
BUSINESS
BOOKS™

NEW YORK   BOSTON

Copyright © 1993, 2006 by Randy W. Kirk
All rights reserved.

Warner Business Books
Warner Books

Time Warner Book Group
1271 Avenue of the Americas, New York, NY 10020
Visit our Web site at www.twbookmark.com.

The Warner Business Books logo is a trademark of Warner Books.

Printed in the United States of America
Originally published as *When Friday Isn't Payday*
First Edition: February 2006

10 9 8 7 6 5 4 3 2 1

Library of Congress Cataloging-in-Publication Data
Kirk, Randy W.
Running a 21st-century small business : the owner's guide to starting and growing your company / Randy W. Kirk.
p. cm.
Rev. ed. of: When Friday isn't payday. c1993.
Includes index.
ISBN 0-446-69618-8
1. Small business—Management. 2. New business enterprises—Management.
I. Title: Running a twenty-first century small business.
II. Kirk, Randy W. When Friday isn't payday. III. Title.

HD62.7.K57 2006
658.02'2—dc22   2005052118

Book design by Stratford Publishing Services
Cover design by Tom McKeveny

This book is dedicated to the huge support group around me that has allowed me the freedom to write and speak. The great love of my life, Pam; my kids, Christian, Brandy, Brian, and Robert; my sons-in-law, Nathan and Casey; my partner of over twenty-five years, Terry Brown; my prayer partner, Eric Snyder; and my friends Brad and Denise Jensen and Max and Amy Ellzey.

There is a much larger cast of friends, relatives, and business associates who contribute in so many ways, large and small. It is they who have provided the grist for this mill.

More than all the rest, I thank the Lord of my life, Jesus Christ, for his blessing on my life.

Be sure to check out a great source of sales tips at www.advertisingspecialty.blogspot.com

Randy W. Kirk, President
American Quality Products
9115-1 Dice Road
Santa Fe Springs, CA 90670
1-800-245-3737, ext. 223
fax: 562-903-0606
web: www.CaliforniaSprings.com

*Press on: Nothing in the world can take the place
of persistence. Talent will not; nothing is more
common than unsuccessful individuals with talent.
Genius will not; unrewarded genius is almost a proverb.
Education will not; the world is full of educated derelicts.
Persistence and determination alone are omnipotent.*

—CALVIN COOLIDGE

Contents

Introduction   1

SECTION ONE
Before You Begin

CHAPTER 1   Why Self-Employment?   9

CHAPTER 2   Do You Have the Right Stuff?   13

CHAPTER 3   What Will It Cost?   20

CHAPTER 4   Basic Budgeting   27

CHAPTER 5   What Kind of Business?   32

CHAPTER 6   Business Types   36

CHAPTER 7   Buying a Business   45

CHAPTER 8   The Partner Issue   48

    Part 1 The Spouse as Partner   50

    Part 2 Other Family Members in the Business   52

CHAPTER 9   Part-Time Possibilities   54

CHAPTER 10   Goal Setting and Success   57

    Part 1 A Personal Evaluation Project   58

    Part 2 Setting Goals   67

    Part 3 Prioritize, Organize, and Internalize   68

SECTION TWO
Opening the Doors

CHAPTER 1   Finalizing Goals   77

    Part 1 Establishing the Basic Blueprint   78

    Part 2 Three-Track Thinking   81

CHAPTER 2   Preparing the Business Plan   83

Part 1   The Business Purpose   84

Part 2   Finding a Location   91

Part 3   Selecting Suppliers   99

Part 4   The Physical Plant   105

Part 5   The Advertising Plan   107

Part 6   Projecting Your Income   116

Part 7   The Break-Even Analysis   127

CHAPTER 3   Legal Requirements   129

Part 1   Enterprise Type   129

Part 2   Business Licenses and Regulations   139

CHAPTER 4   The Grand Opening   142

Part 1   Last-Minute Checklist   143

Part 2   Operating Procedures   144

Part 3   Last-Minute Attitude Check   158

Part 4   The Dress Rehearsal   160

Part 5   The First Day   161

Part 6   Surviving the First Week   166

CHAPTER 5   The First Month   169

Part 1   Training, Training, and Retraining   169

Part 2   Decision Making   170

CHAPTER 6   Months Two Through Six   176

Part 1   The Daily Numbers   176

Part 2   The Monthly Statements   183

Part 3   Dealing with Crisis   188

SECTION THREE
The First Three Years

CHAPTER 1   Why Businesses Succeed   199

CHAPTER 2   Why Businesses Fail   204

CHAPTER 3   Almighty Cash   213

Part 1   Bookkeeping Concepts   213

Part 2 Collection Procedures 227

Part 3 Payables Approaches 238

CHAPTER 4   The Personnel Process   242

Part 1 Bloated Payrolls, the Business Killer 252

Part 2 Final Thoughts on Personnel 253

CHAPTER 5   Building Sales   255

Part 1 Personal Salesmanship 256

Part 2 Sales Management of Others 275

Part 3 Advertising 282

Part 4 Promotion 291

Part 5 Trade Shows 293

Part 6 Using E-Mail and the Web 302

Part 7 Pursuing New Territories 311

SECTION FOUR
Managing Yourself and Others

CHAPTER 1   The Managed Business   321

CHAPTER 2   Managing Managers   325

Part 1 Communicating the Vision 326

Part 2 Leadership 329

Part 3 Compensation Concepts 332

CHAPTER 3   Personal Motivation Techniques   335

CHAPTER 4   If You Discover "It's Just Not for Me"   340

CHAPTER 5   Setting New Goals   343

SECTION FIVE
Managing Your Assets

CHAPTER 1   To Grow or Not to Grow   349

CHAPTER 2   Buying Growth   354

CHAPTER 3   Selling Your Business   359

CHAPTER 4   Selling Part of Your Business   374

Conclusion   377
Appendix: Additional Reading   379
Index   385

Introduction

No knowledgeable person disputes it; the facts are undeniable. Even the federal government has jumped on the bandwagon. The very small businesses of America are the economic engine of the twenty-first century.

The Fortune 500 has seen a net loss of employment, and the mom-and-pop establishments across the country have more than made up for this deficit. There are millions of businesses throughout our nation and the world that have fewer than ten employees on their payroll. Most of these companies were smaller than that in the past, and never will be much bigger. Here is the first amazing fact: **Most have no desire to be any bigger.** And amazing fact number two: **Most of them would not be better off as a result of being larger.** In fact, many of these owners would make less money . . . with more headaches.

If you're reading this book, you're either already in business or are seriously considering taking the plunge. Many in your shoes have the mistaken belief that bigger is better. Many have visions of multistoried office buildings with hundreds of employees scurrying this way and that, all at their bosses' beck and call.

There's absolutely nothing wrong with wanting to own and run a large organization. This book, however, is founded on the premise that there's also nothing wrong with a business whose staff never includes more than ten employees. It's possible to earn well into six figures, or even seven, with a staff of nine. You can sell a small business of this type for millions of dollars.

As an entrepreneur who has founded and operated fourteen

such companies, I can attest that there is virtually no literature that tells an owner/manager how to open such a business, or how to run it. Almost every business book written has in mind an operation made up of hundreds, if not thousands, of employees. A few magazines try to reach this group with at least part of their editorial content. Unfortunately, articles providing basic information and help for the very small business are infrequent and hard to find.

So where does that leave the new business that plans to start and stay small? You may be able to find a mentor in a local service organization or church congregation. Valuable help is available through the chamber of commerce and networking clubs such as LeTip and others. Unfortunately, none of these resources is really going to provide you with the depth of information you need to plan, start, develop, and—when the time comes—divest your business.

I thought about doing this book for almost five years before I started writing in earnest. During that period I wrote two books for the specific industry in which I make my living. Both of these books and the numerous articles I published in trade magazines dealt with one of the most quaint examples of under-ten-employee ownership, the bike shop.

Then one of the businesses I'm involved in broke past the ten-employee level and grew to nearly forty. Plans called for a total of seventy or eighty within the next eighteen months. During this growth I realized that I'd never expected the business to become that large. I'd often pointed out that I preferred the environment of a very small enterprise. It was at this point that I really felt the call to get this book into print.

Running a 21st-Century Small Business is divided into the five clear-cut stages of small business development.

In section 1—Before You Begin—we take a look at what it really means to be an independent businessperson. What is myth and what is reality in terms of finances, hours, and sacrifices to home and hearth? The purpose of section 1 is to provide you with information that will help you make a choice about going into business or not. Section 1 also provides an overview of the types of enterprises that are available and the personality types that offer the best fit.

Section 2—Opening the Doors—picks up after the decision is made to go into business. Presented first is "the plan": a simple, step-by-step procedure for developing a fundamental business plan.

Next, the section looks at some legal considerations. To incorporate or not to incorporate . . . licenses, permits, leases, and insurance. By the time you're through with this section, you'll wish you were an attorney.

Selecting service vendors such as a bank, CPA, lawyer, or insurance agent can be a real can of worms. How do you decide which one to use? How do you work with these folks to get the most out of these relationships?

A major cause of new business failure is inadequate record keeping. Section 2 will explain the fundamental principles of accounting and offer recommendations about how to approach bookkeeping's most challenging hurdles.

For many businesses, the selection of a location can be the most important decision the new owner makes. "How large, how much, and how's the traffic?" are but a few of the elements that go into this important process. Detailed strategies are provided, including how to negotiate with the landlord.

Next, we consider the specifics. What kind of business is it? How do you find out if you have a large enough population to support your new enterprise? What vendors are available to supply you? Have the best suppliers already given exclusives in your preferred neighborhood? How do you establish credit with the sources you'll need to provide your opening inventory, fixtures, supplies, and services?

You've had the grand opening, and everything is perfect. Well, almost everything. There are not nearly enough customers to pay the bills. One of your suppliers was out of product when you called to replenish what you sold at the opening sale. Plus, it's become all too clear that you don't have enough capital to keep going if business doesn't pick up soon.

Never fear! Section 3—The First Three Years—covers just such circumstances. Every aspect of the day-to-day running of a business will be explored. First we'll look at selling, promoting, advertising, and public relations. How *does* a business create interest in its product or services and then *sell* the folks that come in? The first three years will test the new company's ability to do just that.

Clearly, it would be better for your new enterprise if all the t's were crossed and the i's dotted. However, the thing that will kill you fastest is *not enough business*. Therefore, a great portion of section 3 will be devoted to finding customers and selling them.

Even if you manage to do enough volume to take care of your basic bills, bad management can quickly put you in the red. Thus the balance of this section will be devoted to basic management of a small concern. How do you collect money due you? How do you avoid collection from your own vendors without losing them as suppliers? How do you work with banks?

Hiring and firing is a tough area for most new companies unless the owner has had this type of experience in prior positions. Where do you look for employees? What are the techniques for checking applicants' qualifications on the phone? What are the legal aspects? What is the right and wrong way to indoctrinate the new hire? All of these questions will be explored.

Earlier sections explored the area of bookkeeping. However, even if you've taken classes in accounting, you won't be prepared to read and analyze income and financial statements. These tools are sorely underutilized by most start-ups. Potentially, they have the same value to an entrepreneur as a thermometer and stethoscope have to a doctor. If you know how to read the information they give, you'll be able to diagnose the ills of your company and make the necessary changes to bring it to the peak of health. On the positive side, these reports will show you what you're doing right, so that you can do more of it. Section 3 will show you what to look for. Other subjects that will be addressed include outside salespeople, trade shows, international sales, and Internet presence.

Only about 50 percent of start-up businesses will still be around to celebrate their third birthday. If your business manages to survive the stages described in sections 1 and 2, it will have performed far better than the statistical average. It will either be ready to settle into certain patterns that will solidify its customer base, sales levels, and income, or it will be ready to use this base to launch itself into a larger operation.

Section 4 deals with Managing Yourself and Others. The challenge of motivating, training, compensating, and otherwise dealing with your staff is usually the area that requires the most continuing education. Indeed, by this time most of the business is routine. However, there are still plenty of surprises that will come at you from unexpected angles. Your landlord doesn't renew your lease. Your top manager opens in competition with you. The bank tightens up its policies and cuts off your line of credit. A review of the management techniques offered in sections 2 and 3 will help in these situations.

Learning how to manage other folks, however, requires a lifetime of experience and all the book learning you can manage. Each type of employee will be discussed. What characteristics are important for each job? What is the pay scale for that position? What is the protocol for dealing with different issues that will be faced?

One of the most important things this book does is provide insight into how you can create an enjoyable workplace environment. How can you be the kind of employer that people want to work for? How can you put together a team that will outproduce the competition and be happy doing it?

Then there is the business of managing yourself. At this stage of your business you'll be entering an entirely new set of circumstances. You'll no longer be needed to put out the daily fires. You should find yourself needed less in daily management as people and systems become increasingly proficient and professional. *How is that going to affect you?* You're used to being needed for every decision. You've always had a list of things to do that could never be completed.

Will you lose your health over this change? Read the ideas for dealing with this transition offered in section 4, and move into the kind of life that all the hard work was supposed to create. It can be done.

One day you'll wake up and realize that you've created something that has value. It will amaze you, but not nearly so much as it will amaze your parents and your spouse. But alas, it's true. Section 5—Managing Your Assets—covers strategies for holding on to and building this tremendously important possession.

A business that has value should be treated like any other asset. It needs to be protected at least as carefully as your house, your cash, or your coin collection. Section 5 will show you how to do just that.

It's my sincere hope that the approaches discussed in the following pages will help you create a solid business asset—one that can be redeemed for a high return on your investment, should you ever decide to retire.

SECTION ONE

Before
You Begin

1

Why Self-Employment?

SO YOU WANT TO OWN YOUR OWN BUSINESS. You're not alone. The idea of being in business for oneself is as American as apple pie or baseball. It's the rare American who hasn't at least considered the idea from time to time. (This is not to say that the goal is unknown in other nations or cultures. In fact, citizens of Australia and Taiwan have an even higher level of interest in self-employment than do citizens in the United States.)

Many do take the plunge. From selling Avon or Amway to purchasing a McDonald's franchise, from marketing a brand-new idea to hanging out a dentist's shingle, from buying out their boss to opening a hardware store, millions of otherwise intelligent folks give up good-paying jobs and sink their life savings into being their own boss.

What would motivate a person to risk his livelihood, his marriage, and his emotional health? Why would a person want to work sixty or eighty hours per week for little or no income? Who are these entrepreneurs who give up the safe life for a taste of life in the fast lane? What is the big deal, anyway?

Money? The pursuit of the almighty dollar and all that goes with it? Are we a nation of aspiring Donald Trumps? Yes, and no. Many, if not most, of those who choose the path of self-employment expect to make more money than they could as an employee. They're willing to put up with inconvenience and temporary poverty in order to create a high-income position for themselves in the future. Those primarily driven by monetary considerations also generally expect to "get rich." But the lure of excellent pay alone is not appealing enough for most folks to agree to even temporary sacrifices. If it were, we'd see these individuals taking a safer route to the same end, such as furthering their education, job hopping, or going into commissioned sales jobs . . . not starting a business.

Personal independence takes a close second to hard cash in driving an employee to become a boss. This type of individual may find it hard to work for others, or simply want to do it *his* way. Folks who find being employed by others about as desirable as swimming with sharks don't care how successful they are in business. They'll keep the doors open regardless of the sacrifice to self or family. They'd rather be operating a one-man shoe-repair store than be vice president of a $10 million division of a conglomerate. You'd be amazed at how many small retailers fit into this category. You'd be even more surprised to learn how many doctors, lawyers, CPAs, and other professionals make substantially less than their potential income in order to be "on their own."

Among those entering the world of self-employment is the managerial-level woman who has what it takes to run a business, but who has hit the "glass ceiling." That is, while her employer may talk a good game about equal opportunity, and may have made great strides in this area, there's a point above which there is still a sign on the door: NO WOMEN NEED APPLY. Thus the talented and motivated female often finds that the only hope for reaching her full potential is to open her own enterprise.

Another large group of small business owners is motivated by a desire to make a special contribution to the world—one they believe would be impossible to make working for a profit-seeking enterprise. Here you'll find the hobbyist who wants to make sure other model-train collectors in Dubuque have a place to buy, sell, and trade their collections.

Also in this group are the lawyers who wish to provide low-cost legal services to special segments of the population who couldn't otherwise afford a lawyer; doctors, dentists, and other professionals with similar motivation; pastors of independent congregations; founders of specialized schools, cooperatives, and credit unions. The list of those who find small business an outlet for their community-service orientation goes on and on.

Interestingly, this selfless approach often results in much greater financial success than the business founded to create wealth, probably as a result of the tireless devotion that such an enterprise produces. When the primary goal of an owner is making money, it's common to see great swings in the level of desire. When the going gets very rough or too easy, many who have only dollar signs in their eyes lose interest. Those who are pursuing the greater good may feel a stronger compulsion to keep on pushing.

Simply being out of a job has often pushed people into self-employment. This seems to be particularly true when an individual has lost his job due to a merger, an acquisition, a dot-com bust, or changing economic conditions (such as military downsizing).

Having something to prove can be a major motivational factor. A parent, sibling, spouse, or other significant person who is doing well in his own business, or speaks of others who are, could create pressure to give it a try. A rival is making more money than our budding businessman. He sees a small venture as the only hope he has of "keeping up." A son feels that he must keep the family business going, or do it *better* than his dad. This group may be acting from a neurotic point of view, and as such will likely be very unhappy in business. Some of our most successful and well-known businesspeople are very wealthy and very unhappy because their drive comes from this unhealthy direction.

Only rarely does an individual who aspires to a life of self-employment fit just one of these categories. More frequently, there is a mixture of forces at work. For instance, the desire for financial independence coupled with a need to call all the shots is a potent combination. The overriding fact remains that, for whatever reason, many in our population will take a stab at going it alone. There's something very romantic—and very American— about owning your own business.

In this section we'll try to take a slightly less passionate look at ownership. Our goal will be to provide a set of practical guides that will allow you to come to a logical conclusion about whether you should go out on your own. Every attempt will be made to give you an overview of every aspect of the decision-making process.

CHAPTER

2

Do You Have the Right Stuff?

BEING YOUR OWN BOSS will likely be the hardest thing you'll ever do in life. This is not meant to scare you, intimidate you, or even discourage you from trying. It's simply a fact.

Being the boss means making important decisions every day from less-than-complete information and experience—decisions that could destroy the business you've built and all that goes with it. You alone can make these decisions, regardless of the input you might get from employees, partners, spouses, or outside professionals. When all is said and done, it's up to you, and you'll harvest the fruits of your decisions . . . sweet or bitter. This is why we say, "It's lonely at the top."

If you have a friend or relative who owns her own business, she's probably bored you stiff with complaints about the hours she must work, her cash problems, or the loss of a major customer. There's a tendency to see her problems as overstated. Because you have a working acquaintance with hiring, firing, pricing, collections, and lawsuits in your current business, you believe that you have an insight into how tough it really is. *You don't.*

If you run out of cash at home, you borrow twenty or fifty dollars from a coworker until Monday. If the crisis looms larger, you might tap your brother or dad for a thousand bucks until your tax refund comes in. When you run out of cash in a business, where do you go to make a fifteen-thousand-dollar payroll tomorrow morning? How do you come up with thirty thousand dollars to repay the bank today when failure to do so could mean the bank gets your business *and* your home?

When your favorite grocery store goes out of business, you drive a few extra blocks and shop somewhere else. When a supplier of one-of-a-kind merchandise closes, where do you find a new source to make up the 30 percent of your sales that that vendor's merchandise represented? What expenses or which personnel do you cut if you can't find a way to make up the lost sales?

When you make a decision to rent or buy your home, you sign a long-term document that means you have an obligation to pay some amount each month to stay there. If you try to get out of a rental agreement on an apartment, it might cost you a few months' rent. If you try to abandon a mortgage, it will rarely cost you more than your original down payment. When you rent a piece of commercial property, however, you may be signing a document that puts you on the hook for hundreds of thousands of dollars whether you succeed in your business or not.

As an employee you may have complained about the extra work on your desk when your assistant quit to move out of state. You faced this extra burden at least until you could find and train a replacement. Imagine the headaches you'd have if your right-hand person in a three-man shop left to open his own place down the street . . . in competition with your fledgling enterprise.

Now you're sure this is meant to scare you off. Not at all. It's meant to suggest that just as the weak-kneed shouldn't try hang gliding, the weak-minded shouldn't go to medical school, and the weak-spirited should forget small business.

If you have the right stuff, nothing is more fun, more challenging, or more rewarding than being at the controls. There are times when your heart will be in your throat, and times when you'll feel as if you're carrying more than your shoulders can bear. However, there are few experiences in life as exciting as landing the biggest account in your field, or scratching out your first profitable year. There's real exhilaration in knowing that you're creating careers that are supporting families. It feels good to build something, even if it's just a hundred-thousand-dollar-a-year tax-preparation outlet with yourself and one employee.

The very first set of questions you should ask yourself is: "Am I willing to put up with sixty-to-eighty-hour weeks the first four or five years? Do I want to be on an emotional roller coaster for the rest of my career? Do I have the stomach for making several tough decisions every day that might affect not only my own investment, but the livelihood of employees and their families? Is my family ready to cut back financially if necessary?" Then there's a big one: "Am I mentally prepared for failure?"

Now is a really good time to stop. Go back. Reread the last paragraph and think about each question. Unless you can be honest with yourself regarding these questions, your continued reading of this book will be largely wasted. You may protest that you really won't know the answers until you've tried it, and no one could argue against you on that point. However, it's essential that you give the best answer you can, because it is a lead-pipe certainty that you'll find yourself in each one of those circumstances.

Let's take another look at that last one. *Failure!* You *will* fail. Even if your enterprise is a success (and you've certainly already seen the statistics on that), you'll endure many failures on the way to success. Even if you were to follow every idea and approach in this book to the letter, the varieties of circumstances facing a new enterprise are infinite. Business is a process of succeeding from one failure to the next.

Thus, a real measure of the potential of any individual who wants to make it in business boils down to how that person handles failure. Examine yourself in your present endeavors. Do you pick yourself right up after an expensive mistake and keep on keeping on? If the customer says no to your sales pitch, do you still pick up the phone and call the next prospect?

When you work for someone else, you may be able to go into a slump for a few days after a major letdown. If you're on commission, it may affect your income that month. However, unless your sales manager is extra tough, you probably won't see any lasting consequence of being "off" for a few days.

When you own the store, you have no such luxury. If anything, you have to be ready to work harder and smarter after a failure than before. Think hard about this. Don't let your ego get in the way of an honest evaluation. *Do you have the mental and emotional toughness to get back up on the horse immediately after you've been thrown and put the spurs in deep?*

Next let's consider the issue of work habits: Don't believe for a minute that you're going to be successful working forty-hour weeks. For the first few years, expect to spend almost every waking hour either working at a specific task related to your enterprise, or at least thinking about it.

We're not just talking here about whether you have the stamina to put in long hours. The issue is whether you have the willingness to put everything and everybody else on hold until you have the ship afloat. Your spouse and children will be the ones most directly affected, but it will also take a toll on your friends, other relatives, sporting interests, hobbies, and, of course, your TV habits. When you first start out, you'll even have to give up vacations. Not until your company is big enough for you to turn things over to a trusted second-in-command will you be able to afford the luxury of more than a long weekend.

Doubtless, some of you are skeptical. "C'mon," you're saying. "I agree with your premise that I'm not trying to be the next Microsoft. I just want a nice little business that nets me a cool hundred grand a year. Surely I can do that in forty or fifty hours per week and not bring my problems home to the bedroom."

No. No. And no. It just doesn't work that way. Whether you're starting a future General Motors or an ice cream parlor, the first several years are going to require your undivided attention if you have any hope of success. An associate of mine didn't buy my advice; he set up a retail business with the full intention of working nine to six with an hour lunch, five days a week. The company is still in operation today, although my friend now has a 75 percent partner. Worse than that, the business generated no take-home income for five years. One can only guess at the success that might have been attained with 25 percent more effort.

The next question would seem to be an obvious one, but so often this is the very issue that sinks the budding entrepreneur who otherwise has everything going for him. Are you a self-starter? An early riser? A go-getter? Three different questions? No, all three are the same.

Most people need management. They need someone to jump-start their motor when they have an off day, week, or year. They need a mentor to fill in the blanks of their knowledge and experience. They need a patient listener to bounce ideas off of or to complain to. They need a team to help with the brainstorming when the idea well runs dry.

The newly self-employed can kiss all those luxuries good-bye. Your spouse may or may not want to fill some of those roles. Ironically, the spouses who are the most capable of providing help in these areas are usually married to folks who might accept that advice and help from anyone *but* their husband or wife.

Parents, friends, and old business associates might be able to help with ideas during a crisis. There are many kinds of associations you can join that will broaden your knowledge and provide networks of businesspeople similarly situated. The fact remains, however, that you're going to have to do 90 percent of the hard stuff on your own.

There will be mornings when you're certain that someone has put Super Glue in your bed. You'll try to convince yourself that it really doesn't matter whether you open the doors at 9:00 a.m. as dictated by the posted hours. No one is ever there that early anyway.

Try to picture yourself in a retail setting. You arrived at 8:30 a.m. It's now three in the afternoon and the door has yet to open except for the hourly trip you make to the sidewalk to see if the town is still populated. You've restocked the shelves. You've posted all the receipts. You've even taken out the broom and cleaned up the place. You know in your heart of hearts that you should now pick up the phone and find some excuse to call a few customers and offer them a good reason to come in. You consider in your mind a few ideas you've read in trade magazines for improving traffic flow. Unfortunately, selling over the phone and planning promotions are not your favorite thing to do. You have no real experience at either one, and you're nervous about trying your hand at them.

If you can see yourself in the picture above, think long and hard about going out on your own. You're going to have to do *whatever it takes* within the bounds of legality to make your business go when it ain't. If you prefer to be closed on Sunday, but you're not paying the rent, you have to be open on Sunday. If you're in a service business, you'd better join a few organizations like the Lions Club, the Chamber of Commerce, or LeTip even if you're not the joining type. Not only will you gain important information just from joining, but you'll have to be active if you're going to make contacts.

No matter what line you decide to pursue, you're going to have to *sell*. Many, if not most, new businesspeople don't like to sell, have no special gift for selling, and have absolutely no training in selling. Those of you who fit the above description are now arguing out loud with the idea that you must sell your product or service. You're absolutely convinced that your idea is so amazing, and that your future customers are so needful of your stuff, that they'll beat a path to your door based on a three-line ad in the phone book.

You couldn't be more wrong! Nobody ever has—or will in the future—beat the door down to buy any legal substance. If ever there was a product that amazing, the competition would spring up within days to cut short this perfect opportunity.

There are many ideas in this book that will help you immensely if you follow the broad precepts. On the other hand, there are a few "golden nuggets" that are so important, they really do represent the difference between a big success and a bigger failure. Here's the first golden nugget. *Learn to sell.*

Selling is a profession. In its finest form it is at least as difficult as doctoring, lawyering, or pastoring. There is no profession that requires more continuing education. The truly great salespeople are constantly learning new approaches and reviewing the old standards.

You needn't be suave, charming, or brilliant to be a good sales rep any more than those traits benefit a CPA or an engineer. What you need is a good grounding in the specific skills that make for sales success. There are hundreds of books on the subject. Read them. Reread them. Keep them handy. Be prepared to read them again during the first few months after opening. *Nothing happens in business until something is sold.*

Let's review what we've covered thus far. Being your own boss is hard. You'll work harder than you ever have before. You'll need to work smarter than you did as an employee. You'll be the president in charge of everything—including *selling.* You'll be all alone at the very moment when you need a big, experienced team. You'll very likely have to reduce your standard of living, and you may forget what some of your family and friends look like. The question is not "Do I want to attempt this life?" Rather, the question you should ask yourself (with the hope that you'll give yourself a very honest answer) is "Can I do it? Do I have the mental and emotional tools necessary to handle running a very small business?"

CHAPTER

3

What Will It Cost?

THE WORLD IS JUST FULL of wonderful ironies, and the world of small business is no exception. For instance, the primary motive for going into business is financial independence, a state of affairs in which a person, by definition, "no longer has to concern himself about money on a day-to-day basis." So what a twist it is that the good soul who chooses the path of self-employment will spend the next several years thinking about little else besides money.

Unless you're one of the very fortunate few who've already reached the state of financial independence, the lack of money will very likely provide you with your biggest hurdles in the first years of business. Initially, you have to find enough cash to open the doors. A huge percentage of entrepreneurs start their business knowing they're undercapitalized. The rest find out soon afterward.

Later, if you've been able to generate enough cash to keep the place open during the early stages, you'll need to find ways to raise capital for expansion.

Finally, just when you think you have it all figured out, the economy, your business, or both will go into a slump and you'll need a cash fix to bail yourself out.

I've started very small businesses with as little as five thousand in cash and as much as fifty thousand dollars. Neither was nearly enough. I've seen friends start service-oriented enterprises out of their homes that you might think would need very little cash. Within weeks of opening, they found they'd gone through twenty or thirty thousand dollars.

Every book or brochure on start-ups stresses the importance of sufficient capital for both the business and your personal overhead. Most suggest that you have enough funds to pay your personal expenses for six months to two years. *No one ever does.*

In days gone by it was possible, although difficult, for the owner of a small enterprise to get by without knowing too much about financial statements, cash-flow analysis, tax planning, and other tools of the money-planning part of running a business. Hard to believe, but there was even a day when a person could run a fairly big operation without a computer. Even just ten years ago, I knew quite a few owners who were trying to get by without financial and computer skills. They were at a huge disadvantage. In this highly competitive time, you can't afford to give your crosstown rival an inch.

If you have any thought of taking a run at this game, you must get some serious training in accounting, business finance, and computers *now*. There are several good books available, and every junior college and university offers beginning courses in each of these subjects. You'll also get a cursory look at these subjects in later sections of this book. The more you know about money, the better chance you will have of managing it.

So what will it really cost to get started? The flip answer is "All the money you (and any of your friends or relatives foolish enough to lend it to you) have." The thoughtful and realistic answer is "You're probably going to open the doors with whatever you have anyway, so get as much as you can." Section 2 will get into more specifics, but let's take a look at some general ideas of the starting expenses you're likely to incur.

You'll need to determine the legal form your business will take.

The expenses of opening will vary depending on the form you choose.

■ Sole Proprietorship. This approach is the least expensive, but riskiest, way to start out. (We'll discuss other aspects of these legal ideas later. For now, a sole proprietor is a form of business where you are the only owner, and you have not incorporated.) You can probably handle all the legal expenses of starting a sole proprietorship for under two hundred dollars.

■ Partnership. A partnership (which is like a sole proprietorship except that there are two or more partners) will cost substantially more. Most partnerships are simple arrangements where you and a friend or two go into business together. That is where it stops being simple. You need to decide how each partner will contribute to the enterprise in money and time, and how each will benefit in salary, ownership, and other compensation. Decisions need to be made as to who will do what, when, and how. It is also a good idea to know what will happen if one or more of the partners want out. These and other subjects are usually covered in a partnership agreement. Although it is possible to start a partnership without this agreement—and no law requires one—it is, however, a very good idea to prepare such a document to help settle possible disputes later on. A lawyer will charge you anywhere from two thousand dollars and up to prepare this little document. There are books in the library and information online that you could use to help you prepare your own. If you take this route, you would still want an attorney to look it over.

■ Limited Partnerships. This is a business form where there's one partner or group of partners called general partners who are generally active in the company. Another group called limited partners are merely investors. This form has some characteristics of a partnership and some of a corporation. The legal costs associated with beginning a limited partnership would range from five to fifty thousand dollars. This form of business is associated with enterprises that are more sophisticated than most first-timers are going to try.

■ Corporations. The best approach for most new firms is going to be incorporation. It is not very expensive, and there are many benefits. Depending on whether or not you use a lawyer, and varying somewhat based on the complexity, you can handle the legal expenses of a new corporation for one to five thousand dollars. (If you're planning to offer stock to the public the cost will be closer to fifty thousand.) There are two types of corporations, Sub "S" and "C." There is no difference in cost between these two types.

As for licenses, fees, and taxes, this category of start-up expense will vary greatly depending upon the type of business you intend to enter. There are ways to reduce these specific expenses. Section 2 provides you with thirty years of experience at *legally* beating the system.

At a minimum you can probably expect to pay one hundred dollars in unavoidable levies to the various governments that will have their hand out. If you're planning to open a professional office or a highly regulated operation like a restaurant, your total outlay in this category could run easily into the thousands, or even tens of thousands, of dollars.

Office supplies and basic equipment will cost at least two thousand dollars. You'll need to print letterhead and business cards. Most new companies will need to purchase a computer, an all-in-one printer, and miscellaneous office supplies, as well as establish an e-mail address and create a basic Web site. Today it's complicated and expensive to set up phone lines. You may also need to leave deposits with the utilities and set up online accounts with UPS and FedEx.

Fixtures could hit you the hardest of all. Manufacturers need production equipment, installation of electrical and plumbing systems, shelving, tools, and shipping supplies. Wholesalers will find it hard to operate without shelving, a UPS scale, shipping tables, and quality dollies. Retailers can easily spend five to ten thousand or more on display cases, wall displays, specialty equipment such as clothing racks or jewelry cases, and mood-setting items such as carpet, paint, and lighting.

Service industries may have even greater outlays in the fixture department. Dentists, doctors, and veterinarians have huge outlays for the tools of their trade. Beyond that, there may be even more expense for waiting-room furniture, patient record supplies, and uniforms. These same kinds of outlays await lawyers, CPAs, interior decorators, and others who are service providers.

Next on the list is facilities. Many small businesses are operated out of the home, but for most types of enterprise this just isn't practical. This is an extremely important area. Many young companies that go under in the first year do so because they can't make the rent.

If you need to rent a space for your firm, you'll have to figure an initial outlay of at least first and last months' rent plus any leasehold improvements (changes made to the building for your type of business). Since you're just beginning, it's likely that your landlord will be looking for three months' rent to move in. All the issues raised here are subject to negotiation, and section 2 offers plenty of ideas on how to reduce your rent and your up-front payout to the landlord. For this aspect of your open-the-doors cost you'll want to figure anywhere from five hundred dollars for a seven-hundred-square-foot warehouse space in a rural area with no leasehold improvements to twenty thousand dollars for eighteen hundred square feet in a major urban retail setting with minor build-outs. (Please don't confuse this range with the different issue of monthly rents. This is what it will cost you to move in.)

Yes, it *is* starting to add up. Unfortunately, we haven't come to the really big ones yet—inventory and receivables. Some businesses keep no inventory, and there are few companies that can get all of their customers to pay cash on the barrelhead. For the rest (almost all) of us, these two items usually represent the biggest numbers on the balance sheet.

Example: An extremely well-run retailer may be able to "turn" his inventory four times per year. This means that the store will sell four times its average inventory (in dollars, at cost) each year. To briefly explain, let's work through an example. If a store stocks an average of five hundred dollars in product and sells that product at a 50 percent margin (buys the product for $1 and sells it for $2), and is able to turn it four times, it will have $5,000 at 50 percent margin ($10,000) times four turns, equaling $40,000 in sales.

Since there are very few retailers who could make it on $40,000 in sales their first year, let's use $100,000 as the first-year sales goal instead. Second, a 50 percent average margin is a good goal for most general retailers (with many exceptions). But that markup is also unlikely the first year due to probable discounting to attract customers. Let's use a 40 percent margin instead. Finally, an inexperienced retailer is not going to turn his product four times. Let's be conservative and use three turns. One hundred thousand dollars in sales after three turns equals $33,333 after a 40 percent markup, which means $20,000 in average inventory.

Our retailer in the example may be able to get some help from his suppliers in allowing credit terms for payment. Unfortunately, unless you have a great personal balance sheet, most suppliers are not going to offer trade credit to a start-up. They'll want to ship to you at least once or twice on a COD basis before offering you a small credit line.

Manufacturers and wholesalers have the double capital burden of carrying inventory *and* "carrying" their customers' receivables. Today, the companies who carry receivables can expect to get paid forty-five to sixty days after shipment (exceptions in both directions abound). Thus, if you hope to do $300,000 in sales your first year (a modest goal for most wholesalers and manufacturers), you can expect to carry $300,000 divided by 12 months in a year ($25,000) multiplied by 1½ months (average time from sale to payment), resulting in $37,500 in receivables. The money that you "loan" to your customers is *cash* you won't have available to spend on new inventory, payroll, or the rent.

There are many other potential items to consider in arriving at the starting capital necessary to open the doors. Some are: an advertising budget for a grand opening and ongoing marketing; outdoor signs; a down payment on vehicles; an accountant's fees and software for setting up a bookkeeping system; special bonds for certain industries; computers.

Finally, there's the question of staying power. How many months of operating expenses are you going to put aside as a hedge against missed sales expectations? You're going to have to pay fixed overhead expenses such as rent, payroll, payroll taxes, and utilities even if no customers succumb to your terrific sales pitch.

Depending on the type of business, you should probably have about three to six months' worth of hard expenses set aside, including enough money to cover your personal expenses for the same period. For a single individual starting a service business out of his apartment, this may be only a few thousand dollars. For a married manufacturer with children to feed and a payroll to meet the amount could total tens of thousands of dollars.

CHAPTER

4

Basic Budgeting

WHAT DOES ALL OF THIS ADD UP TO? The best way to find out is to construct a budget. If you decide to go forward with a career as a business owner, you'll be constructing lots of budgets. Happily, this is the least difficult of all financial documents. It is really little different from the kind of budget you use at home.

Of course, it's possible that many reading this don't have a household budget, and wouldn't know how to create one. What follows is a very simple budget for starting a small retail establishment.

I'll use a fictional bike dealer as our example. Most of what will be covered would pertain to all types of small enterprises. For many of you, some of these amounts may seem small, but they're representative of the time and the place in the example.

Jimmy wants to open his new shop in a suburb of Dallas. He's worked for an established bike store for a couple of years (very good idea), and feels he's ready to go out on his own. He has savings of $25,000, and he has an excellent credit rating. He's single, but dating, and shares an apartment with a roommate.

Jimmy was making $1,850 a month as a manager for Smith and Sons Pedalrama. After taxes and $300 per month for his savings account, he has been spending about $1,200 on personal expenses.

Jimmy decides it would be a very good idea to see just how little he can get by with for the first year after he opens. He starts with a personal budget.

Item	Amount
Rent	$ 350
Food	150
Car Payment	70
Gas/Repairs	60
Car Insurance	70
Telephone	25
Gas	30
Electric	35
Water	15
Clothes	40
Entertainment	50
Charity	10
Gifts	35
Household	25
Medical/Dental	50
Payments	25
Misc.	60
Total	$1,100

After taking a look at his checkbook and tax file, and charting his cash expenses for a month, the above budget emerges. Jimmy is able to cut $100 a month from his spending. However, he's unable to see how he can save anything beyond that without giving up his car or moving back in with his folks. He decides to use this amount as a basis for his first six months in business to see if his savings will hold out.

Next, he constructs a projected budget for opening the doors.

Item	To Open
Legal	$ 150
Office Supplies	75
Office Equipment	150
Store Fixtures	2,500
Shop Tools	700
Rent	3,000
Build-Outs	2,500
Inventory	15,000
Advertising	400
Accounting	450
License/Fees	150
Telephone	300
Utilities	100
Signage	600
Total	$26,075

Right away Jimmy can see he has a problem. His opening expenses are going to be $1,075 higher than his total savings. He won't have a cent left to pay expenses for the first month of operation, or any income to himself. This is exactly the kind of information that you'd expect good budgeting to provide. With these findings in hand Jimmy can now become a manager. He can make decisions. His first decision is to go ahead and look at the operating budget for the first six months, anyway (see page 30).

It's evident from this budget that the conservative way to open this business is with capital (real, hard money, cash dollars) of $50,000. It's rare that anyone is that conservative, however. In fact, a more common approach to the above would be to open the doors with the $25,000 available and borrow the balance. Typically, entrepreneurs such as Jimmy would try to open even if they had only $10,000 cash. The balance would come from credit extended by suppliers, friends, relatives, and MasterCard. Opening

Item	To Open	Month 1	Month 2	Month 3	Month 4	Month 5	Month 6	Total
Legal	150	25	25	25	25	25	25	300
Office Supplies	75	25	25	25	25	25	25	225
Office Equipment	150	0	0	0	0	0	0	150
Store Fixtures	2,500	0	0	0	0	0	0	2,500
Shop Tools	700	50	50	50	50	50	50	1,000
Rent	3,000	1,500	1,500	1,500	1,500	1,500	1,500	12,000
Build-outs	2,500	0	0	0	0	0	0	2,500
Inventory	15,000	0	0	0	0	0	0	15,000
Advertising	400	150	150	150	150	150	150	1,300
Accounting	450	100	100	100	100	100	100	1,050
Taxes	0	0	0	0	0	0	0	0
License/Fees	150	0	0	100	0	0	0	250
Dues/Publications	0	20	0	0	30	0	0	50
Payroll/Payroll Tax	0	0	0	1,000	1,000	1,000	1,000	4,000
Interest	0	0	0	0	0	0	0	0
Postage	0	20	0	20	0	20	0	60
Telephone	300	50	50	50	50	50	50	600
Utilities	100	75	75	75	75	75	75	550
Shows/Travel	0	0	0	0	500	0	0	500
Signage	600	0	0	0	0	0	0	600
Personal Needs	0	1,100	1,100	1,100	1,100	1,100	1,100	6,600
Total	26,075	3,115	3,075	4,195	4,605	4,095	4,075	49,235

a business with such a bare minimum of invested cash and a great dependence on borrowed funds is defined as leverage.

There's only one problem with leverage. When you're trying to move a ten-thousand-pound boulder with a ten-foot lever your success is based less on your skill at boulder moving than it is on your weight. To make certain this concept is fully absorbed: The ten-thousand-pound boulder is the prospect of your success, the lever is the credit extension that must be paid back and usually comes with interest (expense), and your weight is your own investment.

The real point of this exercise, though, is to give you a formula that will enable you to determine just how much cash you'll need to open your doors. *Going through this process is a fundamental step you must take in the decision-making process.*

CHAPTER

5

What Kind of Business?

ONE OF THE MAJOR BENEFITS of being in business for yourself is the ability to choose a job that suits you perfectly. True ☐ False ☐

Clearly, the above statement is true. We all have the ability to make that selection. Unfortunately, few ever do.

The most common reasons a first-timer has for selecting a given business are:

1. He works in that industry now.
2. He's worked in that industry in the past.
3. A relative has offered him a chance to take over a going concern.
4. An associate has talked him into selling A. L. Williams, Shaklee, Tupperware, etc.
5. He goes to an opportunity fair and a salesperson talks him into parting with thousands of dollars to start his own print shop, car wash, or hamburger stand.
6. He's an active or past hobbyist in that field.
7. He's always dreamed of owning that type of establishment.
8. Someone he knows is doing well in a similar business in another town.
9. An idea hits him.
10. He can buy an existing business for a bargain.

The preceding list certainly doesn't cover every possible situation, but each reason stated has one thing in common: by themselves they're lousy reasons for going into any business.

The next few pages will help you with an intelligent approach for deciding which way to jump. It could help you avoid years of wasted time and huge amounts of wasted greenbacks.

WHAT DO YOU LIKE TO DO?

It may be that the idea that an individual should enjoy her work was something dreamed up by the baby boomers while they were going through college. In any case, it has been so reported. Horrible as it is to imagine, there is evidence that past generations may not have concerned themselves very much with the question "Will I like it?" in choosing their vocation.

There are two reasons a person would *not* want to earn a living doing something that he or she truly enjoys. One: a belief that turning an avocation into a vocation would destroy the enjoyment of the first. Two: a worry that if the job is too enjoyable it will mean too much time spent working and not enough time spent with spouse and children.

Where there is smoke there is fire; thus, I would agree that there is potential for either of the above to come true. However, the potential benefits far outweigh the possible pitfalls. Getting and staying motivated is a critical ingredient in any career. It's a whole lot easier to "keep on keepin' on," even when things are really bleak, if you really enjoy what you're doing.

The challenge here is to figure out what you enjoy doing. It's one thing to recognize that you're good with your hands or really enjoy music. It's quite another thing to consider the other elements that go into making a career based on those interests.

For example, let's take a look at a field crowded with hobbyists turned professionals: computers. You really enjoy poking around on a computer. You're better at it than anybody you know. You have a roomful of equipment, programs, and manuals. You subscribe to a stack of industry publications, and you belong to two computer clubs.

It's *likely* you can succeed in a business related to computers. The question is . . . which one? Are you really interested in what makes the machine tick and probing the depths of programs? In that case you might do well as an independent consultant helping other businesses implement specialized requirements for their systems.

Maybe you're primarily interested in applications. You may be able to make it as a programmer, inventing ways a computer can help with tasks, and writing software that gets you there.

Another possibility is that you're most intrigued with the latest products being offered for personal or business use. Every new item that comes out makes you drool. You might find success as a retailer of computer products.

Maybe every Saturday morning your house is filled with neighborhood kids wanting to help you play with your computer. The thing is, you're happy to help them. You're as excited as they are by their explorations into the world of electronic information. Could a computer school or camp be in your future?

So far, we've looked at the enjoyment issue on two levels. The job gets a little tougher as we look at level three. If you were to go into that type of business, what would you really spend your time doing? The computer school provides a great example.

What you enjoy is working with computers, and working with kids and computers. A computer school could provide a great outlet for those interests, but running a computer school would entail far more than that. Call the owner of a computer school in a town far enough away that he won't feel reluctant to give a potential competitor ideas and discuss what really goes into the job. It might look something like this.

Activity	Percentage of time used
Teaching Kids	35 percent
Selling Parents	15 percent
Hiring and Training Teachers	10 percent
Administration	30 percent
Planning Curriculum	10 percent
Designing Advertising and Promotion	5 percent

The first thing you notice is that the total is 105 percent, and that is probably an understatement. The second thing you notice is that you'll spend only about 45 percent of your time working with computers and/or with kids. You may get some additional computer time as part of your administrative duties, but it's hardly the same. You'll get computer and teaching involvement as part of hiring and training teachers, but will you love working with adults in this environment as much as you enjoy helping the kids?

Then there is "selling parents," or how about "designing advertising and promotion"? Do you really want to do all these things? You probably won't be able to hire a person to do them in the beginning. Maybe you never will. Is there another business that you could create to give you the good parts without the bad parts?

How about designing tutorial programs that would let kids teach themselves? To do this effectively you'd have to work with kids to make certain your system is working. You'd spend another large part of your time writing programs and tutorials. The rest of the job would require selling your output. If you're not much of a salesperson, and don't want to become one, it's possible to find agents to sell for you.

Now you can begin to see that it's possible to design a business around your particular interests in an effort to make your work fun and interesting. Of course, no matter how perfectly you match this enterprise to your personality, there'll still be tasks that you don't particularly like to do. The idea is to keep these to a minimum.

6

Business Types

THE NEXT FEW PAGES WILL LOOK at broad categories of industries and services so as to acquaint you with the wide range of opportunities available to match your needs with a specific business.

Manufacturing. Did you ever stop to think about it? Everything has to be made by somebody. Some things are obvious, like cars and refrigerators, but someone also manufactures the door handle and the lock on your car. Some other company makes the keys and the little pins and springs inside that lock. Another company fabricates the machine that puts the lock together.

To succeed as a manufacturer you'd want to have some affinity for machinery and knowledge of certain aspects of the raw materials specific to the type of manufacturing in which you have an interest. It would also be important to know how to motivate factory workers. Most manufacturers also understand about cost accounting and enjoy finding methods of doing the job better, faster, and cheaper.

Selling the output of a factory takes many forms, but the owner will usually be actively involved in sales activities. The potential client list of this category would include an OEM (original equipment manufacturer). In this type of arrangement the output of one factory is sold to another for a component part of the second factory's output. In our example above, the springs, pins, and keys would be OEM parts for the ultimate lock manufacturer, and the lock would be an OEM part for the car manufacturer.

Another customer for a factory's production is distributors. The use of a distributor allows the manufacturer to deal with fewer customers than if that factory were to sell directly to the distributor's customer. By taking this approach, the factory owner can concentrate his resources on making product rather than fielding a large sales force and managing a large accounting department.

Some makers would rather sell directly to retailers. Some call this "eliminating the middleman" (the distributor). The customers here could range from the local mom-and-pop retail store to Wal-Mart.

A big market for manufacturers is the government; federal, state, and local. If you decided to sell to this market, you'd want to have an interest in such pursuits as exacting contract writing, meeting rigid specifications, and dealing with bureaucracies and bureaucrats.

Some companies that fit into the category of manufacturers sell directly to the consumer or, as he is sometimes called, the end user. This is true for the maker of anything, from handicrafts sold at a swap meet, through producers of certain computer programs that sell through their own mail-order lists, to producers of specialized equipment, such as robotics or respirators, that sell to factories or hospitals.

Wholesale distribution. Called variously wholesalers, distributors, jobbers, or feeders, these individuals are the middlemen of business. They generally don't manufacture anything, although some may put their own brand or label on products made by others. Their customer is the retailer, large and small. They may also sell to some end users and to government agencies.

The wholesaler must have special skills, such as warehouse management, purchasing, and collections. Generally, he will also be fielding a large sales staff made up of poorly paid salespeople. It takes talent to find and motivate salespersonnel in any case, but it's particularly difficult when the financial motivation is lacking.

Sometimes the wholesaler's success derives from the specific product lines it carries. This may occur when a wholesaler has an exclusive for sought-after products in a specific territory. In most cases, however, the successful distributor is one who maintains a high level of service combined with a competitive price for products readily available from competitors.

Manufacturers' representatives. In this business, you operate as an independent commissioned sales representative for one or more manufacturers. Many manufacturers don't want to invest in maintaining their own sales staff. This is partly because quality salespeople command large salaries and thus create a big fixed overhead. It also has to do with independent manufacturers' reps having ready access to the customer. A company that fields its own salespeople must spend valuable time and effort to find and develop customers on its own.

There are few small businesses riskier than that of the rep. If he doesn't do a good job for a company he represents, he'll be terminated. Even if he does a great job, there's a chance that the company will decide it can perform the sales function less expensively with its own sales force. In the meantime, the rep must constantly maintain relationships with existing buyers and work hard to build new relationships with an ever-changing buyer lineup. To make matters ever more interesting, all this risk is taken on a commission basis (where the rep is only paid based on how much he or she sells). To add insult to injury, it is sometimes difficult to collect commissions due.

To enter this field you need aggressiveness tempered by great charm. You must be a top-flight professional salesperson. If you're to grow beyond a staff of one, you'll need excellent skills in sales management and bookkeeping.

Sales reps fall into the same categories as the manufacturers they serve. They'll sell to original equipment manufacturers (OEMs), distributors, dealers, end users, or government.

Retailers. This is probably the most familiar category to the average person. Almost every store on the boulevard is either a retailer or a service provider. In a general sense, the operation of a retail store is a perfect job for the jack-of-all-trades. The owner of such a shop usually holds down every job at one time or another, including janitor.

The most important skill that a small, independent retailer can possess is salesmanship, but sadly, it's frequently missing. Other important skills include purchasing, store layout and design, inventory management, and hiring and training of clerks. The retailer must be prepared to be open seven days a week, fifty-two weeks a year. Finally, the successful retail store owner must be a good promoter. She must be able to create traffic (customers walking into the store) as inexpensively as possible. Ads in the Yellow Pages, window banners, sidewalk sales—these are but a few of the countless methods employed to entice the consumer to drop by and check out the merchandise.

Service providers. This group may be the most diverse of all. Restaurants, print service providers, doctors, lawyers, beauty salons, and tax preparers all fall into this category. Their customer may be anyone from the individual consumer to other businesses or the government. A print shop is a good example of a service provider who has a customer base of just about everybody.

Most of the members of this group are trained and licensed in a special skill. In addition, the small shop must have all the abilities mentioned above in the retailer section. On top of all of that, these folks commonly provide their service on credit, so they must also be good at collections. As a rule, they're not.

Retailers and service providers who hope to enjoy their life in business should like interactions with the public. They should have a strong desire and need to be of help to perfect strangers. Individuals who make their customers feel that they're really on their side and desirous of sending them home with exactly what they need will have great success and happiness as a retailer or service provider.

Those who depend on traffic for a living must also expect to deal with days or weeks when there is little or none. If you're the type of person who goes stir-crazy if you don't have a clear-cut task always awaiting, you may wish to avoid retail and service-type enterprises. The best personality for this type of business is the go-getter who can effectively use dead time to come up with ways to create traffic on future days.

The building trades. It might seem logical to call a home builder a manufacturer, an architect a service provider, and a building-materials supplier a retailer. It would, but it isn't a tidy fit. This is a completely different world. Very few folks just decide one day that they'd like to become a contractor. This industry requires you to come up through the ranks. It is one of the few places where you'll find the guild system still in effect, with future owners doing their apprenticeship out on the construction site.

If ever there was a type of work that needed owners who love their job, this is it. You either fit in at the construction site or you don't. It isn't absolutely necessary that your hands are rough and calloused and that you have a perpetual tan, but it doesn't hurt.

When you're in this business, you don't get the contract because you have the best salesman. Sometimes you don't even win a contract on the strength of your reputation for good work. Most of the building industry uses a bid system, wherein the lowest bid wins. The balance of your success or failure may rest on whether you're a member of the "good ole boys' club."

Multilevel marketing. Here we have the army of individuals who fill the ranks of independent sales workers for such organizations as Amway, Avon, Fuller Brush, Shaklee, Mary Kay, and Tupperware. Most of these businesses are run on a part-time basis and are highly structured activities where the supplier of the merchandise provides a complete set of materials, samples, and training.

To run this type of enterprise you generally don't need a formal organizational form (such as a corporation), a special business location, or fixtures. There's also generally very little, if any, financial outlay for product. Since the risk is very low, the reward opportunity is fairly low as well. Only a superstar will make more than ten or fifteen dollars per hour for her actual sales effort.

The real money in most of these organizations is the establishment of a "downline" (other independent salespeople recruited by you whose sales result in an override or commission to you). This is called multilevel marketing. There are any number of persons who've started a multilevel business on a part-time basis while holding down another job or working as a stay-at-home parent. Some of the most successful have turned investments of under one hundred dollars into millions, with thousands of people working under them in their downline.

There exists a broad range of individuals who can find success in the multilevel marketing world. It offers an opportunity to those who would be pleased to pick up an extra couple of hundred dollars per month by selling products to friends and family. This type of enterprise may also offer the perfect challenge to the hard-driving individual who is not afraid to stop perfect strangers anywhere to convince them that they can get rich selling that product line.

If you're the second type you'd need to be prepared for the following: (1) Recruiting and motivating individuals who're not professionally trained and may not care about earning more than a little spare change; (2) preparing and running sales meetings heavy on enthusiasm and motivation (in other words, you'll do best in this area if you like to lead the singing at church or have an enthusiastic attitude that you can share from the podium); and (3) doing most of your work on evenings and weekends, because that's when your part-timers are most likely to be available to attend meetings and workshops.

In the area of multilevel marketing be careful to ensure that you're joining a legitimate organization. Based on current law as this book is being written, the primary difference between a responsible multilevel marketing group and one that is not is as follows: The responsible organization is in the business of selling product. The illegitimate group is in the business of selling distribution agreements.

You can generally determine which is the case by looking at two aspects of the contract: (1) If the cost of joining the organization is high or requires a very large outlay for samples, supplies, or fixtures, you may want to look more closely at this company. (2) If you're able to buy into a high distribution level, rather than starting as a salesperson and moving up in the organization by recruiting others to sell, you should investigate very carefully before going further.

Franchises. A business form still very popular today is the franchise. A franchise is an exclusive territory purchased by a prospective businessman from a company that has established a successful model business. The company (called the franchisor) proceeds to duplicate that model by using independent owners (the franchisees) rather than owning their own locations.

Franchising is used for a wide variety of business types, but is probably best exemplified by fast-food stores, real estate offices, convenience stores, print services, and greeting card outlets.

The benefit of franchising is that you're given a blueprint of exactly how to proceed with the business. A quality franchisor provides help in site location, store layout and design, planning a grand opening, co-op advertising, management classes, and bookkeeping aid. This gives the franchisee a leg up on success, since many of the pitfalls have already been discovered in the test locations. The new franchisee doesn't have to lose precious time, money, and energy plodding through those same problems. *As a result, the success rate for franchise purchasers is dramatically higher than for start-ups using any other approaches.*

Unless you're dealing with a McDonald's or other well-known

franchisors, there *are* a number of potential problems that come with using this approach. Many successful businesses believe that they can easily duplicate themselves across the country by starting a chain of franchises. What they don't realize is that franchising is like any other enterprise. It has its own unique skill and temperament requirements. Just because a person has put together a fantastically successful ice cream store doesn't mean she'll automatically have the ability to establish a successful national chain.

Even with the noblest of intentions, it's all too common for the franchisor to fail to train the management of the new locations properly, not perform as promised on advertising, and even fall short of producing enough product for its member stores. Unfortunately, too, there are more than a few franchisors who've recruited folks to open locations where the entire deal was a fraud from the outset. In other words, you should use the same amount of care in approaching franchising as you would with any major purchase . . . and then some.

Many studies have been done on franchising because there is a great deal of money to be made by everyone concerned. One of the most interesting conclusions to result from these studies concerns the type of person who is likely to be most successful with a franchise. It has been determined that individuals who have backgrounds working in big corporations have the best chance. This is because they're used to working within a framework dictated by some impersonal third party. They're also good at following directions to the letter without questioning.

On the other hand, the person who has worked in a small office or plant, or who had a business of his own in the past, does not do as well. These individuals are too independent. They want to do things *their* way and are offended by having to take orders from those above. This is especially true if the orders don't square with how the franchise owner sees things.

Another major issue with regard to franchising is the cost. First, the cost of purchasing a territory can be very high indeed—

$10,000, $20,000, or even more just for the right to open a store under the franchisor's name. Next, the start-up costs will usually be higher than would be the case for an independent store. This is because the franchisee must follow all the requirements of the contract. A quality franchisor will have set very high standards to ensure a high success rate. Finally, the business must pay an ongoing fee to the franchisor. This fee pays for the continuing privilege of using the name, management training, and joint advertising and PR. This monthly amount might be anywhere from 5 percent to 15 percent of sales, depending on the services rendered.

For the person with the right personality, plenty of start-up capital, and a cautious approach to learning about the franchisor, this entrepreneurial experience can be very satisfying, personally and financially.

CHAPTER

7

Buying a Business

MANY WHO DECIDE TO GIVE UP a steady paycheck for a dream pursue that dream by purchasing somebody else's used one. It's possible that they may be buying a nightmare. Even if the current owners tell you the truth, the whole truth, and nothing but the truth, you may still find yourself in all kinds of traps that neither you nor the old owners ever imagined.

Key employees might leave. Important customers may have been buying from the company because of the personality of the owner rather than the quality and service. Once you take over, these customers may decide to shop around. Equipment that has functioned perfectly for decades may wheeze to a stop the second day you own it. These are but a few of the problems you may face even if you do a fair bit of research and your seller is perfectly honest.

But should you fail to investigate the business from top to bottom, or should the seller be adept at keeping key information out of your hands (for example, a major new competitor is about to begin producing product), you may be finished before you start.

Finally, there is a sleeper issue that has recently surfaced in some new research. The failure rate for newly purchased businesses is almost exactly the same as the failure rate for startups. The reason for this should be obvious. There is very little difference between the two types of businesses from the stand-point of the new owner's ability to succeed. She either will or will not have the necessary skills; be willing to put in the needed money, time, and effort; and/or be blessed with good luck. These three elements have more to do with whether a new business suc-ceeds than the rightness of the idea or the length of time the idea has been tried.

The kind of person best suited to taking over a going concern would be one who likes to buy fixer-upper anythings: cars, houses, furniture, whatever. When someone has decided to sell their busi-ness, there's a reason. That reason probably has something to do with the current owner's age, health, or interest level. It may also have to do with the prevailing business climate for the company's products or services. The buyer's job is to hit the ground running so that he can hold on to as much as possible of what the former owner did right. Then the owner must quickly evaluate how it may be possible to fix the things that are broken.

It's also critical that the purchaser be a good listener, and be willing to be very open to the advice of the departing owner. Good ongoing communication between the old and new owner is one of the most important ingredients for success in a takeover. In this respect following the lead of the old management is not unlike entering a franchise situation. If the new management wants to travel their own road from the start, or fails to use the experience of the old team to help them around the potholes, they'll have to endure the same learning curves experienced when building a company from scratch.

The financial aspects of purchasing an existing enterprise can have great advantages over the start-up. It's often possible to buy out the old owner for less than it would cost to open a new opera-tion. Often you'll be able to get the business for the cost of inven-tory or less.

In addition, the seller may be willing to "take back paper." This means that he may be willing to let you pay some or all of the purchase price over time. He may do this to facilitate the sale or to take advantage of tax breaks.

If you're patient, you can find a real deal. There is no end to the examples of people who've taken over excellent businesses for no money down and little or nothing later. They were able to get such a deal, for instance, just because the retiring owner liked them and felt they would be good to the customers and employees. So spend some time in the search phase of this approach and you could win big.

CHAPTER

8

The Partner Issue

SHOULD YOU OR SHOULDN'T YOU take a partner? Do you want or need the help in skills, management, or money? Is there enough potential income to make two, three, or more of you independently wealthy? Are you ready to deal with this type of relationship?

The question of partners is probably more personal than any other. Taking on a partner in business is not very different from taking a partner in marriage. In fact, you'll probably spend more hours per week with your office "spouse" than with your marriage partner. You'll certainly communicate more. You're likely to fight more. Plus, if things don't work out, the decision to end a partnership may be more difficult and more emotionally trying than ending a marriage.

With that said, involving a partner can make great sense in business. Everyone needs someone to motivate them and to hear their ideas and honestly evaluate them. Brainstorming is twice as productive when you have two brains, and both have a commitment. How comforting it is to feel there will be someone to pick up the slack if you're sick or just in a slump. These roles can be nicely performed by the right partner.

In addition, a good partner can bring needed management skills with him. He may also have contacts, customers, or product lines that he can deliver to the new company. Clearly, the partner adds productivity. Each partner should be able to produce as much as you do.

In general there are some economies of scale. The rent, phone, and electricity will not double for two partners over what they would be for each one if they were operating independently. Two (or even three) partners may be able to share a secretary, book-keeper, and other staff workers that would not be affordable for a sole owner.

What kind of person is suited to be a partner? All owners, but especially those who decide to have a partner or partners, should have the kind of personality not easily intimidated by the talents of others. Said another way, you should seek a partner who is as good as or better than you. *You must be willing to accept that this person is as good as or better than you!*

The second skill you'll need is the ability to trust. Notice again the similarity to marriage. You can't be looking over your partner's shoulder all the time. To the extent that your partner picks up on any mistrust on your part, it will influence her to begin to hide things. She may also return the mistrust in kind. Lack of trust and faith in the other partner is a sure path to disunity and the eventual demise of the partnership.

Moreover, one of you must be willing to give ground. It's even better if both partners possess this ability. At the same time, there can be only one head of any body, one ultimate authority. You have a better chance of winning the lottery than of running a successful business in which two or more partners have identical authority. This is not to suggest that there can't be a pure sharing of *power* fifty-fifty. It only means that each partner must have areas of authority where, when there is a dispute, one partner has the final say. The situation may be likened to the biblical approach to marriage where the two partners are completely equal, but the man is the head of the house. A critical element to remember about both the business and marriage partnership is that the decision maker has the responsibility to make that decision in light of the other partner's needs.

Finally, in a partnership situation you must look for a balance of skills and thinking. There is far greater potential when partners bring varied skills and ideas to the table. If the owners are too much alike, it's possible to end up with redundancy that reduces the potential for productivity gains. Take, for example, a situation in which both partners in a law practice specialize in personal injury, both prefer to represent plaintiffs, and neither is particularly excited about management. It's clear that they haven't increased their potential client base through their association. Nor have they gained a critical skill—management—necessary to run a successful practice.

In the above example, it would make better sense to seek out a partner who has an interest in the management side of the business. A partner who was either a defendants' specialist in the same field of personal injury, or who specialized in a different, though related, area would also be a good choice.

Part 1
The Spouse as Partner

It can and does work! Possibly you even know a couple who've had a wonderful forty years of marriage and also built a nice business together. But the pitfalls are numerous.

On the negative side, the couple will end up spending most of their waking hours together. The romantic says, "How can this be negative?" Reality tells us, though, that no matter how much two people like each other, there is a limit to how much time they can be together without driving each other nuts.

Dr. Joyce Brothers has said that it will help even the strongest relationship if each spouse takes a full day off from the other every fourth day.

Strain is put on a married couple in a partnership situation simply because there are more reasons for conflict. It's one thing if you can limit your disagreements to how to spend the household budget or how to raise the kids. It's quite another if you must reach consensus on whether to expand into new markets or whether to fire Jennifer.

The positive side of the equation clearly outweighs the negative for the right couple. Involvement of both spouses gives each a complete view of the decision-making process, the ups and downs, and the pressures on the other spouse. There will be less question of who's making a contribution and fewer opportunities for distrust, especially since the opportunity for untrustworthy behavior is limited.

Another big benefit is that a couple who share common goals have a significantly better chance of success in marriage. Starting a business is often equated with having a baby. The struggle of bringing a child to adulthood is bound to bring the parents closer together—so, too, with a business.

Who should try this approach? First, both spouses must genuinely love and respect each other. Second, there must be a clear line of command at home, and an even clearer understanding of that line of command in the proposed new business. Like the partnership situation discussed above, equality of *power* is understood, but *authority* must be allocated.

Both partners must be able to make a real contribution. There can be big problems if one spouse feels that the contributions are unequal. That is not to say that they can't have greatly unequal skills or talents. However, each must feel that his or her skill or talent is truly needed by the firm, and that both partners are giving a full effort. Surely this is true for partners who are not married. It's at least as critical, if not more so, for husband and wife.

Part 2
Other Family Members
in the Business

The general rule: As much as possible, family members must be treated as well as, but not better than, other employees with the same position. This is for the family member/employee's benefit as well as for the benefit of the other employees. Favoritism has a way of cutting both ways; the morale of the other employees will be greatly affected, and those who are favored will be on the defensive about their privileged status.

Whether the family member is a cousin or dear old Dad, he'll be a better and happier employee and you'll be a much happier employer if the ground rules are clearly established in the beginning and firmly enforced during the term of employment.

These general rules change very little if the family member is also a minority owner (has a smaller percentage of ownership than the largest shareholder, or partner). If you're to be the boss, you must be *the boss*. In you rests all authority, even that which has been delegated. Related partners may feel that, because they have an investment and they are working in the business, they have special authority. If you agree to those strings in the beginning, so be it. (You'll regret it later, but then money does have its price.) You and your family member partner will be better off, though, if you both agree that during the business day he will be treated like anyone else—no better . . . and *no worse*.

Which brings us to another issue. Some family members are treated much worse than others in the business. A father may be trying to toughen up his son. A daughter may use the opportunity to give her mother as good as she got. A brother may continue a pattern of bullying that was present in the parents' home. These kinds of activities will be even more negative than the bestowing of privilege. They will create a great deal of tension that will pervade all the activities of an otherwise well-run company.

So, if you're going to bring your spouse or other relatives into the business as an employee or partner, do your best to leave the family relationship at the door. Conduct your office relationship in a businesslike manner.

CHAPTER
9

Part-Time Possibilities

I FEEL AS IF I COULD WRITE an entire book on the part-time enterprise. There are millions of folks out there in the business arena making or losing a little money "on the side." Very few of these efforts are serious, and thus they are doomed to be no more than generators of loose change. The few people who are truly serious will suffer greatly from failure to give their undivided attention just at the time when the business needs it most.

Here we'll deal only with the situation in which an individual starts a business on a part-time basis with every intention of going full-time just as soon as there is enough business to justify leaving the old, paying job. While it's possible to start an enterprise this way (it's done all the time), this is by far the most difficult and risky method. It will be all-consuming of your time and energy, even beyond that of the full-time start-up, but it can work.

If you're thinking of taking this approach, ask yourself, "Is this really necessary? Could I work at my job a few more months and put aside enough money to start up full-time? If I wait, and then devote one hundred percent of my personal resources to going out and getting clients, could I build the business fast enough to cover my overhead?"

If you honestly evaluate these questions and still feel driven to start up part-time, you may want to consider the following types of businesses that lend themselves to that approach.

Some retail. Retail operations where personal service is not that important may allow you to hire unsupervised individuals to take care of the shop while you're at work. Ice cream parlors, card and gift shops, self-service gas stations, convenience stores, and others fall into this category. Certainly, you must have trustworthy help or incredible accounting systems to ensure that you are the sole beneficiary of each day's take.

Personal service businesses. Managing an answering service, bookkeeping, consulting, selling real estate, and leading seminars or self-improvement classes can all be pursued in available time. This is not to say these enterprises wouldn't be better off with your undivided effort, only that they are better suited to a part-time launch than a barbershop or a real estate brokerage. Note how a real estate agency (listing and selling homes) is fine for part-time, whereas a brokerage (which employs agents, advertises listings, and so forth) is not.

Craft manufacturing. Tens of thousands of people create art or craft items that they sell to friends or at swap meets, art fairs, or on eBay. It's not such a big jump from earning a steady extra income through such a pursuit to offering your bestsellers to retailers, wholesalers, mail order catalogues, or even major mass marketers.

Multilevel marketing. The pitch you'll hear from such multilevel marketers as Shaklee or Amway is that you can start part-time and work up to full-time. The fact is, it probably wouldn't pay to work at one of these enterprises full-time at first. You should, however, be willing to work just as hard at this as you would at a business in which you'd invested tens of thousands of your hard-earned, after-tax dollars. If you don't, you're not going to make more than pin money.

Franchises. Many franchises are designed to be managed by absentee owners. If you decide to open a franchise while still working your old job, make certain you have an understanding employer who'll let you take a few hours off here and there to handle emergencies. If you plop down fifty or sixty thousand dollars for a franchise, you're not going to want to feel awkward having to leave your "day job" to tend shop when your key manager has an auto accident.

10

Goal Setting and Success

THERE IS A RULE OF THUMB that those who write and speak about motivation, sales, and goal setting have all come to follow. They are not based on any study or science, but are borne out by years of experience.

1. Only about 10 percent of highly motivated individuals who see themselves as on the fast track to success have a clear idea of what kind of financial future they want. In other words, they know they want to be successful, but have only a vague idea of what that means to them.

2. Only a third of those have the guts to write it down. Somehow, this group knows intuitively that writing it down gives it a higher degree of meaning, including a greater degree of commitment as well.

3. Those who write down their goals are always at the top in earnings and accomplishments. They have clear ideas of what they want and are much more successful than those who go with the flow, but do not achieve at the same level as those who commit goals to writing.

Part 1
A Personal Evaluation Project

If writing down clear goals and objectives is so important to future results, why don't those who desire to maximize their futures do so? Some don't know how to. Some are afraid to. Some just never slow down long enough to take the time. What follows is a comprehensive approach to self-evaluation and goal setting. If you take the time to carefully go through this process, you'll set yourself up for major success in anything you do.

What you're going to engage in here is a "personal inventory." It's not a test. There are no trick questions or trick answers. But it may be the most difficult assignment you've ever undertaken. In order to get useful results, it will be necessary for you to take a look deep into your own heart, soul, mind, and spirit.

It's imperative that you find a totally quiet place where you'll have no interruptions for at least two hours. I know this is hard in many homes, but if necessary, rent a hotel room, or find a secluded spot in the park.

HOW I SEE MYSELF

Take out a spiral notebook or other writing pad that you can keep forever. Open to page 1 and write at the top of the page: HOW I SEE MYSELF. Now create two columns. On the left write POSITIVE. On the right, NEGATIVE. Under POSITIVE you should write a list of at least twenty positive things that you believe about yourself. Under NEGATIVE you should put the negative that seems to be the natural result of each positive item. The list might look like this:

HOW I SEE MYSELF: PART I

Positive	Negative
I am a happy person.	I can't relate to unhappy people.
I am an optimist.	I am not always realistic.
I have an even temperament.	I never experience big highs or big lows.
I have a good sense of humor.	I use it to gloss over serious issues.
I am creative.	I am absentminded.
I am hardworking.	I don't tolerate those who aren't.
I like to lead.	I like to control others and the turn of events.
I feel self-confident.	I can be cocky.
I make an excellent first impression.	It commonly doesn't last.
I love my work.	The parts I don't love I put off.
I love God.	I feel frustrated about not being spiritual enough.
I like to develop things that have potential.	I like to control people and events.

Now it's time to reverse the process. Begin first with the big negatives in your life. Write down at least ten. As you did above, now write the positives that might flow from these negatives. This second list might look like this:

HOW I SEE MYSELF: PART 2

Negative	Positive
I don't feel attractive.	I have done well with the opposite sex anyway.
I am opinionated.	My opinion is often sought.
I am very absentminded.	People look after me.
I am too competitive in noncompetitive arenas (discussion with spouse, etc.).	This is the same competitiveness that helps me in sports and business.
I haven't many good friends.	It is largely due to my attention to my family.
I dominate conversations.	I am an interesting speaker.
I am superficial in most relationships.	I am capable of giving some attention to many friends and associates.

I truly hope that you're now sitting in that secluded place with two hours to spare and your pen and notebook ready. If not, please don't go on. This is the time to put a place marker in the book and close it until you are in a position to do the above exercise.

It's human nature—and I am just as guilty as anyone—to look at the exercise just outlined and think such thoughts as: "I don't need to do that," or "I'll read on a little further and come back to this later," or "I wonder what he's driving at. I'll read on and check out the analysis first. Then I can decide whether I should take this test."

This is not a test. It is a very personal inventory of your feelings about your strengths and weaknesses. There is no grade and no cute list of what kind of person you are based on your answers. But if you'll go back and follow the directions to a T, you'll have your eyes opened up about who you really are. *Please! Stop reading now! Go back and do the exercise!*

* * *

With what I hope is not unfounded optimism, I'm assuming that at least 3 percent of you actually followed the most important piece of advice in this book and took a personal inventory. I use the 3 percent figure on purpose. The 3 percent who took the inventory are the same 3 percent who'll work through the rest of the exercises that follow. They're the very same 3 percent who'll eventually write down their goals. Yep! They're the 3 percent who'll do many, many times better than those who didn't have the courage to go through the self-analysis.

Now that you've completed the personal inventory, go back and take a look at all the negatives in both Part 1 and Part 2. Put a big 1 next to the negative that bothers you the most. Repeat this procedure for 2 and 3. Now put a line through those negative aspects that aren't that significant, or that you know you'll never consider changing. For the few that are left, decide whether they should have a #4 and so on, or if you should put a line through them.

Your chart should now look something like this:

HOW I SEE MYSELF: PART I

Positive		Negative
I am a happy person.		~~I can't relate to unhappy people.~~
I am an optimist.		~~I am not always realistic.~~
I have an even temperament.	3	I never experience big highs or big lows.
I have a good sense of humor.		~~I use it to gloss over serious issues.~~
I am creative.		~~I am absentminded.~~
I am hardworking.		~~I don't tolerate those who aren't.~~
I like to lead.		~~I like to control others and the turn of events.~~
I feel self-confident.	4	I can be cocky.

I make an excellent first impression.		It commonly doesn't last.
I love my work.	2	The parts I don't love I put off.
I love God.	5	I feel frustrated about not being spiritual enough.
I like to develop things that have potential.		I like to control people and events.

HOW I SEE MYSELF: PART 2

Negative		Positive
I don't feel attractive.		I have done well with the opposite sex anyway.
I am opinionated.		My opinion is often sought.
I am very absentminded.		People look after me.
I am too competitive in noncompetitive arenas (discussion with spouse, etc.).	6	This is the same competitiveness that helps me in sports and business.
I haven't many good friends.	7	It is largely due to my attention to my family.
I dominate conversations.	1	I am an interesting speaker.
I am superficial in most relationships.		I am capable of giving some attention to many friends and associates.

What you've done above is to completely define yourself in your own eyes. If you've really thought about this in depth, your positives and negatives probably don't look anything like the above. Your list is probably longer, and maybe you've made some side notes.

You've also given yourself a blueprint for personal improvement. You've indicated those parts of your life that you'd really like to improve—parts about which you *care* enough to improve. The first rule of changing something about ourselves is that we have to want to make the change. Often, though, that list of negatives rolling around in our psyche is so ill-defined and so long that we don't want to think about changing any of it. What you've done here is sharpened the clarity of your list and shortened its length. You've made it manageable. Now it will be easier to make improvement.

You've accomplished something else as well. By defining your negative attributes and then checking off those items that you don't care enough to change, you've greatly reduced your stress level. You've given these items up. You no longer have to carry them around with you.

On the positive side, you've admitted to yourself that you do have some wonderful characteristics. There are things about you that make you lovable, capable, and worthwhile. Now that you have a clear understanding of what your best features are, you can better direct the planning of your future. You can focus on the kinds of opportunities that will take advantage of those things you do best.

The next set of exercises is a bit easier than the last, but in some ways digs even deeper into the hidden parts of your being. If you've followed the instructions with regard to the above and have received the benefit that most do from taking the time and effort, you'll find that the same diligence applied to the following will yield similar benefits.

Once again, it's critical that you find two hours or so of quiet, uninterrupted solitude. You'll need your spiral notepad, pencil, and the same willingness to be open and honest with yourself. With these next exercises you'll feel intense internal pressure to put down what society tells you you should. Resist this with everything you possess. Put down your real feelings. You have nothing to lose and everything to gain.

As with the last exercise, please stop reading at this point until you are able to set aside the time to do it right.

THE LOTTERY

You come home from work and settle in to watch the evening news. You absently pick up your lottery tickets to see if you have any matches in this week's game. As the newscaster reads off the numbers you notice that you have two matches . . . then three, four, five, six, and even the bonus. You can't believe your ears or your eyes, but as the anchorman repeats the numbers each and every one comes up the same as on your ticket. With equal parts of disbelief and excitement you realize that you've just won three million dollars. After confirming the numbers with your spouse during the seven o'clock news, you begin to believe that it's possible.

After considerable shouting, dancing, and kissing, not to mention a few phone calls, you sit down to consider how you will spend this incredible surprise. That is the exercise that follows. However, unlike the real lottery, you've just been handed three million dollars in cash, tax free. Write down the top ten things you would do with the money. (You don't have to stop with ten, but write down at least ten. Begin now. Don't read on.)

Wasn't that fun? Almost as fun as actually getting to spend it. Okay, not quite. Next, go back and put numbers next to each item in order of priority. In other words, 1 would be the item you'd want if you only had enough money to purchase one thing. Your ranking should have nothing to do with how much each entry costs. You have enough to purchase one thing. Make that 1. Now you have enough to purchase two things. Put a 2 next to the additional item you'd buy if there were enough funds for two. Continue this process up to at least ten.

Again, if you were thoughtful and honest about your selections, you probably have some new insights into who you really are. Let's go on to exercise four.

THE GENIE

You are out for a stroll along a totally secluded beach on the north shore of Oahu, Hawaii. You look down and notice a piece of brightly colored metal protruding through the sand. As you uncover it, you notice it is some kind of ancient lamp. As you brush the sand away, a genie appears from nowhere in a puff of smoke. (Feel like you've heard this story somewhere before?) The genie tells you that he is very grateful to you for releasing him from the lamp, and as a show of gratitude he will grant you three wishes. But you trick him; on the third wish, you ask for eight more wishes. He is outraged, but has no choice but to comply.

Part of the bargain is that you have to tell the genie all ten wishes right now. Take up your pencil and paper and write down those ten wishes. If it isn't obvious to you already, these will probably be different from the lottery as they are not restricted to things you can buy. Do not read on until you have written down these ten wishes. If you wish to list more, you may.

If you haven't begun to have some new insights into your heart, soul, and mind by this time, you're either being dishonest with yourself or you're dead from the neck up. (There is one more possibility. You may have already been part of the 3 percent who know all this about themselves already.)

As with the lottery exercise, go back now and put numbers next to each entry in the order of their importance to you, without regard to their likelihood, cost, or any other criterion. Simply ask yourself which of these things would you most appreciate, which second, and so on.

Having done that, you should have just enough time left in your two hours to complete the following exercise.

THE ENCYCLOPEDIA

It is the year 2100. You're having a quick game of Super Mario Brothers 584 on your three-dimensional video game set. You're doing this in heaven. You have long since passed away.

Saint Peter comes over to you and interrupts your play. He wants to send you on an important assignment down on earth. You agree and are instantaneously transformed into a librarian in Springfield, Illinois. You have plenty of free time on your hands as you begin your assignment. You decide it would be interesting to look yourself up in the encyclopedia, and see what history has to say about you.

Beginning now, fill at least a full sheet of paper with what you'd want to find in the write-up of your life in the encyclopedia many years after your demise. Think it through carefully. What would the article say about your career? Your family? Your contributions? Your admirers and detractors? Remember, this doesn't have to have anything at all to do with the life you're leading now. You're to write down what you'd *like* to find written about you.

As with the previous assignments, finish the exercise before continuing to read.

Wow! Are you getting excited yet? Is it time to take a serious look at how you have been conducting your life? Your two hours are undoubtedly up by now. If you have the time, you may wish to continue on into this next section. If you're out of time, you'll need to schedule a third two-hour slot for the final set of exercises.

If you're married, you may wish to have your spouse complete these same exercises. For you to have the best chance at creating a new beginning for yourself, you need to have your spouse along for the ride. Sure, there's a risk. When both of you are totally honest about these things, you may find out that you have many different desires and that your priorities don't match very well.

It's better that you both become aware of these differences, rather than keep these feelings to yourselves. How many partners are doing their best to attempt to make their spouses happy, when they're simply guessing as to what would truly make them so?

Once you each have an opportunity to discuss the hopes and dreams of the other, each of you can begin to share and take a bit of equity in the goals of the other. Once a person has some ownership, it is amazing how they begin to help rather than hinder their loved one in reaching the goal.

At this point you need to be relaxed and alone. You should have with you your notebook and pencil, and be ready to be open and honest with yourself this one last time. If you're ready, read on.

Part 2
Setting Goals

Quickly reread what you've written under How I See Myself, The Lottery, The Genie, and The Encyclopedia.

Now put at the top of the page MY PERSONAL GOALS. Write down as many as you want, but make them realistic and make sure you're willing to sacrifice to attain them.

They can be big things like becoming president of General Motors, or small things like losing ten pounds. They can be about any part of your life. They can be trips you want to take, children you want to have, or even the kinds of things you want for your kids or your spouse. You can list personality changes you wish to make or athletic achievements you want to pursue.

There is no time frame on these goals. Write them down even if you may not begin to attempt them for ten or twenty years. The longer-term goals are the more important ones.

Try to write fast and free. Don't be afraid to write down something you're not sure will stay on the list. You may want to try to put down twenty-five, fifty, or even one hundred items. There will be plenty of time later for revisiting this list and setting priorities.

Now is the time to stop reading and write. Please don't read ahead until you have written down every goal you can think of.

You're now a part of that elite 10 percent that has given a great deal of thought to what it wants out of life. You fit into an in-between group that has written down its goals. You're poised to be ten times more successful that those who have done neither. There are but three easy steps to take to join the very top 3 percent who have a clear set of written goals.

Part 3
Prioritize, Organize, and
Internalize

First, prioritize. Go back over the list and put a 1 next to the item that is the most important to you, a 2 next to the second most important, and so on. As you're doing this, eliminate those items that you know you'll never attempt, or for which the reward just wouldn't be worth the effort.

Now organize. Create at least two lists: one for your career, and one for your home life. You may wish a third for your community aspirations. List your goals in priority order under each heading, and leave about ten lines after each goal. Finally, create a brief outline under each goal showing what you'll have to do to accomplish the goal. For a final touch, put a date after each of the items, indicating the deadline you've set for the completion of each goal. Your page should now look something like this.

My Personal Goals

1. I want to be in a position to work or not work and not be concerned about the financial aspect of that decision by the time I'm fifty.

   A. I'll need to have $2 million in liquid net worth.

   B. I'll need to prepare myself for a life where work is not my life.

   C. I'll need to find a method for achieving the financial part in the twenty years I have left.

   D. I believe I can raise half of the $2 million through sound conservative investment of 10 percent of my income each year.

   E. I believe I can raise the other half through the sale of an enterprise that I plan to open by the summer of next year.

2. I want to live in Hawaii on the island of Maui three months of every year, starting five years from now.

   A. My business will have to be able to get along without my presence; I'll have to be able to conduct business from there.

   B. I'll have to have the wholehearted support of my family and my business associates.

   C. I'll need to buy a condo or home within three years and arrange to rent it out the balance of the time I'm not occupying it.

3. I want all of my kids to reach adulthood without having tested drugs, become sexually active, and with their religious beliefs intact. I also desire that they all attend college.

   A. I must have my spouse's and kids' agreement in these goals.

   B. They should be written down by the kids as personal goals.

   C. I'll keep the kids in private schools where I can maximize my knowledge of—and input into—their schooling.

4. I want to lose fifty pounds in the next five months and keep it off.
   A. I'll have to select a weight-loss system within two weeks.
   B. I'll need to budget for the cost of that system.
   C. I'll have to ask for the cooperation of my spouse and family.
   D. I'll need to discipline myself to do an hour per day of exercise.

Business Goals

1. I want to build a business that will provide me with great personal satisfaction, $150,000-per-year income, and a salable asset worth $1 million in cash by the time I'm fifty.
   A. I must first decide exactly what business I wish to pursue.
   B. Then I must raise the necessary capital to open the doors.
   C. I must prepare myself with the skills to enter that business.
   D. I must work with my family to assure that everyone appreciates and agrees with my entrepreneurial choice. They must understand the potential sacrifices and how each of them will be affected.
2. I want to raise a minimum of $50,000 before I open the doors. If the venture that I choose requires more than that, I'll find a partner.
   A. I need to save $1,500 per month to reach that goal.
   B. I need to draw up a list of potential partners.
3. I want to have an impact on the industry that I choose. I'm not interested in merely providing a standard product or service. I want to do something new and different.
   A. I'll have to invest in knowledge of that industry in order to discern what is new and exciting, and what is not.
   B. I'll have to have the guts to go with my intuition.
   C. I'll have to pick an industry where my abilities will allow me to have an impact.

4. I want to learn all I can about selling and computers before I open.

    A. I need to sign up for a computer class.

    B. I need to purchase a computer.

    C. I need to see if my current employer could use my potential computer skills.

    D. I need to purchase several books and tapes on selling.

If you've completed this section and feel good about what you've done, you have only one last step to take. You need to internalize your decision. You need to make it your own. You have to believe you can do it and dial in the desire to make it happen. How do you do that?

VISUALIZE

This time you need to find a quiet spot for only thirty minutes to an hour. Once you've done so, continue to read.

Lie down or get as comfortable as you can while sitting. Read over all of your material with special emphasis on your goals. Now, close your eyes and imagine the result of having achieved those goals. Think about every detail. What does it feel like to drive up to your own company in the morning and greet the employees who are supporting their families because of the jobs you're providing?

What does it feel like to produce products that you later see in the marketplace? Imagine, in detail, the excitement of landing your first really big contract or having to pay taxes on your first profitable year.

Take an imaginary walk on the sand in front of your home in Maui. Drink in the tropical breezes. Feel the warm surf on your bare feet.

It's a good idea to repeat this process very frequently. Your author finds himself indulging in this daydreaming (a sport for which I was roundly criticized as a child) just before falling asleep. I will think about even the most minute details of the steps in my overall goal and the excitement of reaching the summit.

Okay. Lie back and daydream. As usual, it's totally against the rules to read on until you've completed this exercise.

My heartiest congratulations to those of you who've completed each and every step. You still have a lot of work ahead of you. You'll have to show more discipline than you've ever shown before. But you're now positioned to be *one hundred times* more successful than the average member of your peer group.

A FEW MORE THOUGHTS ON GOALS

1. They don't have to be grandiose to be meaningful. They need only be important to you.
2. That you set a goal and fail to achieve it should in no way be seen as a failure. Setting a goal and not trying to achieve it . . . that can be considered failure.
3. Goals are not set in concrete. There's nothing wrong with changing them as frequently as your situation changes. However, each change should be thoroughly considered.
4. Publicize your goal. Tell your soulmates: your spouse, your best friend, and your partner. Some may be critical or jealous or skeptical. Your job is to use every comment made by these well-meaning associates to hone your goal. Even the least objective statements may have a kernel of substance that might help you to consider strategy changes.
5. Don't let naysayers get in your way, though. There are two main reasons you're telling them your plans. One was covered in point 4. The other is that you'll be more motivated

to complete what you've started once you've told the world what you plan to do. Therefore, unless someone points out a fact that you truly hadn't considered before, let the negative folks have their say, and then move on.

6. Make certain that you don't allow the goal to own you. You must own the goal. There are many things in this world that are well worth doing or having, but none of them is worth giving up your soul. You must be in control of your destiny. If you allow money, fame, or success in reaching your goals to take over your life, you'll end up being one miserable individual. Keep each part of your life in perspective, and you can find real happiness.

Opening the Doors

1

Finalizing Goals

IF YOU'VE READ THROUGH SECTION 1, you understand the importance of goal setting. At this point you have probably set at least one goal: you intend to open a very small business that you expect will stay small. And you've probably selected the kind of business you intend to enter.

If you haven't yet made those two determinations, the following material will have very little meaning to you. If you're still undecided as to the type of enterprise, there's only one way to decide; and that's to research those that hold interest and make a decision. In going through the following exercises, you may change your mind about decisions you've already made. However, it's very unlikely that anything you read in this section will help to direct you to a first decision about enterprise type. You may wish to return to section 1 for some broad ideas of some available options.

Part 1
Establishing the Basic
Blueprint

It's necessary at this point to fix on the details that will allow you to accomplish your goal. The questions below will help you create a solid business plan.

1. What kind of business have you decided to enter? Be as specific as possible. For instance: "I intend to open a dog and cat hospital," as opposed to "I want to be a veterinarian." Another example: "I've decided to be a wholesaler of contemporary art prints," rather than "I'm going into the art business."

2. By what date do you intend to open? Give an exact date. __/__/__

3. What are your primary motivations for starting this business? Some possibilities follow, but it's very important that you reach deep inside and find your own reasons. You'll very likely have more than one. Number these in order of importance.

- **A.** Financial independence
- **B.** Professional fulfillment
- **C.** Independent work environment
- **D.** Maximize personal potential
- **E.** Exercise total control
- **F.** Become famous
- **G.** Prove something
- **H.** Increase earnings
- **I.** Create wealth
- **J.** Be accepted
- **K.** Sell new idea
- **L.** Losing existing job
- **M.** Topped out in existing job
- **N.** Special opportunity
- **O.** Security

P. Location not possible if employed

Q. Pressure from _____

R. Take over family business

S. Buy out present employer

T. No choice (Why? _____)

4. How much money per year do you desire to earn from your new business? First year $_____ Second year $_____ Third year $_____ Fourth year $_____ Fifth year $_____

5. What net worth do you wish the business to reach? By the end of the Fifth year $___ Tenth year $___ Twentieth year $_____

6. By what other criteria will you judge the business to be successful? Again, here listed are some possibilities. Fill in your own.

A. Leader in the field

B. Dollar volume per year (list specific goals)

C. Number of customers, clients, patients, etc. (be specific)

D. Passing a going concern to my children

E. Being recognized as an important concern

7. As best as you can judge, which of the following elements are already in place and which will you have to obtain before you can open?

Element	In place	Not in place
A. Partners, if any	___	___
B. Finances	___	___
C. Education or training	___	___
D. Personnel	___	___
E. General location (city)	___	___
F. Family support	___	___

8. For each of the above that is "not in place," select a deadline for putting that element in place. This will ensure meeting your timetable for the opening date above.

You've now established a basic blueprint for action. Now it's time to make certain that you're not so wrapped up in your business goals that you've forgotten the rest of your life.

The following questions may remind you of some that you've seen before in section 1.

1. What are your top three personal goals for your lifetime?

2. Indicate the times by which you hope to achieve each of these goals. For instance:

    A. My most important goal is to reach financial independence for my family. I define this as having a liquid net worth not including my personal residence of $1 million. I hope to achieve this by my fortieth birthday.

    B. My second most important goal is to create a family environment that will result in my spouse and me enjoying a lifetime of marriage together, and my children reaching adulthood with a minimum of pain for them and us. This goal does not have a completion date as such, but the result should be fairly clear by the time my youngest is eighteen.

    C. My third most important goal is to provide a lasting contribution to my community. My plan at this time is to open a small group home for troubled youth. I'd hope to achieve this about the time my youngest leaves home.

3. Of course your goals look far different from these, but they give you a possible approach for constructing them. The next question becomes: Are any of your business goals in direct contradiction to your personal goals? If they're in perfect harmony, you're a very fortunate individual. If not, now is the time to resolve any differences.

One way to resolve them is to eliminate one or the other of the conflicting items. Many individuals who have the energy to consider the life of an entrepreneur also find that they have so many goals that there's a constant conflict. There just aren't enough hours in the day to create a great little business, give plenty of love and devotion to the family, be a pillar of the community, be active in three or four sports activities, and still find time to write a novel. Thus it may be necessary to give up one or more of these ideas.

Another method is to put off something that can wait. I've had the goal of taking a year off to travel and gather my thoughts. This is a dream that will have as much validity in ten years as it has today, but will be far more practical then than now.

You may merely wish to modify some of the conflicting plans. Becoming the best golfer at your club within five years could take huge amounts of time away from your business just when it needs you most. Moving the date of your goal to ten years may allow you to devote single-minded attention to your business for the first five years, after which you can begin your run at golf greatness.

Part 2
Three-Track Thinking

A final thought as you put the finishing touches on your life plan. There are many components that go into determining whether you can maintain your equilibrium while undertaking a challenge as great as business ownership. One of these I call "three-track thinking."

There are those who would advise you to set a single course and stick to it no matter what happens. That advice is appropriate for your marriage, but not for the very small business. You need to keep your options open and close at hand. For example: You've just decided to open a computer repair business specializing in Compaq PC's and compatibles. You have three years' experience with this type of work and believe that you can run the business out of your home. You've begun to accumulate the needed equipment and your current employer has announced plans to close up his operation and retire in three months.

It would be natural and normal for you to assume that you'll just take over his customer base, keep your overhead low, and enjoy good profits from day one. Unfortunately, one week before you open, your old boss loses half his wealth in an uninsured apartment fire, and he is forced to stay in business.

If you're a one-track thinker, your old boss's decision will cause you much despair. The pie will be cut in half at best. At worst, you may be unable to capture any of the business loyal to your ex-employer. In addition, you feel a certain loyalty to your boss and feel uncomfortable competing with him.

Three-track thinking works like this. When you make the decision to open a computer repair store, you also consider other similar kinds of repairs. In this case that might include a different specialty (Apple) or a different electronic product (faxes, copiers). You also research the customer base for Compaq repairs beyond your current company's customer list. Finally, you investigate other employment opportunities as an ultimate backup.

Being prepared with plan A, B, or C doesn't mean that it will be completely painless when an unexpected roadblock appears. It does mean that you'll sleep better at night knowing that you do have options.

It's possible and desirable to use three-track thinking in almost everything you do in virtually every area of your life. This method of dealing with life's little surprises is particularly useful when you have a hint of a storm brewing. However, the expert practitioner will have one or more parallel tracks to divert to for every important aspect of his business.

2

Preparing the Business Plan

IT'S POSSIBLE TO OPEN AND OPERATE a successful new enterprise without first preparing a formal business plan. It's also possible for a brain surgeon to successfully remove a malignant tumor from your skull without first taking X-rays and spending hours in consultation to determine how to do the job. But would you want that doctor operating on you? If the answer is no, then you also don't want to have someone running your business who hasn't gone to the same trouble and more to prepare for that job. The someone we're talking about is you.

The business plan is not just a document to look at later to make certain you've followed a certain path. It's more a method of thinking through each aspect of your business in an attempt to work through as many problems as possible before they occur. You may, indeed, find it instructive to refer to your plan from time to time after you're open to see if you've forgotten an important aspect or taken an unintended direction. The real value, however, is in the preparation.

Most of the rest of chapter 2 is devoted to a series of questions to which you should know the answers long before you open your doors. Each question is accompanied by commentary designed to help you make decisions about that question. In many cases you'll need to do research in order to respond properly. The more thought, calculation, and research that you invest in this section, the greater the chances for a successful launch of your new enterprise.

Part 1
The Business Purpose

Until now you've been thinking about goals, hopes, and dreams having to do with your personal life and career. From this point forward you will need to *shift your thinking*. You're now the president, chairman of the board, and senior partner of a separate, legal entity. (No, I haven't skipped ahead. Even though you haven't yet created this business, you should begin thinking as if it were already in existence.)

As the leader of this new concern, it's your primary responsibility to steer your ship on a course that is most likely to get it safely to harbor. Now you must concentrate on the needs of the business. *These are likely to be different, though hopefully not at odds, with your own specific goals.*

For instance, the primary reason you may have started the business is to achieve economic independence. It's unlikely that the best goal of the *business* is to make *you* independently wealthy. The goal of the business is more likely to be selling the most widgets possible at a price that will allow you to cover overhead and make a profit.

Your personal goal may be to retire by age forty. Your reason for going into business may be to have an outlet for your creative energy. You can be certain that if the purpose of your business is to achieve either of those ends, you're destined for failure. A more appropriate business goal might be to provide very-high-quality print services to local businesses at bargain prices.

With that lengthy introduction out of the way, it's time to create your business purpose. Here is a list of questions that will help you to define it. As with the exercises in section 1, you'll benefit most if you write out the answers to each of these questions *now*.

1. What product or service will you be providing? Be specific. Rather than "the grocery business," say "convenience store with gas pump." Instead of the general category of "law practice," say "general legal practice with a specialty in personal injury."

2. At what level in the distribution chain will you be? Manufacturer, wholesaler, jobber, rep, retailer, business to business, or other?

3. Describe your quality and pricing approach. A few examples might be:

A. Cutthroat prices on commodity products until I'm established, and then increase to industry norm.

B. Highest-quality products with prices to match.

C. Unique products that should command prices slightly higher than competition.

D. Service and quality will be as good as anyone's, but specializing in discounting and volume.

The list could go on and on. What is your approach going to be?

4. What geographic boundaries describe your territory? Also indicate whether this is by choice or imposed by contract. For instance, a retail business may figure it can reach a five-mile radius. A wholesaler may be expecting to reach a three- or four-state area. A manufacturer may see the world as his oyster (though the manufacturer's rep may be limited by her contract to a certain area). A manufacturer may have licenses that restrict his selling area. A franchisee almost certainly has certain boundaries beyond which he may not offer his product or service.

5. *What special niche do you plan to fill?* This is one of the most important questions you will answer in section 2. That being the case, we will now take a brief detour to look at this issue in detail.

The dictionary defines niche as, "A place suitable for a person or thing." As part of your mission statement, you'll want to find the place in the field you're entering that is suitable for you. However, you'll have much greater success if you take the concept of "niche" one step further. You'll want to find a place that is unique, separate, and distinct from others providing similar goods or services.

Why is this so important? Because it will give you something to talk about when you're selling your product. Because it will allow you to charge more than the competition if you can find a need that is not currently being met. Because it will give you an opportunity to become the "leader" in that specific way of doing business. And, as we'll show later, leadership is a big asset to a company.

You don't have to have a niche to be successful. If you're a super-successful salesperson and plan to function as a manufacturer's representative, you'll probably do just fine if you can find a few good factories to represent. You might really become something special, however, if you offer those same factories representation in India besides your normal three-state territory. That would be a special niche.

You might think that a doctor would be hard-pressed to come up with a niche. How about opening at 6:00 a.m.? Or making house calls? One of my friends made a small fortune as one of the first doctors to specialize in sports medicine.

In other words, if everyone else is selling price, sell service. If your competition is well known for quality and service, but his prices are out of line, come in with some really hot pricing. If the rest of the market is selling your product in basic black, offer yours in color. If color is the current rage, you may find that your customers would love to eliminate inventory and go back to black.

Potentially you can create a niche out of almost any element of your business. Does anyone currently sell what you sell by phone? How about by e-mail, eBay, or through a Web site? Do other manufacturers sell your product only to distributors? Maybe you should try selling it direct.

Packaging, advertising strategy, promotions, even a new can set you apart from all the others.

One of the best niche plays of all is to have protected merchandise. That is, to have products or services that no one else can sell due to the protection of patents, trademarks, copyrights, or proprietary information. One of the companies I used to manage will only rarely consider a new product line that isn't protected by one of these devices.

For instance, if your competition is selling a notebook for $1.99 and it has a plain yellow cover on it, you may be able to sell an identical notebook for $2.49 just because it has a cute picture of a famous, lasagna-loving cat on the front. Sure, you'll have to pay a royalty for that, and it may cost a few cents extra for the four-color cover. However, the difference won't come close to the normal margin of profit on $2.49, and no one else will be able to offer that notepad to your customer. In reality, you'll have created a minimonopoly.

One of my companies was once selling a bicycle security cable that every competitor in town also carried. We asked the manufacturer to make one for us that was one foot longer, and to restrict his sales of that product to our company since we'd suggested the idea to him. We then showed our customers that this extra foot was a benefit. Within a few weeks, we'd sewn up almost all the business in that product. We'd created a niche.

Your special niche doesn't necessarily have to be highly creative. Maybe you're just the best there is at your task. Another of my friends decided to make some extra money hanging wallpaper. There was nothing special about her part-time business, except that she was immensely talented at installing wallpaper. With very little effort she was soon swamped with business.

Unless you're quite certain that you can build a reputation around your special skills, don't count on craftsmanship alone. Possibly my friend the wallpaper hanger would have even grown faster had she also let the word out that she could finish any job within forty-eight hours. When people decide to paper their home, they want it done *now*. This could have been a very successful niche.

A classic niche is "filling a void" in the marketplace. In 1989 we began producing water bottles. No one was manufacturing a water bottle in the United States for sale to the wholesaler. Those that were being produced domestically were sold direct to retailers. Our customers were having to purchase their water bottles from Taiwan and Europe. By filling this void we were able to capture close to half of the business in our market the first year.

Our overwhelming success in water bottles wouldn't have been possible if there'd been other manufacturers making bottles for the wholesaler. We moved into the niche and saturated it. With our domination of the category, we've also made it very difficult for a competitor to move into our territory.

Many businesspeople have opened their doors believing that a great location is all that is needed to bite off a chunk of the market. Although location can be extremely important to the success of certain business types, only rarely does this element alone propel a business to success. For instance, owning a food concession at an airport or ballpark may be a great niche, but you still won't be the only concessionaire. You'll still need to offer something special to get folks to come to your stand.

There's no reason you can't have more than one niche. Every additional successful niche you find will make your business grow and prosper. Let's return to the example of the doctor. He might build an incredible practice by specializing in sports medicine, getting a famous athlete to endorse his clinic, and producing a newsletter that offers tips for preventing injury.

As a final example, let me tell you about one of the greatest niche players I've ever seen. There is a nationwide chain of grocery outlets known as Trader Joe's. The basic concept of Trader Joe's fits our definition perfectly. In this day of grocery stores that are larger than football fields and offer thousands of items, Trader Joe's are usually under three thousand square feet and sell little else than gourmet items including beer and wine.

The story doesn't end there. Many of the wines have been specially purchased by the company. They might buy all of a given lot, and then put Trader Joe's brand on the label. Next, they hand out or mail out a newsletter . . . wine that has been specially chosen, and that you can only buy at Trader Joe's.

There's more. They do the same thing with cheeses and with products as diverse as peanut butter and ice cream. Oh! Lest I forget, the original owner, Joe, developed such a reputation for his knowledge of wine and cheese that he was asked to do short segments about these topics on the local radio in Los Angeles, where the franchise started. You can only imagine the value of those free spots on Los Angeles radio programs.

What will there be about *your* business that will set *you* apart? Why will your potential customer arrive at your door rather than your competitor's? What is so special about your offer that you'll be able to take business away from others who've been in business for decades?

A final secret about niches. You may not have to continue to offer this special approach forever. Frequently, after building his business to a certain level, a price discounter will begin slowly to raise the price. Special hours may begin to be trimmed back. Less profitable products or services might be eliminated.

You must be careful when you do this. You don't want to kill the goose that laid the golden egg. You'll also want to make certain that you're still giving your customers a very good reason to trade with you instead of your rivals. This could even mean establishing a new niche to replace the old. For now, however, as you prepare to open your doors, develop as many unique approaches to offer your customer in product and/or service as you can think of. There may be an expense associated with some of these. Therefore, you'll want to weigh the expense against the expected benefit. Of course, you must also weigh the expense against your ability to pay.

Now is the time. Write out each and every special niche you will occupy.

After you've answered the preceding five questions, you should be prepared to write out your formal statement of business purpose, or mission statement. This should be a concisely written description of your overall approach. It may be only one sentence. It surely shouldn't be more than three.

As an example, here's a mission statement for one of the companies I helped establish, AC International: "AC International is a marketing company that manufactures for sale to wholesalers and mass retailers a line of high-quality, unique, protectable bicycle accessories that enhance the bicycling experience."

The first thing you notice about this statement is that AC International is a marketing company. The company may be a manufacturer as is stated in the next phrase, but the emphasis is on marketing, not manufacturing. It would be just as easy for a company to be successful with that phrase reversed: "ABC Company is a *manufacturer* that *markets* for sale . . ." However, these two companies would be as different as night and day.

The marketing company emphasizes product design, packaging, methods of distribution, and advertising. The manufacturing aspect of its business is a part of the overall marketing strategy. The company may be manufacturing in order to achieve lower cost, control over delivery of the finished product, or protection of trade secrets.

The manufacturing company orients itself toward certain types of manufacturing capability. It then looks for markets where its capacity can be sold. It will usually do only enough marketing to move product out the door, and count on its customers to provide packaging, advertising, and distribution.

The next phrase simply states who the customers are.

The final line describes the niche. Our company seeks products that are unlike any other. These items should be protectable by patents, trademarks, copyrights, or proprietary knowledge. The product category is bicycle accessories. AC International is not dividing its attention into other areas.

Last, we lay out our goal of "enhancing the bicycling experience." This slogan appears on our advertising and packaging. It's how we want to be perceived by our customers. We're not merely selling any product that comes along. We're trying to make a statement with these products.

Your mission statement may have all of these elements, only some of them, or you may say it in a totally different way. There's no right or wrong way to put down these ideas. The two important things are (1) that you write down a mission statement and (2) that you think about this statement so thoroughly that you can say it in one or two sentences.

You will receive far more benefit from the rest of this section on creating a business plan if you've written out your mission statement. It's possible that you'll change your original statement by the time you've finished section 2. You may also revise it further as you move toward your opening date. There's a good likelihood that it will change again after you've been open a while. However, as was the case with your goals, the fact that this statement may change does not invalidate the reasons for going through the process of developing it.

Write out your mission statement now.

Part 2
Finding a Location

Much of what you've accomplished until now has been done in your mind and on a piece of paper. Next we begin to attack those elements that will require research, field work, and interaction with others.

Location is a critical factor for retail stores, personal services, and restaurants. Don't, however, underestimate the importance of site selection for many other businesses.

You should be prepared to spend more time, money, and energy on this issue than almost any other. Recently, a friend wanted to open a clothing store. She believed she'd located a great storefront and entered into negotiations for a lease. While this was going on, she started making purchases of the next season's fashions.

Unfortunately, negotiations broke down on that store. She immediately started looking for an alternative. The clothing she'd purchased would be delivered in sixty days. With so little time she was forced to compromise. She took a marginal store that had poor parking access and no foot traffic. Six months later, she had a stack of bills and no business.

The following are criteria to consider in selecting a location. Some of these may not apply to your type of business. Even so, carefully evaluate each one.

TRAFFIC

On the surface this would seem to be the most obvious issue of all. Now let's take a look below the surface.

Certain kinds of businesses can benefit from traffic, vehicular and/or pedestrian. Your decision-making process must take into consideration: (a) Do you need traffic? (b) What kind? (c) How much rent are you willing to pay for various levels of traffic? (d) How do you maximize your location's advantage to bring the traffic into the store?

Most businesses open to the general public can benefit from traffic. By contrast, businesses who cater to a limited clientele or who have no reason for customers to walk in shouldn't pay extra for a location that offers good traffic.

Many service providers such as doctors, lawyers, advertising agencies, or auto insurance brokers seem to think that the prestige of a top-floor office in the town's tallest building is best for them. They might find that they'd attract quite a bit of walk-in traffic if they were to relocate in a ground-level storefront on Main Street.

There are many different types of traffic. If you were interested in opening a sandwich shop, you'd want to have a location where many clerical workers and middle managers would see you. Executives and factory workers don't go to sandwich shops. Neither do Mom and the family.

If you're opening a fancy restaurant, you probably don't want to locate in an industrial center. You need traffic at night to fill up your restaurant, and industrial areas turn into tombs at night. You want to be where middle- and upper-class folks can see you and get to you conveniently for dinner. This might mean a corner strip mail in an upscale residential area, an area that features other nighttime entertainment, or an upscale shopping center.

Yours is not the only business that wants to maximize certain kinds of traffic. Where there is competition for a scarce commodity, those who desire that commodity must be willing to pay a premium to get it. Your next decision is: How much extra money for how much extra traffic?

I wish I could give you a wonderful mathematical formula for determining how to make this decision. I haven't seen one, nor can I imagine how to derive one. Advertising is similarly vague. You know it will benefit you, but it's very hard to know how much to spend.

If you depend on foot traffic, I don't think it's possible to underestimate the importance of the quality and quantity you need. Being on the second floor of a second-rate mall will be death for your ladies' shoe business when there are three others on the first floor. However, you might survive on the second floor if yours is the only vitamin store in that mall.

Vehicular traffic is a much harder call. A fast-food restaurant might have an almost exactly proportional volume of business to the volume of traffic. Knowing this, it might negotiate the lease accordingly. A furniture store competing for the same location may not be able to expect an exactly incremental increase based on pure traffic. They may have to rely more on local advertising and mailers to produce customers.

If traffic is a consideration, you'll want to learn as much as you can about the type of traffic you can expect at the various locations you are considering. A shopping center manager will usually have figures. An industrial real estate agent will usually have numbers supplied by his client. *Get your own!*

Buy an inexpensive counting device, go to the location, and count. Stop people and take a short survey. Those folks who're willing to stop will give as much as five or ten minutes of their time. You'll want to determine who they are, why they shop here, and whether they have any need for what you'll be offering. You'll need to survey at least a hundred people for the results to have validity.

PROXIMITY TO CUSTOMERS

If you rent used cars to people whose auto is in the repair shop, you'll want to locate your business near auto repair shops. This may seem obvious. Less obvious might be this example. If you're a wholesaler selling locksmith supplies to lock and key shops in a five-state area, where do you locate to be close to your customers?

After some investigation (including asking your future customers' advice) you'd probably decide to locate in the traffic center of a large urban area. Why? Locksmiths often need product *today*. If you're located an hour away and your competitor is two hours away (in the suburbs where the rent is lower), you're going to get the job. As this customer comes to rely on you for the rush job, you're likely to get his regular business as well.

A manufacturer such as AC International, which sells to wholesalers, has no reason to be close to customers. Others who fall in this category would be mail-order companies, import-export companies (they may need to be close to a port), or television production companies.

NEIGHBORHOOD

Shopping for a business home is in many ways like shopping for a home for your family. You'd prefer to be in a nice, clean, crime-free environment. There are advantages to being close to needed services such as restaurants, print services, office supply stores, and the post office. I never realized the value of a public library until we located six blocks from one. Personal need may play a part. You may want to be near certain kinds of recreation or within a certain commute time. You hope you'll never need it, but it may be worth a few extra dollars per month to be near police and fire services.

Some of the above may be critical. Is your customer going to come to a known high-crime area just to do business with you? Will you have difficulty attracting the kind of employees you need if the commute time from that kind of residential area is an hour or more? If you plan to project a high-tech image, will you be able to overcome a low-tech neighborhood? What about the neighbors? A little bit of research might show you that the arcade on the corner is going to attract certain clientele that will not help your business. If you're going to be in an industrial area, are there neighbors who might create environmental concerns? I used to live next to an agricultural college. When the wind blew in the wrong direction . . . need I say more? Noise, odors, unsavory visitors, bitter contests for available parking, and dangerous activities are a few of the things you may want to be on the lookout for before signing a long-term lease.

GOVERNMENT AND LOCATION

Local governments are not all alike. Some are quite enthusiastic about business. Others are downright inhospitable. You may be the type of person who naturally follows all the rules to a T, enjoys working with government employees, and filling out forms. If you are, you're not the typical entrepreneur.

When I was in the rental car business, I had two locations. Each had an office trailer, a sign, and a space to do minor repairs. In one city, we were able to open without any permit other than a business license, which took half an hour to secure.

In the other city, we had to have a variance to be in the rental car business at all. Our sign was not in adherence to code, for which we were cited within six weeks of opening. The trailer also required a variance, and we were told the two-year variance would not be renewed. We would have to arrange to build a permanent structure within two years.

A good industrial real estate agent should be able to tell you something about the government attitude toward your enterprise type in the various cities you're considering.

PARKING

Several times, I've seen friends and associates open in locations where parking was a clear problem. "Oh," they assured me, "it may affect business a little, but the rent is cheap. Besides, look at this visibility." The rent was cheap because there was no parking. The result in every case was disaster.

Now that you know some of the elements that go into the decision about location, how do you go about finding the perfect spot?

Here comes another one of those golden nuggets: *Use a commer-*

cial real estate broker. Yes, there's a chance you could save a few bucks by dealing directly with a landlord who doesn't have to pay a commission. But there's a greater likelihood that the landlord may try to take advantage of you without a real estate agent there to help you.

You find a commercial real estate broker the same way you find any other service provider. Start with networking. Then try the Yellow Pages and the local chamber of commerce. Interview several brokers. Each one will provide you with invaluable information about current market conditions. Some may have differing opinions. The combination of those opinions can be quite eye-opening.

Like all agents, commercial real estate agents will stress how important it is that you deal with just one. They will provide great arguments about how everyone has access to the same listings. They'll tell you how embarrassing it is to have two different agents making inquiries about the same property for the same client.

Forget it. Let them think they're exclusive if it will make them feel better, but you should have at least two agents working. No one can have complete knowledge of anything so complex as the commercial real estate market for a given area. Even within a small geographic area, different agents have brought me vastly different options when they've been presented identical criteria. You need all the information you can possibly get for this important decision. Use two agents.

If two is better, is three best? Maybe. There probably is a point of diminishing returns, but until I've located an excellent property, I continue to interview new agents. I may not actually send more than two or three out looking, but I keep my options open.

As we'll discuss later, always remember that the commercial real estate agent is usually also working for the landlord. The agent has certain responsibilities of disclosure due you, but you must maintain a certain wariness at all times.

Remember, also, the experience of my friend with the clothing store. Have a backup location in mind until you sign the lease, and don't make other irreversible decisions.

Once you've selected your location, write it up in your business plan. List the strengths and weaknesses. What do you expect the location to do for your business? What were your reasons for selecting it? What are the drawbacks that you hope to be able to overcome? How will you take advantage of the positive aspects of this site?

Before we leave this area, let's evaluate the last question. You've worked hard, analyzed the choices, and you can't imagine having picked a better spot for your new enterprise. You're a CPA specializing in corporate taxes and you're located right next door to the biggest corporate law practice in town. Maybe you're opening a bookstore, and you've taken a lease on the closest retail store to a major campus. Maybe your location stinks, but the rent on your restaurant is the envy of every other restaurant owner in town.

Your work, location-wise, has just begun. The CPA could merely hope people will see his name on the door as they come to visit the attorney. Or, he could go next door and work out some deals with his neighbor. The neighbor might agree to something as simple as leaving business cards on the reception desk, or something as complex as selling each other's services.

Let's look at the bookstore situation. The owner will not maximize her extra expense for the rent on that incredible location if she merely puts up an attractive sign. She needs the nicest sign ever. As big as the local law will allow. She should also consider a sandwich board on the sidewalk, sidewalk sales every day, and/or students handing out fliers in front of the store to maximize the advantage she's paying for.

And what about our restaurateur who's accepted cheap rent instead of great location? He should have the extra money to rent the largest and best-located billboard in town to tell folks who he is and where. He should offer to those who find him a free meal each time they come back and bring a new friend along.

We'll talk at length in later chapters about promotions, signage, and other methods for finding customers, but these are usually specific to your decision about location. For now, simply add to your business plan the methods you can think of to take advantage of your great new site.

Part 3
Selecting Suppliers

Who will supply you? If your business will be primarily aimed at supplying product rather than services, nothing is more important than your sources of supply. Most service providers must pay attention to supply as well. However, the products and services they must purchase are usually widely available and very price competitive.

For example, a taxicab company will need to purchase or lease some cabs, and will certainly need phone and communication equipment. It will also need oil, gas, and repair services. The quality and cost of each one of these could substantially affect the profits of the company, but each of these items can be readily purchased from other suppliers if necessary.

Most retailers, on the other hand, build up certain brand names and become known by the brands they carry. If that major vendor has supply problems, does not maintain a competitive posture in the marketplace, or cuts you off due to poor performance or bad credit, you could be out of business in short order.

Wholesalers, importers, and many manufacturers are in the same position. Our manufacturing company, AC International, had been in business just three years when the raw material required to make our product was discontinued by a major chemical company. We believed that it was the only product that would work. It had been part of the formula that accompanied the manufacturing instructions when we took over the company. We were *panic stricken*!

Fortunately, we were able to find another source, but we were out of production for almost a month in the middle of the season. This happened, of course, just as we were finally turning the corner on profitability.

I could provide you with a list of such instances from my personal experience, and then another one ten times as long from the experiences of friends and acquaintances. Golden nugget: It's the opinion of this author that *suppliers are more important than customers*. I have a saying that I pass on to my employees and associates: "Customers are easy; vendors are hard!"

Let me give you an example from my own business. As mentioned before, AC International makes bicycle water bottles. They're of high quality. Our price is right. And our customers want us to supply them. We haven't had to *sell* any bottles. Our customers are lined up to get them.

Initially, we were going to buy all of our bottles from a job shop. This manufacturer said he could make 150,000 bottles per month. We took orders for that many. Our supplier delivered only 40,000 the first two months, and we were no longer in the business of taking orders for bottles. We were now in the business of handling customer complaints. Not only were we failing to realize the sales we could have had in those months, we were making our customers angrier by the day. Additionally, we were opening the door wide for competition to take advantage of our inability to ship.

Your suppliers can make you or break you. You'll have to select many of your most important suppliers before you even open your doors. How do you make a good judgment about this critical issue?

Product vendors are generally judged on four criteria: quality, price, delivery, and terms. It's rare that you'll find suppliers that will rate at the top of their class on all four. Thus, you'll have to make trade-offs and arrive at the optimum for your kind of business.

For instance, if you're in a one-man auto repair shop, you must be able to get any part for the one car you're working on in one day. You care about price, but you'll gladly pay a good bit more to get it today rather than next week.

The wholesaler of televisions to local TV retailers will probably be more concerned about the terms he gets from the manufacturer. It will be very expensive for him to maintain a large inventory of TV sets. He may continue to carry a line that has some quality problems if he gets ninety days to pay.

It's time for you to come to a few conclusions for your own enterprise. In this part of your business plan we'll deal only with suppliers who provide goods and services that are integral to the product or service you'll be selling.

1. Rate the four criteria by which vendors are judged on a scale of 1 to 10. For instance: Quality 9; Price 10; Delivery 6; Terms 8.

2. Now take each of your top four products or services and rate the vendor performance that you need for each. An example for a bicycle shop might look like this:

Bicycles:	Quality	8	Price	8	Delivery	9	Terms	10
Clothing:	Quality	10	Price	7	Delivery	7	Terms	10
Locks:	Quality	9	Price	7	Delivery	8	Terms	7
Tools:	Quality	10	Price	5	Delivery	5	Terms	2

3. Some or all of the products, services, or raw materials you need may have very limited sources of supply. Make a list of those items that you believe may be available only from one source. For example, when I owned the used car rental business, there was only one insurance company in the United States that was insuring used rental cars. That was an important negative in my business plan.

4. Is there anything you need where it would be important to have a name-brand supplier? If you'll be selling computers, can you make it without Compaq or Apple? Make a list of these situations.

5. Now begins some very hard work. Begin to compile a list of companies that could provide you with the needed resources for your business. Use the Internet and Yellow Pages; industry magazines, buyers' guides, and trade associations; library references such as the Thomas Register; the local chamber of commerce; U.S. Department of Commerce listings; and every other method you can come up with to prepare a comprehensive list.

6. Begin with the most important product. Get on the phone. Call the company and ask to speak with a salesman. *Do not write a letter asking for information and do not use the e-mail on the "contact us" page of their Web site;* either will get lost in the shuffle. The salesman is the guy who stands to gain the most from your new account. Tell him you're getting ready to open in his territory and you'd like to get together for breakfast some morning.

Why breakfast? It won't take him away from his selling day. Use the breakfast to find out whether his territory has any neighborhoods where his product is not getting enough exposure. Learn all you can about the strengths and weaknesses of his company. Find out what it takes to qualify for credit terms, and how much merchandise he thinks you'll need to open up your operation.

See if he'll introduce you to a couple of his best accounts—ones that are located far enough away from your territory that you wouldn't represent a competitive threat to them.

If possible, try to arrange a tour of the supplier's facilities, and an opportunity to meet the salesperson's superiors. Even the owner.

Without waiting for your first choice of supplier to implement all this, move on to other potential suppliers and repeat the process with as many as you have time for. The more of this you do, the more likely you will be to secure vendors that can help make your business.

7. In the case of those companies that don't have field representatives, and that are too far away to visit in person, have them send you all the information possible. Also, don't be afraid to take the time to gain as much information over the phone as you can.

8. Create a notebook where you write down extensive notes on your visits. Start a library of the catalogs, brochures, and price lists that you pick up along the way.

9. By now you've surely begun to make certain decisions about your primary suppliers. Write up each one in your business plan. Indicate what they'll supply and describe their strengths and weaknesses.

10. Where necessary or desirable, enter into formal contracts with your preferred suppliers. Indicate in your business plan the contracts you've secured and what the terms are.

Some of your preferred vendors may not be prepared to supply you. They may have territory problems. They may not be inclined to sell to new businesses. They may not like your credit standing. If you run into this situation, and you feel it's important to have this supplier as a part of your team, you'll need to turn into a salesperson.

It's the rare occasion where a good salesperson won't be able to persuade a company to sell him or her product. That's not to say that anyone can get a McDonald's franchise in a location where contracts and covenants preclude it, but most situations aren't that cut and dried.

Selling yourself to a vendor isn't that hard. What they want from you is simple: high sales volume and fast payment. If you can convince the decision maker that you'll give them these two things, you'll seldom have any trouble getting the lines you need.

Generally, the vendor salesperson has the power to decide whether or not you become a customer. The credit department will take over when it comes to whether or not you'll get credit, and how much you'll get. If you've selected a vendor that you think may be tough to sell, call the salesperson again to set up another breakfast.

Begin your discussion by assuming his willingness to sell to you, unless you already know that this meeting is to overcome his decision not to. Ask questions that would imply that you'll be doing business together: "If I give you an order today for seventeen hundred widgets, when can I expect delivery? Has your credit department had a chance to examine my credit application yet? Will you waive the freight on my first order?"

If the salesperson balks at this approach, and says that he's either unsure of adding you as a customer or not inclined to, it is time to begin selling. Enthusiasm is all important. At this point enthusiasm is all you have. You can't prove your ability to move mountains of product, and you have no track record for paying your bills. Bring to the fore every bit of excitement you can muster and make this person believe he's going to make money with you. You are going to feature his product in your store, in your brochures, on your Web site, and in your Yellow Pages ad. You'll carry a full range of his product, not just cherry-pick the line. You might even offer to carry his products exclusive of his competition for the first year.

If you've selected a location, take him to see it. Provide him with as much information about your plan as he'll listen to. Ask him if he has other ideas as to how you can make this a mutually profitable deal.

After you have finished your pitch, make sure you *close*. Ask him if he is prepared to supply you. If the answer is no, call his boss. What do you have to lose? The salesperson may not like that you've gone above him, but if you don't get the line, that sales rep can't hurt you.

If you strike out with the sales manager, and the line is important enough, go to the president. Many company owners are more aggressive about opening new accounts than the sales force. (Maybe the sales force is on straight salary, and they just see your account as extra work. Possibly the salesperson has a favorite buddy close to your proposed location whom he is trying to protect.)

After you've exhausted every avenue, put this matter in the tickler file for later. If the line is important enough, you'll want to try again in six months or a year.

How many vendors will you need? Is it possible to have too many? You need to have as many suppliers as necessary to provide you with the full range of goods and services you need to do business and to have adequate backup for those hard-to-get resources. You may also want to have competitive suppliers on a number of items that are commonly available to make certain you're getting the right price.

It's definitely possible to have too many vendors. Each vendor represents a cost to your purchasing and bookkeeping departments. In other words, for each supplier there will be a sales rep calling who'll take up the time of the person in charge of buying that line. This has a cost equal to the lost opportunity of what that person could have been doing to add sales or profit if she had not been with the salesperson. Also, each supplier will be sending you invoices. Each invoice must be posted and eventually paid. This will cost you bookkeeping time and the cost of checks, envelopes, and stamps. To the extent that you are slow paying, or there is a disagreement about your account, there will be additional time spent working these things out.

In business today there's a great emphasis on reducing the number of suppliers, and I would agree that a business should be wary. However, I would argue that it's better to have too many than too few. It's very hard to sell out of an empty store.

At this point in your business plan you will want to list your primary suppliers and provide a short paragraph on each as to their benefit to your business.

Part 4
The Physical Plant

We've already discussed the selection of your business location. A related but distinct issue is determining the size and layout requirements of the facility.

For many types of enterprises this should also be a multipart plan. To illustrate this, let me use as an example a typical whole-sale distributor.

Blake is a supplier of small parts such as electronics devices. His new business will supply these to retailers in a city of three million. Later he hopes to expand to the whole state and beyond.

Depending on size, it's not impossible for Blake to set up operations in a garage. A step up from that would be a ministorage warehouse. Because the parts are small, he should be able to warehouse quite an inventory in a very small facility. An additional advantage to such a first location is that he can rent month to month and not commit to a long-term lease.

Blake may want to include in his business plan this type of warehouse along with the rent and terms. He might then predict a sales level at which it will be necessary and affordable to move into a larger unit. Possibly the second location would include four hundred square feet of reception and office space, and four thousand square feet of warehouse with a loading dock.

He may expect that he'll occupy that facility for three years until sales reach $1 million, at which time he'll move to a ten-thousand-square-foot building. Blake's intentions might even include purchasing this unit.

Whether or not you go into this kind of detail about your future plans, you do need to produce a list of "needs" for your first facility. You may also want to create a "want" list. Do you need a loading dock? Do you need a sprinkler system because of the type of inventory you will carry? Do you need carpeted floors? Two bathrooms? Lots of window display space? Two-twenty electrical service? High ceilings?

How much space do you really need? It's very easy to put yourself in a situation where you're in business to pay the landlord. Unless you have unlimited funds, you'll do well to start off with the minimum amount of space possible. Then be willing to move a time or two if your sales goals are met.

There are times when this advice won't apply. If you'll have a large investment in fixed equipment such as in a restaurant or a manufacturing plant, you may have to take a risk on a larger space. The cost of moving these types of enterprises dictates moving less than might be the case for a retailer, wholesaler, or service provider. (How much can it cost to move a tax preparation office?)

Golden nugget: *Don't burden your new business with more overhead than it needs in space rental.* Start small and build as necessary.

Add to your business plan as much detail as you think is necessary concerning your physical plant, along with any up-front costs necessary to implement your plan.

Part 5
The Advertising Plan

Your business plan should include how you intend to approach the complicated issue of advertising. The issues that should be addressed include:

1. How much will you budget for advertising the first year?
2. What basis will you use for determining your budget in the second and ensuing years?
3. Whom do you expect to reach with your message?
4. What advertising media will you use to reach your audience?
5. What message do you expect to convey with your campaign?

It's the rare business that can build beyond a meager beginning without advertising. At the very least, most businesses should have a presence in the Yellow Pages and on the Web. At the other end of the spectrum, entertainment firms such as nightclubs or movie theaters have to spend a good portion of their start-up money getting out the word that they're in town.

If your business depends on the Yellow Pages, you may wish to plan your opening around the date of the distribution of the next issue. I've heard many tales of—and have twice experienced—the incredible difference in business that can occur the day the phone books are delivered. If you open shortly after the cutoff date, and have to wait a year for the next edition, you might not be in business to enjoy the benefit.

In determining your advertising strategy, begin by writing down again, in detail, who your customers are. Are you selling to consumers, dealers, OEMs, the government? Are you selling in a five-zip code area, citywide, across a five-state region, internationally? Are your customers a certain age and sex, or do they fit into some other special group?

It's important to realize that you may have more than one type of customer who needs to be reached by your message. Take the case of a manufacturer, for instance.

A manufacturer may be selling to a wholesaler, who in turn sells to retailers. The retailer finally sells the same product to a consumer. The manufacturer ends up having at least five customers to whom it will be advantageous to deliver information about the product.

He must sell the buyer at the wholesale level. If the wholesale buyer isn't convinced about the need for your product, the retailer and consumer will never have a chance to make a decision. At this level it may also be important that the buyer's supervisor and/or the owner of the company is also knowledgeable about your product and feels confident it can be sold.

Next in the chain is the salesperson who represents the wholesaler. If she doesn't take the time to show your item, or is not convincing when she shows it to the dealer, you may find your product bottlenecked at the wholesale level.

The wholesale sales rep's job will be made easier if the owner or buyer at the dealer level is already aware of the product when she walks in. Thus you may wish to advertise to this level also.

It does little good to persuade the retailer to purchase your item if his salesclerks don't know why the consumer would ever want one. This clerk represents the fourth link in the chain.

Finally, if the consumer visits a retailer and is already primed to buy, you can create some real excitement that may be translated all the way back up the distribution chain. If the dealer sells out quickly, you can be certain that he'll reorder. If he reorders, the salesperson will spread the word to his other customers as well as to his fellow sales clerks. If the wholesaler quickly empties his shelf, he may place a larger second order.

As a manufacturer I often wish I had the resources to reach all five of these levels at once. Unfortunately, it would break the company's back. As a result, each year we must decide which of these levels is the most important to attack.

One year we may spend most of our ad dollars on trade magazine advertising. These ads are designed to reach the wholesale buyer, his salesperson, the dealer, and his clerk. However, if we want to be certain to reach the wholesale buyer with a message that is not appropriate for the dealer, we'll more likely use direct mail.

In the bicycle industry, another year we might allocate most of our ad budget to consumer magazine advertising. In our industry, the dealer and wholesale personnel also read these special-interest magazines. However, if we're specifically trying to reach the consumer, we might also try in-store merchandisers such as brochures or displays.

Write into your business plan a list of "customers" to whom you need to communicate your message.

The following is a list of media that are available, with a short paragraph about each. The Appendix will suggest some further reading that can provide more depth.

The Web. Today, a Web presence can be the most important advertising avenue for any business. And the good news is that you can get a lot of bang for a very few bucks. A rudimentary Web page can be constructed by any fifteen-year-old that will give your customers a place to see your story and pictures, descriptions, and prices of your basic product or service lines. And your own Web address can cost as little as $100 per year. Or you can participate in one of hundreds of groups where your Web site hosting is free, but you pay for other services.

Your Web page is so important that for many businesses, it exists before the business opens. You can test the water and see how many hits you get, even before you have a location or phone number. See section 3 for more on Web and e-mail marketing.

In addition to your own site, there are many ways to advertise on the Web. Industry associations often have sites where you can be listed for free. Other for-profit organizations might offer some free listings in hopes of getting you to pay for upgrades and placement. Paying for placement in search engines or paying services to help you get better exposure on search engines are other avenues of using the Web.

E-mail. We all hate Spam! Or do we? Our company now sends out 50,000 e-mails each week to our customer base, and we are always working hard to add new names. It isn't actually Spam, because we have permission to send these ads, and we offer an opt out for those who've had enough. In this author's opinion e-mail has had the greatest impact on business efficiency of any invention in fifty years. It is fast and cheap to communicate with our customers, vendors, sales force, and even our bank.

You will almost certainly want to create your own e-mail database of customers willing to receive updates, sales, or new product information from your company. In addition, there is very likely one or more services in your industry that will e-mail your information to their database of opted-in companies or individuals. Much more on this in section 3 on Web and e-mail marketing.

Trade magazines. Almost every trade has specialized magazines, newsletters, and/or buying guides that are distributed to members of the trade at very little or no cost. The cost of advertising in these publications is usually very low. Do some research into how well read the trade publications in your industry are. One may be quite popular, while another may go right into the trash.

Specialty magazines. These range from slick four-color magazines to four-page newsprint club papers. Often, use of them will enable you to reach the consumer of your product or service more efficiently. For instance, if you're selling professional ice skates, you'll be better off advertising in a magazine read by professional ice skaters as opposed to, say, *Sports Illustrated,* which is marketed to a more general audience. There is a wide range of pricing for this type of magazine, depending upon circulation and quality of the publication.

General interest magazines. You will want to consider such magazines as *People, Business Week, TV Guide,* and so on only if you have a product that appeals to the majority of the public, and if you have a national distribution network. It's rare indeed that the owner of a business with fewer than ten employees will want to risk the cost of an ad in these publications. The cost of a single page can be tens of thousands of dollars.

General circulation newspapers. Local or regional retailers and service providers may do very well advertising in newspapers that serve their customers. Newspaper advertising is fairly expensive, however. Additionally, you, the advertiser, are competing for the reader's attention with a lot of other advertising.

Outdoor advertising. Billboards, bus benches, and other outdoor media are a much overlooked method of getting exposure. It's possible to get into this in a big way or a small way. One friend of mine took only a single ad on one bus bench near his retail store with excellent results. Many restaurants off the main drag use a billboard on the main drag to direct potential diners to their location.

A variation of outdoor advertising would be your own signs and window displays. If you expect to attract traffic because of your store's location, buy the biggest, boldest sign you can afford (and that the law will allow). If you have a window display, spend some real time and effort making it attractive and *interesting*. Don't be afraid to make your window display a bit weird. You want to attract attention! Otherwise, why spend the extra money on that great location?

Mailings. Among the least expensive ways (even in the days of ever-increasing postal rates) of reaching your specific customer with a very specific message is the mail. You can buy lists of prospects broken out by almost any criterion you can imagine. It may seem far-fetched, but you should be able to buy a list of all the single folks between the ages of twenty and forty, with above-average incomes, in the five closest zip codes to your business. Look for sellers of such lists in the Yellow Pages or online under "Mailing Lists."

You should also build your own list. After you're open, have every customer who walks through the door add his or her name to your mailing list. You might do this with a guest register, a drawing in which the customer must fill out an entry blank to win (the prize doesn't have to be that big), or by having a detailed sales receipt. Radio Shack has used this approach to build up its mailing lists for years. Also, use this method to get an e-mail address and permission to send them information.

You may also be able to reach your customer through a "stack" mailing. I'm certain you've seen the little stacks of postcards that come to you in a plastic-wrapped package. It costs you only a few cents each to participate in that kind of mailing program. Check with the trade and consumer magazines in your industry for help in locating companies that do this type of mailing. Check for listings with Standard Rate and Data. Larger libraries should have a copy or you can search online.

There are companies that are in the specific business of doing mailings for other businesses. They can help you design your piece; sell you a list; and print, fold, address, and mail the item on their bulk-rate permit. Again, you should be able to find help for this in the Yellow Pages under "Mailing Services."

If you are a manufacturer or wholesaler or otherwise deal on a regional or national level, there is usually a list supplier that specializes in your industry. Check with your association or an industry buyer's guide.

Radio. Like the local newspaper, radio offers a way to get your message to a broad spectrum of people in your territory. And you can get great bang for your buck in the less-sought-after time periods. The salesperson for the radio station is often an accomplished copywriter who may be able to help you write your ad for free.

Television. Cable television has created an opportunity for even the smallest business to take advantage of the advertising power of TV. There are packagers who'll provide you with everything from the script to airtime purchases for a set fee. You may find TV to be especially appropriate for your grand opening or other special sales situations. Contact your local cable television station for suggestions as to suppliers of these services.

Trade shows. Most manufacturers and distributors aren't considered to be "in the business" if they aren't attending some of the special trade shows offered by their industry. My own experience has shown that it's possible to give the impression that you're much bigger than you really are by taking a large space and doing a good decorating job.

Consumer shows. Local businesses that serve consumers also have opportunities for shows. These may be special-interest shows like a home show or boat show. They might also be more general exhibitions put on by the local chamber of commerce, or as part of a county fair.

You might also be able to put together your own exhibit at a local mall. You may not be able to afford a shop in the mall full-time, but you may be able to take a kiosk during a peak season for your type of product.

Public relations. Frequently referred to as free advertising, PR can be many times more effective than paid advertising. If you can come up with a special-interest story about your business that the media will latch on to, it can provide a dose of credibility. People believe editorial ink more than they believe advertising.

Publicity stories are usually easier to place in trade publications. Most will publish a short release about a new product, change in location, or appointment of a new salesperson. Use this venue as much as possible. It isn't absolutely free since it takes time to write a release and a few dollars for photos, but it's far more cost efficient than paid advertising.

Premiums. Pens, calendars, notebooks, clocks, and many other products can attractively display your name or logo, and at the same time make an attractive gift for you to give to your customer. Premiums such as these represent a low-cost, but potentially very effective, way to get your message to a specific group of customers.

I've made several mentions of AC International's entry into the water bottle business. A large proportion of our sales is made to companies who want either to sell or give away bottles with their name, logo, and/or message on the side. For less than two dollars apiece, a dealer can give customers who've purchased a bike a bottle that has the dealer's store name and phone number emblazoned on the side.

With this range of possible advertising venues in mind, you'll now want to begin to decide what approach to take to get your message out. Part of that process will include whether or not to use an advertising agency.

Unless you've had substantial advertising experience, have access to someone who does, or like to burn up your money with no idea of whether or not it will bring results, you'll need the help of a professional advertising agency. Even in the best of situations advertising is not an exact science. You can hire the best, follow their directions exactly, and still not get the results you hoped for. However, well-planned and -executed advertising can produce remarkable results.

When you're starting out and don't have much money for advertising, it's difficult to attract a large, well-established agency. Using the recommendations of others, the Yellow Pages, the Internet, or chamber of commerce, you'll want to look at the qualifications and portfolios of several agencies before making your selection. If nothing else, these interviews will teach you a great deal about how advertising works.

There are two kinds of agencies. Most of the larger ones are full-service, meaning that they can handle every aspect of the campaign from concept to paste-up and placement. Smaller agencies, by contrast, specialize in one or another portion of the business. In the early stages of your development you'll want an agency that is versatile enough to make an intelligent suggestion as to the best media for you to use. Once you've decided how much money to allocate to each category, you should ask the agency's account executive some serious questions about the agency's ability to develop the actual ad.

For instance, a good agency will tell you if you need to spend 25 percent of your budget on outdoor advertising, even if it hasn't had experience in this area. Then it will help you find someone who does.

With respect to advertising, you should set specific goals that you want to achieve. Maybe—over the course of a six-week campaign—you want to increase the number of people walking through your door by 35 percent. Possibly you want 30 percent of the people in your market to be able to identify you and your product within one year. Fifty new clients with opening orders of five hundred dollars or more within six months might make you happy.

Tell the advertising agency what your goal is. They should honestly tell you whether they believe advertising can achieve that goal. If you fall substantially short of your plan, and assuming you have not interfered with the agency's suggested approach, it is very likely the fault of the agency. Consider a new one.

At this point in your business plan you'll want to describe the advertising plan that you have for your opening. Possibly you'll want to include some rough sketches of the concept. Indicate the budget, the media, the frequency, and, above all, the goal.

Next, include a statement of the method you'll use to appropriate advertising money for future budgets. Possible approaches might include a percentage of last year's sales, a percentage of projected sales, a dollar amount that seems affordable.

It's important to remember one major limitation of advertising. The best campaign in the world will get the customer to try your product, service, or store only once. Ultimately, what keeps the customer coming back is quality and service.

Part 6
Projecting Your Income

Before getting into the meat of this section, I'd like to drive home two points:

1. Do *not* plan to lose money your first year. Do not even plan to lose money your first month. I can't tell you how many ill-conceived business plans have been created that offer investors nothing but losses for the first year or three.

2. Do *not* plan to work for *free* for the first year. If you don't take a salary for your efforts, you're kidding yourself about the success of your enterprise. If you currently make $40,000 per year and your business breaks even in its first year with you taking no salary, the company has really lost $40,000. If you take $50,000 a year after that, you will be back only to even at the end of five years.

Charge your company a reasonable amount for your services. It's not unreasonable to take a small cut from your previous salary, but don't work cheap or for free. In section 1 I showed you a budget that I felt you'd understand since it was similar to a household budget. The budget that you'll now be shown is a more appropriate way to evaluate and plan a business. It's called a profit-and-loss statement, or income statement.

Business is based on percentages. Using the family budget

approach, you have no analytical tools. That method is commonly referred to as "running your business out of the checkbook": If there is money in the bank, everything is okay. If you don't have money in the bank, you must be doing something wrong. Even if that were true (which it isn't) this simplistic method wouldn't tell you where to make changes. To put money in the bank, you would be just as likely to cut highly productive employees as consider a price increase.

The percentage method helps you to determine whether a lay-off or a price hike is likely to produce the optimum result. Using the income statement method that follows, it's possible to analyze each aspect of your business to determine where you need to make adjustments.

DEFINING THE TERMS

Gross sales. The total amount of income generated from all sales activities. This would include such things as sales of merchandise, services, meals, buildings, rentals, or commissions. It's restricted to those items that represent your regular business activity. It would not include, for instance, income from the rental of extra space in your facility, or interest income on a savings account.

Cost of goods sold (or services delivered). The total cost you have paid to make the goods or services in your gross sales ready for sale. The cost of raw material, labor, machine time, and overhead would be an example of the costs of goods sold for a manufacturer. If the product wasn't ready for sale until it was packaged, then it would be necessary to add the cost of packaging materials, labor, and associated overhead to complete the packaging.

In a service business most of the costs derive from labor and overhead. There's an important difference between the two. A dental assistant, for example, is part of the cost of services, not the general overhead.

Gross profit. When the cost of goods is subtracted from the gross sales, what is left is the gross profit. If you buy ten apples for $1 apiece (cost of goods = $10), and sell all ten for $3 each (gross sales = $30), you are left with a gross profit of $20 ($30 – $10 = $20).

Overhead. Those items that are required to support the activities of the business, but not necessary to the production of the product or service. Bookkeeping, office expenses, administrative payroll, commissions, royalties, advertising, and other such expenses fall into the category of overhead.

Fixed overhead. Those portions of the total overhead that tend to remain the same regardless of total sales. Rent, office payroll, phone, depreciation of office equipment and furniture, postage, and office supplies are some of the items that represent the fixed overhead.

Variable overhead. Expenses that are more generally seen as a percentage of sales or that can be quickly adjusted to varying sales conditions. Sales commissions, royalties, and product liability insurance are examples of the cost of doing business that are generally seen as a percentage of sales. Advertising, promotions, research and development, and travel might be viewed as expenses that can be quickly cut or expanded, depending on specific circumstances.

Net profit. The result of subtracting all overhead, both fixed and variable from gross sales. (Also known as the "bottom line.") In our apple cart example above, you may have paid two dollars to rent the cart for the day, and a 10 percent commission to the salesperson. Thus you would have had a total overhead of five dollars (two dollars in fixed overhead and three dollars in variable). This would leave you with a ten-dollar profit for the day (fifteen dollars gross profit minus five dollars in total overhead).

The following formula should be memorized, dissected, and thoroughly understood before you open your doors:

Gross Sales
   – Cost of Goods (or Services)
   = Gross Profit
   – Overhead
   = Net Profit

Here is the income statement of a very basic retail operation.

Gross sales	$1,500	100%
Cost of goods	900	60
Gross profit	600	40
Overhead		
Variable		
Advertising	75	5
Commission	45	3
Fixed		
Rent	150	10
Salary	90	6
Phone	60	4
Postage	30	2
Total overhead	450	30
Net profit	$ 150	10%

Each item is shown as a dollar amount. Then the amount is restated as a percentage of gross sales (e.g., salary is 6 percent of gross sales).

As sales increase or decrease, it's possible to see how some of these line items change relative to one another by watching the percentages change. In the following example, we see what might happen if sales doubled.

Gross sales	$3,000	100%
Cost of sales	1,800	60
Gross profit	1,200	40
Overhead		
Variable		
Advertising	150	5
Commission	90	3
Fixed		
Rent	150	5
Salary	90	3
Phone	60	2
Postage	30	1
Total overhead	570	19
Net profit	$ 630	21%

Overhead increased a few dollars, but dropped dramatically in percentage of gross sales. This resulted in a substantial increase in profit.

Most businesses are far more complex than the above example. Let's revisit each of the basic definitions covered thus far in part 6, and add a little meat to those bare bones.

Gross sales. Sometimes referred to as gross revenues to provide a broader-based classification, this is the total dollars received in any given period (day, week, month, year) from any source. In an uncomplicated business this might represent all the receipts from the sale of products or services. In some businesses there may be income from both sales of products and delivery of services. Examples would be a locksmith who sells locks and also repairs them; an optometrist who examines your eyes, but also sells glasses and contact lenses; or an appliance store that sells you a stove and offers installation at a charge.

In these instances it may make sense to break out the sales from products on one line and the revenue from services on a separate line.

A portion of your revenue might not really belong to you. For instance, if you must charge sales tax, you are merely holding the money for the government. This amount must be subtracted from gross sales.

Other amounts are commonly subtracted from this first figure. Discounts, returns, sales taxes, and other credits are usually shown on the second line, since these are amounts that reduce your gross revenue.

Cost of goods sold or services delivered. This line can become quite complicated. Accounting and tax rules are forever changing concerning what is and what is not a cost of goods. In general, this amount is how much you paid for the goods that you sold in this period.

If you didn't carry inventory from period to period this would be easy to figure. If you purchased $550 in product on day one of the period and sold all of it before the end of the period for $1,000, it wouldn't take a computer for you to know your cost was $550 and gross profit was $450. Life is not so simple, however. Let's say that you have $120 worth of inventory at cost left at the end of the period. Now your cost of goods was $550 minus $120, or $430. Your sales were still $1,000, so your gross profit is now $570.

In the real world you also started with inventory. Continuing with the same example, let's say you had $75 worth of inventory at the beginning. Now your cost of goods would be: beginning inventory plus purchases minus ending inventory, or $75 + $550 − $120 = $505. There is still no change in your sales, so $1,000 − $505 = $495, which is now your gross profit.

Other things affecting cost of goods include freight-in (cost of shipping product from supplier to you), labor to prepare the item for sale, and any other charges directly related to the sale of the item. A very complicated gross profit analysis for products might look like this:

Gross sales		$11,000	100.0%
Less: Discount		800	7.3
Returns		300	2.7
Adjusted gross sales		9,900	90.0
Cost of goods			
Beginning inventory		$ 2,400	
Plus: Purchases	$6,100		
Freight-in	550		
Direct labor	2,350		
Less: End inventory	−6,800		
Cost of goods sold		$ 4,600	41.8
Gross profit		$ 5,300	48.2%

Later, you'll see that if you are losing money, an increase of 5 percent in your sales price will result in $550 more gross profit and a gross profit percentage of 53.2 percent. That assumes that you still sell as many units. You could achieve the same result by buying the product for about 9 percent less or reducing the labor cost necessary to make it salable by $550. You could also do a little of each. Thus you can begin to see how this system allows you to make management decisions.

Please note: All the above references are only to those items that you purchase and inventory for resale. When you buy a workbench or a computer, it is not included in "purchases" or in inventory.

Gross profit. What kind of gross profit percentage do you need for your business? The answer may be as low as 5 percent or as high as 70 percent depending on the kind of business you are in. Here are a few examples:

Retail hardware store	33–40%
Italian restaurant	66%
Manufacturer of consumer goods	50%
Auto retailer	10%
Parts wholesaler	28%

For more information about the appropriate profit margin for your industry, call the trade association or the editor of one of the trade magazines. In many industries there may even be statistics available on what others are doing.

PROFIT ANALYSIS FOR A SERVICE BUSINESS

How should you use this approach if you are in a service business? In the simplest example, you are the sole service provider. Figure out how many hours per month you spend actually providing that service or in direct preparation for doing so.

For instance, you are an auto mechanic. You work seventy hours per week. Out of this, however, you spend twenty hours in administrative tasks having nothing to do with servicing cars. You do count, however, the time you spend calling or driving around for parts, cleaning up, and explaining the bill to the customer.

Therefore you are spending fifty hours providing services. You are paying yourself $700 per week, for a total of seventy hours of work. An easy calculation shows you are earning $10 per hour. Fifty hours at $10 per hour means that your cost of service is $500. Your cost-of-service analysis would look like this.

Gross sales	$1,500	100.0%
Cost of services	500	33.3
Gross profit	$1,000	66.7%

Again, this can become more complicated by taking into account discounts and items directly related to the delivery of the service. In the case of the auto mechanic, the cost of service could include rags, lubricating greases, or other items not billed specifically to the customer.

PROFIT ANALYSIS FOR A COMPLEX BUSINESS

If you're selling two or more very different kinds of products that result in dramatically different margins for each, you may wish to separate them on your statement. This is also true if you offer dramatically different types of services, or a combination of product sales and services.

For instance, our primary company, AC International, has six different profit centers that are separately shown in the gross-profit analysis. Each one is evaluated according to its own purchases, freight factors, inventory changes, labor factors, and service components. By breaking the company into these six parts we're able to evaluate each on its own merits, rather than guessing that each is carrying its own weight. If any part is not contributing to profits, we can make appropriate adjustments specific to that portion of the business.

General and administrative overhead. The costs of doing business that are not directly related to the cost of goods fall under the category of general and administrative overhead. Under this category, place everything from telephones and rent to office salaries and payroll taxes. Those items that do not necessarily increase or decrease as sales go up or down will be shown in the budget as a dollar amount. Those items that generally fluctuate in accordance with sales will be shown as a percentage.

For instance, generally rent, casualty insurance, and trash service will be the same month after month. Thus you would put these items in at their dollar amount.

Salaries, telephone, postage, depreciation, and other similar categories may change from month to month and might even increase or decrease in a pattern similar to sales. However, in most cases, it is harder to predict these amounts by using a percentage of sales than if you project a dollar amount.

Line items that are commonly shown as a percentage would be commissions, royalties, utilities (for a manufacturer), product liability insurance, freight out for those giving freight allowances, phone expense for phone sales operations, and advertising.

Your statement for general and administrative expenses might look something like this (assuming $20,000 in sales):

GENERAL AND ADMINISTRATIVE EXPENSES

Office salaries		$3,300	16.50%
Payroll taxes		330	1.65
Rent		1,250	6.25
Utilities		350	1.75
Interest		550	2.75
Travel		200	1.00
Office supplies		200	1.00
Depreciation		600	3.00
Commissions	6%	1,200	
Freight-out	1%	200	
Advertising	5%	1,000	
Insurance	1%	200	
Total general and administrative expenses		$9,380	46.90%

If your sales of $20,000 in this example had generated a gross profit of $10,000, you would now subtract the general and administrative expenses from the gross profit ($10,000 − $9,380) and you would arrive at the profit for that period of $620.

Finally you would want to include an amount for income tax. This is shown after the net profit and is subtracted from net profit to produce the final line on your budget: "Net profit after tax."

For most individuals the first projected income statement they will want to construct will be their ideal budget. It will project sales as realistically as possible given the prospective owner's knowledge. The cost of goods and gross profit will reflect information supplied by the trade or from the owner's personal knowledge.

The other expenses will be shown at the highest amount within a range of expectations.

Let's take a minute to make that last paragraph concrete. You are going to open a retail auto-parts store. You can imagine in your dreams or nightmares that the monthly sales might range from $100 to $100,000 in the first twelve months. You've talked to owners of similar businesses, the local trade association, and the sales representatives from three prospective suppliers. From these you would narrow the realistic sales number to a range of $10,000 to $60,000, but the consensus seems to be in the range of $20,000. If you want to be very conservative in your approach, you might even use $15,000.

Further investigation shows the cost of goods sold averages about 66 percent, leaving a gross profit of 34 percent. You might figure that your cost of goods could be a little higher in the early going in that you may not buy as well as an experienced dealer. You may also find yourself discounting to your customers in the early going to keep from losing a marginal sale. Thus you may want to figure your cost of goods at 70 percent.

If you already have a location, you know the rent. If not, you will have to make your best guess. If you are certain that you will employ one clerk at $1,000 per month and you will pay yourself $800, you can show an exact figure there. Most companies will figure payroll taxes at around 10 percent of payroll. Now you have that figure. Earlier you were supposed to arrive at a formula for advertising. Put that one in.

Continue the process until you have what will represent your best guess as to what the company will actually do in each category. This becomes your working budget, the one to which you will compare each month's actual figures.

Part 7
The Break-Even Analysis

The break-even analysis takes the information that you have compiled in your income statement and looks at it backward. Given your best guess at the costs of doing business, this analysis asks the question: If these are my actual costs, what volume of sales must I do to break even (no profit and no loss)?

For this example we'll assume a company that has figured their dollar amount of general and administrative overhead (sometimes referred to as fixed expenses) to be $1,000 per month. Their percentage amount (also known as variable expenses) of general and administrative overhead is 15 percent of gross sales. Their cost of goods is 40 percent.

Our question now becomes a formula that might look something like this:

Gross sales	$X	100%
– Cost of Goods	–.40X	–40
Gross Profit	$.60X	60%
– variable expense	–.15X	–15%
– fixed expense	**– $900**	**–45**
	$0	0%

Note that fixed expense had to be 45 percent for net profit to be 0 percent.

We now have one line (in bold letters) that shows the relationship between the percentage amounts and the dollar amount. $900 = 45 percent. Thus we can create the equation $X/$900 = 100%/45%. After employing some freshman algebra we arrive at the formula X = 90,000/45 or X = $2,000. Thus you have determined that this business would have to produce $2,000 in gross sales during this period to break even. We would also be able to determine that if the fixed expenses stay fixed, this owner can expect to make a profit equal to 45 percent of every additional dollar he sells.

To arrive at your break-even without going through all the algebra, remember to divide fixed expenses in dollars by fixed expenses in percentage. The result will be the gross volume of sales needed to break even.

At this point produce for your business plan a projection of income statements for the first year by month. Also produce a break-even analysis. You may also want to produce income statements for years two and three if you expect more than 10 percent growth in each year.

CHAPTER
3

Legal Requirements

Part 1
Enterprise Type

You'll need to decide before opening the business what form your business will take. As mentioned in chapter 3 of section 1, in the United States there are four approaches available. In other countries it will be necessary to check with local resources to determine the choices offered.

Sole proprietorship. Most very small businesses use this enterprise type. It is the simplest from a tax and legal standpoint. In many cases part-time businesses using the sole proprietor approach will not even segregate their personal financial affairs from their business income and expenses. While this is not the best way to run any company, it is possible.

In general, the steps for establishing a sole proprietorship include:

A. Determination of a name. If you're not going to use your own name as the business name, you must file a "fictitious business statement." The government requires this filing so as to put your vendors and customers on notice that you are the responsible party behind the "fictitious name."

In most jurisdictions, this filing is accomplished by publishing certain information three times in a general circulation newspaper. If you will open your daily paper to the beginning of the want ads you will see a section titled something like "legal notices." Most papers publish new fictitious business statements every day. However, if you don't see any in today's paper, it is possible your local news vendor publishes these items only once a week. A quick call will determine their policy and prices. If you decide to use your own name, it's not necessary to file this statement. For instance, a professional firm named John Doe and Associates would not need to file. However, John's Baby Furniture would. If you're not certain, it's better to file.

B. Next you should open a checking account in the company name. The bank will require a copy of your fictitious business filing before they'll open the account. It is not absolutely necessary to have a separate checking account, but it's highly recommended.

C. If you will have employees, you should apply for a federal ID number. You can use your Social Security number in a sole proprietorship, but it doesn't cost anything to get a special number for your business.

D. In most states you'll need a sales tax number. This is the way that the state identifies you for the purposes of collecting sales taxes from you, your customers, and your vendors. You'll need this number regardless of the type of business you'll be running or the enterprise form you select. Your vendors will require this number in order to sell you items tax free that you intend to resell.

Generally, the state will ask for a cash deposit to ensure your payment of future sales taxes. If you sell only to other businesses who have sales tax numbers, you won't have any tax liability, and thus—in most states—you shouldn't have to make a deposit.

However, if you'll be selling to consumers, end users, or others who must pay a sales tax for the products or services you provide, then you'll certainly be asked for a deposit.

Most entrepreneurs are optimistic and somewhat proud of their enterprise. As a result, when the clerk at the sales tax office asks you to provide an estimate of your first quarter's or year's income, there is a tendency to give a high figure. The amount you state will be used to determine the amount of your deposit. In other words, the more optimistic you are, the more out-of-pocket expense you'll have.

A better approach is to come up with the lowest estimate that you think will be believed. If the clerk doesn't agree with your number and attempts to have you increase it, there's no rule against continuing to argue your position. If the difference of opinion is great enough, you may even want to involve a supervisor. The clerk's job is to get the largest deposit possible. Your job is to pay the smallest amount possible.

Please understand. This in no way affects your future tax liability, only your immediate cash flow. And remember, this general rule of not overestimating your income applies to *all* deposits you might make.

The positive aspect of the sole proprietorship as an enterprise type is that it is uncomplicated and inexpensive. The negative is that you have unlimited personal liability for the debts or other liabilities that may arise in running the business. You have less flexibility in your tax matters. In addition, you may find it more difficult to raise capital. Addressing these issues one at a time, the most important by far is the matter of unlimited personal liability.

You may or may not currently own a home, substantial savings, stocks, bonds, or other commercial paper. If you don't now, you certainly intend to build such assets in the future. You may even intend to own a vacation home, boat, jewelry, or art. As a sole proprietor, everything you own is subject to being seized by your business creditors.

Here are two examples of what can happen. Let's say that you currently own your own home, which is worth $150,000, and it has a mortgage of $70,000. You also have stocks and other holdings worth $25,000. You intend to open the business with your savings of $20,000. After six months in business, you decide to close down due to continuous losses. You are out of cash and owe suppliers $40,000. You signed a lease that has eighteen months to go at $500 per month. You also failed to pay employee tax deposits of $10,000.

Your vendors, the landlord, and the government will go after your home, stock, and anything else that isn't nailed down to collect the $59,000 you owe. And they will have every legal right.

In case number two, you go into the business with every penny you can scrape together. You live in an apartment and drive an old, beat-up VW. Five years later you are very successful. You have net assets worth $500,000 in addition to the book value (assets minus liabilities) of the business. One of your customers has an accident using one of your products. The manufacturer is out of business. You are the retailer. The customer successfully sues your business for $2 million. Your insurance pays the first million. Your business is able to come up with another $250,000. Your customer may next go after every asset you own personally.

This liability exposure is true for sole proprietorships, partnerships, and the general partners in a limited partnership. Only through incorporation can you escape this potential disaster.

Regarding the tax flexibility issue, 100 percent of the income of the business is taxed at the rate applicable to the owner as an individual. Under tax law in 2004, there is a slight advantage over regular corporation taxation. Of course, the government is always changing the rules, so consult your attorney or CPA to determine the current situation.

Regardless of the small current advantage in actual tax percentages between sole proprietorship and corporations, the real problem for the sole proprietor is the lack of flexibility. The owner of a corporation will have an easier time writing off certain expenses that may be perceived as personal or partly personal in a corporate tax return than will her counterpart in a sole proprietorship. In the second instance the small business return is part of the owner's tax return. With a corporation, it is an entirely different filing. We don't mention these issues of scrutiny with any intention of suggesting illegal tax avoidance. The point is, in a sole proprietorship situation even appropriate write-offs will get a tougher look in the owner's personal tax return.

A sole proprietor also has fewer options for pension, profit sharing, and employee benefit programs. Many of these have substantial tax advantages, but are available only to corporations.

Additionally, you may not be able to raise funds as easily with a sole proprietorship. Banks and other financial institutions who lend to companies prefer that the owner's liability be limited to the net worth of the business, as in a corporation. Why? Because, unless the corporation is rock solid, the bank will also ask for a personal guarantee from the owners. Then it will be the only entity that can attempt to take your personal assets if your company fails. In the case of a sole proprietorship, *all* creditors would have access to the owner's personal assets.

You are also limited in raising funds from others. The only method available is loans. Only through the other enterprise types can you raise money by offering ownership.

Partnerships. A partnership is identical in every aspect to a sole proprietorship except that everything is split among the partners. Thus, the personal liability will now extend to any partner. Creditors or individuals with judgments against the company can now attempt to get satisfaction by attaching any or all the partners' assets.

The partnership does file a separate tax return, which helps to make expenses easier to claim. However, the same tax-advantaged programs (pensions, profit sharing, and so forth) that are unavailable to the sole proprietor are also unavailable to partnerships.

When it comes to raising money, the partnership has an advantage in that banks now have potentially greater assets to use as collateral to secure loans. They will ask for personal guarantees from each partner. In addition, partnerships are often used as a method to raise capital by adding owners. If your partnership now has two individuals owning 50 percent each, it may be possible to entice a third partner to bring extra money into the business by giving up part of that ownership. For instance, you may need fifty thousand dollars. A potential investor who likes your business says he is willing to put in the funds for 40 percent of the business. This would leave you and your original partner with 30 percent each. It is possible to do this as often as you like. There is no limit to the number of partners in a partnership.

Limited partnerships. This form is much like a regular partnership except that only the "general partners" have unlimited liability. The "limited partners" (investors) have their liability limited to the amount of their investment. The determination of who is a general and who is a limited partner is decided solely by the partners. And generally, limited partners are not actively involved with the day-to-day running of the business.

Corporations. The second most popular form of enterprise is the corporation. It provides the ultimate protection from personal liability and the maximum amount of flexibility. In addition, the small corporation may be the least scrutinized form of business by government or tax authorities. The corporation generally has a wider range of ways to raise funds. Finally, the corporation enjoys the widest range of opportunities for special tax benefits.

A corporation is owned by its stockholders. There may be one stockholder holding all the shares, or there may be millions of shareholders holding various amounts of shares. Without going into details that are far beyond the scope of a business this size, I should point out that it is also possible for corporations to sell various classes of shares with various rights and preferences. For the very small business, we can limit our discussion to two types of simple corporations: the regular, or "C" corporation, which is taxed directly by the IRS; and the "Sub S" corporation, where the earnings are passed through to the stockholders, who must pay the tax personally.

Both of these forms limit the financial exposure of the owners to their actual investment and any value in the corporation beyond that investment. This is the single greatest advantage of a corporation. However, the shareholders can lose this protection if they don't completely separate the affairs of the corporation from their own personal affairs. They must also be certain that the amount of the original investment is clearly adequate to protect the public and the vendors from the likely activities of the corporation.

Let's examine these two concepts in reverse order. When a state grants one or more individuals the privilege of opening a corporation, it is only willing to shield the individual owners from personal liability in return for an expectation that the corporation will be able to adequately cover that exposure by itself.

Take, for instance, a company with an investment by the owners of five hundred dollars that incorporates to manufacture a new drug. It is unlikely that the owners could shield their personal assets from a future lawsuit. Someone who is harmed as a result of taking the drug would very likely be able to "pierce the corporate shield," and make a claim against the individual shareholders. This is because they have inadequately "capitalized" the business for its business purpose.

For most very small businesses, an initial investment of between five to a hundred thousand dollars would show the proper intent to adequately capitalize the firm.

The second problem is with intermingling of assets or affairs. It is perfectly legal for a sole proprietorship or partnership to run its business out of the owner's personal checkbook, and for the owner to use personal and business assets interchangeably (as long as the percentage of use is shown for tax purposes). In the case of a corporation it is critical that the business have a separate checking account and treat all aspects of that corporation as distinct from the owner's personal activities.

The owner must account for any financial transaction between himself and the corporation, including payment, loans, or sales of assets from one to the other. The corporation must be seen in all ways to be a separate and distinct entity from the owner. If not, there is the potential for creditors or judgment holders to "pierce the corporate veil" (show that no real separate entity existed) and go after the shareholders' personal assets.

Taxing authorities will also have problems with mingled accounts and assets. By failing to clearly distinguish between those things that are owned personally and those that are owned by the corporation, management risks losing depreciation allowances and other tax advantages.

Raising cash is another major advantage of the corporation. Through the sale of shares, the corporation can raise capital from outsiders at any time. Each time the company sells additional shares, the current shareholders lose a percentage of their ownership. This is referred to as dilution. However, it is not uncommon for the remaining percentage to be worth more than the larger undiluted share. This would be because of the additional capital that was raised by the sale of stock.

It isn't possible just to sell stock in a corporation any way you see fit. There are many rules as to how to proceed. The states are the only entities that have the right to grant corporate status. Therefore, each state establishes its own rules concerning how the corporation is formed and what procedures must be followed to sell stock.

Corporations may also borrow money from institutions or individuals. Very small businesses usually document these borrowings in the same way that individuals would. They use a standard loan agreement. For larger companies or amounts, the corporation can issue bonds. As with stocks, these securities can be issued only according to rules established by the state in which the company is incorporated or in which the corporation wishes to sell the bonds.

If your business becomes successful, you'll undoubtedly be looking for ways to deprive Uncle Sam and other taxing entities of as much of your money as you can legally achieve. The corporation is the easy winner in this department.

Later sections of this book will detail some of the more complicated profit-sharing, pension, and retirement plans. Many of these are available only to corporations.

In regular "C" corporations, the company, not the individual, pays taxes on its earnings. If the corporate tax rate is lower than the rate the owners would have had to pay, the owners are able to shield themselves from taxation. The business may "retain" earnings up to a point that the taxing authority believes reasonable for that type of enterprise. If the company keeps holding these tax-sheltered earnings beyond this "reasonable" level, the government will treat any additional earnings as if they had been distributed to the shareholders. The corporation must then pay taxes on these amounts.

This is where the double taxation of the "C" corporation comes in. Whether the earnings are actually distributed (in the form of dividends) to the shareholders *or* deemed to be distributed, the shareholders must now pay taxes on this income. The corporation pays tax on the income. Now the owners are taxed on what is left.

It may seem as though this would never be a good idea. However, there are ways to avoid this double taxation. The working owners may pay themselves a "reasonable" salary and bonus. This is deductible to the corporation. You may be able to take all or almost all the profits of the "C" corporation as salary. It may be more than you think you are worth and still be seen as reasonable.

You can capitalize the company with the minimum amount you believe is "reasonable." If the company needs more money, you can lend your own funds to the corporation. The interest you earn is deductible to the company. Later you can pay back the loan. Of course, this principal passes back to you without tax. If you had capitalized the corporation at a higher level instead of using this loan technique, you would not have received tax-advantaged interest. Additionally, if you wanted to take out your original capital it might be seen as a dividend. In any case it would require the transfer of stock that would reduce your ownership if there was more than one owner.

The corporation can also lend you money. All these loans need to be clearly documented, and the company must charge you reasonable interest. However, once again you have been able to take some of the retained earnings out of the company without being taxed.

In many cases, the very small business is better off with a "Sub S" corporation, so called because it falls under Subsection S in the federal tax code. This form combines the advantages of a corporation with those of a partnership.

As long as the owners follow the rules of the federal tax code and their local state corporation code, the company will receive all the benefits of limited exposure offered to the "C" corporation. "Sub S" companies may also take advantage of some of the tax-advantaged pension, profit-sharing, and retirement plans enjoyed by a "C" corp. Others are not available.

The exciting part of the "Sub S" is the elimination of double taxation. In this form, a company passes through its earnings or losses to its owners. The corporation itself pays no taxes. (Actually, some states have a special tax for "Sub S" companies.)

Businesses that are expecting losses often use this form so that the owners can write off these losses. This is not possible in a "C" corp. If you have ten owners holding 10 percent each, and the company loses $100,000, each owner can write off $10,000 (as long as they have invested at least $10,000).

Be careful, however. If you have stockholders, or even if you are the only stockholder, a profit will result in a taxable event for all the owners. This is true whether or not the company pays out any cash (called distributions in a "Sub S"). For instance, if the company above makes $100,000, each shareholder will have $10,000 in regular income for that tax period. If she pays 25 percent tax, she will owe $2,500. If the company doesn't pay out at least that amount, the taxpayer will still owe it . . . and will have to pay it out of pocket.

It's possible to switch your enterprise type. You can do so almost as often as you wish. Of course, each change means costs in money, time, and paperwork. It's not uncommon for a company to start out as a simple sole proprietorship with commingled bank accounts and assets. As the business grows, it may move to separate its affairs from those of its owner. Down the road there may be a need for a working and/or financial partner, at which time the partnership form may be used.

As the company becomes successful and begins to accumulate assets, the partners may feel it is time to incorporate. They might start out as a "C" corporation, but later desire the tax benefits of the "Sub S."

Unless you are a tax expert, you should probably get some advice from a CPA or an attorney as to which enterprise form best meets your needs now. You will also want to ask that question again from time to time as your business grows and changes.

Add to your business plan the enterprise type that you will use, the reasons for so choosing, your planned initial capital, and a list of partners or shareholders, if any.

Part 2
Business Licenses
and Regulations

You will usually need a business license. This is a requirement of the city or county where the enterprise will be located. You will almost certainly need this license if you plan to operate out of a commercial facility such as a storefront, office building, or warehouse. You may not need a business license if you have a home-based business that provides professional services, such as a manufacturers' representative or business consultant, or if you are part of a multilevel organization.

When you begin to research your location, you'll see the major disparity in business climate from city to city or county to county. Some are very eager to have businesses of your type locate in their area. You may be bringing jobs for their citizens and additional tax revenues for their coffers. In these cities you may find that getting a license is a ten-minute exercise in filling out a form and paying a small (under one hundred dollars) fee.

Other cities exhibit an antibusiness attitude. In these jurisdictions you may find yourself wading through a substantial bureaucracy before being issued your license. This might include a site inspection by the building department and/or the fire department. You may be required to prove financial standing. You may be provided with a list of dos and don'ts concerning signs, parking, carpooling, hours of operation, and much more. You may also find the initial fee to be abnormally high.

The hoops through which you may have to jump at the city or county level also depend on the type of business you plan to open. Most retailers, wholesalers, and service providers won't be faced with major red tape.

However, if you intend to open a restaurant, manufacturing company, or auto repair business, the story will be quite different. You will find legal requirements and restrictions on everything from the type of materials and equipment you can use to the number and size of restrooms you must provide. These rules and regulations may affect your decision on location. Therefore, you should check out the requirements of likely cities for your type of business before you begin to seek a location.

Because of the endless list of regulations, their common

appearance of arbitrariness, and the low likelihood of enforcement, it is common for business owners to press forward with their plans without carefully evaluating those parts of the local laws that may apply to them.

Clearly, there are plenty of small business owners who know the laws and interpret them in the most favorable light given what they want to accomplish. While not taking a position on the ethics involved at this juncture, I'll simply say that it is good business practice to make such decisions carefully.

For example, a major retail headache today is sign rules. You are paying a great deal of money for a great location, and you want to be able to shout your store name or other message from your walls, window, and rooftop. Most cities now have lists of rules concerning what you can and cannot do in this regard.

The most practical approach to planning your signage in this environment would be to read a copy of the local sign code before you begin thinking about a possible design. Hopefully, you or your sign maker will be able to conceive of a sign that will accomplish your goals within the rules of your city.

If not, you are faced with a choice. You can go to the city with your plan and ask for a variance. Depending upon the city and the type of variance you are seeking, you may or may not be successful. Your other option is to go ahead with your sign and see what happens. This is dangerous because you risk trashing an expensive sign. On the other hand, the violation may go unnoticed or unenforced for years.

If you know that you will be operating in a gray area where it is unclear how the ordinance is intended, *and* you feel it is very important to your company to push into this gray area, you should probably do so without asking the city first. Bureaucrats are predisposed to say no. They also like to bog you down in endless paperwork and commission meetings. If you are truly operating in a gray area, try to avoid this messy and expensive process.

CHAPTER
4

The Grand Opening

THE BALANCE OF THIS SECTION and the entirety of the next section deal with the beginning of your business. Many of you are purchasing or taking over an existing business. Thus the business will not be experiencing its grand opening or its first week. However, it will still be *your* beginning, and you'll be encountering a lot of things for the first time. Therefore most of the following applies as much to you as it would to a start-up.

There are two kinds of grand openings. One is a special promotion called a "Grand Opening." If you've established a business that depends on walk-in traffic, you'll undoubtedly want to use your opening as an excuse to have a grand-opening promotion. Whatever you do, *don't do this on your first day*. You'll have plenty of time to do this promotion after you've worked out the kinks of your operation and had enough time to properly plan such an event.

The other grand opening *is* your first day of business. This chapter deals with the second type of grand opening. Put on your seat belt. You are about to begin the ride of your life.

Part 1
Last-Minute Checklist

Wow! If you'd only known it would be this much work just to get to opening day! Let's check off the list of things you should have done before opening your doors for the first time.

1. Created a simple business plan that includes your mission statement, your strategy, and your budget.
2. Secured a location.
3. Contacted vendors for the products and services you will need and established their willingness to supply you.
4. Hired the necessary staff for the opening.
5. Determined the business form you will use and taken care of the necessary legal requirements to establish the business.
6. Secured the necessary government licenses, permits, etc. At the top of the list would be business license, sales tax permit, tax ID number, and any special licenses or permits specific to your type of business.
7. Purchased and installed the necessary equipment and fixtures. You may need to plan the purchase and installation of your phone, fax, and computer lines months in advance. It is a complicated and time-consuming project.
8. Opened a checking account and established a banking relationship.
9. Secured firm delivery dates for your opening inventory. Don't forget forms, stationery, and other incidentals necessary to the conduct of business (such as pens).
10. Established contact with potential customers or clients through advertising, mailings, or personal calls to let them know you are about to open.
11. In some instances you may wish to have secured orders or contracts in advance of opening.

12. Contracted for Yellow Pages advertising if appropriate.

13. Determined your operating procedures: such things as hours, pricing procedure, purchasing method, invoicing procedure, terms and conditions of sale, warranties and guarantees, return authorizations, bookkeeping system, and filing.

14. Created your Web page and established your e-mail information. Contacted search engines and other services that direct customers to your Web site.

Let me guess that you were doing just fine until number 13. While no amount of planning will result in every base being covered on day one, there is much you should do to appear professional and to avoid losing sales and profit needlessly.

Part 2
Operating Procedures

HOURS OF OPERATION

Now it is time to make a decision. You don't want to needlessly limit your hours of operation. However, you can only personally work so many hours per day. An employee can be hired to expand the number of hours the business is open. However, there is a cost for that. You'll want to carefully evaluate whether there is enough business during those times to justify the wages and other overhead costs incurred by staying open.

You may be able to substantially expand your hours of availability to your customers with an answering machine, a cell phone, call forwarding, a fax machine, e-mail, and your Web site. Every time I've started a new business, my first business card has included my home phone. I probably haven't received more than a few dozen calls at home as a result, but it sends a message about my commitment to serving my customer.

PRICING PROCEDURE

Again, we have had some discussion earlier about how to price. Retailers generally need to double cost for items under twenty dollars. Service companies generally must triple their labor cost. Wholesalers look for average margins around 30 percent. Whatever approach you use it is important that, before opening, you formalize your pricing policy. This should be done in such a way that anyone involved in sales or invoicing knows exactly what to do.

Pricing includes discounting. Are you going to offer discounts for volume, cash terms, or to match the competition? If not, you will want to provide your sales team with a rationale for "why not." For instance, you might prefer a one-price-fits-all policy. Customers who want to place large orders may feel that they deserve a price break, but you can tell them that your policy ensures that an even larger competitor will not be able to buy better than they did.

Whatever your pricing and discounting policy, it needs to be formalized. Put it in writing. Discuss it with each person who will have contact with customers or billing. Provide them with the necessary resources to double-check a price if the normal system (price sticker, computer, etc.) isn't available.

PURCHASING

If all goes well, by day two or three you'll need to start reordering some items. First, you'll need to establish the criteria that determine when it's appropriate to reorder. Generally, this is a function of cost, volume of usage, order minimums, lead time, and terms.

You may be selling 5 drinking glasses per day that cost you fifty cents each, take three weeks from order to delivery, and must be ordered in fifties. Since it takes three weeks for delivery, you might want to maintain a maximum inventory of twenty-one days (assuming seven selling days per week) times 5 glasses, or 110. In addition you could establish a standing order for 50 glasses each ten days. If you didn't experience a major variation in your usage, you would range between 60 and 110 in stock.

Other things could radically change this formula. You may average 5 per day, but the most common order size is 100. In this case you may wish to maintain at least 200 in stock and another 100 on order. This way you'd rarely miss a sale due to being out of stock. On the other hand, your customer may be used to waiting two or three weeks for this type of product. In this case you may only wish to order the next 100 each time you sell 100 or more.

Your supplier may also offer discounts for volume either in the form of a direct off-price discount or through free freight for purchases above a certain size. Some suppliers offer dating terms (buy now, pay in sixty, ninety, or more days) at certain times of year. This may allow you to carry more inventory than usual.

In any case, you need to establish a policy as to who orders what. This can be by product category, amount of purchase, or other criteria, but it is extremely important that someone have the responsibility and the authority to order more product. This should be one of the most systematic aspects of your business. Some items might need to be monitored daily, others weekly, and some only monthly or as a special need arises.

The other side of purchasing policy has to do with follow-up. You'll learn soon enough that not all vendors will ship as promised. It may take longer and/or you may not get everything you ordered. This can result in lost sales and major aggravation. Call the vendor the day after you place the order to confirm the availability and ship date. In critical situations, call again on the day before shipment to confirm that the product will be leaving on time and in the quantities promised. Someone needs to be responsible for this follow-up.

INVOICING PROCEDURE

The way you invoice your customer reflects on your entire business. Other than the business transaction (product or service) you provide, the sales slip may be the only lasting impression you'll make.

From your first day of business you should be providing a professional sales slip, personalized with your company name. If you're a retailer, your sales register receipt should have your name on it. If you're using handwritten receipts, don't use standard forms from the local stationery store. Have forms printed with your name on them.

Manufacturers and wholesalers should always use typed or computer-generated invoices on custom invoice paper. Make certain that your pricing is clear. Make it obvious what your terms are. If you want your customer to take the early-pay discount, compute it for them so they can see the actual amount saved. Point put the date by which payment must be received to earn this discount.

Make certain that your customer gets the invoice . . . and *fast*. You should send out an invoice the very same day that the product is shipped or the service rendered. The sooner your bill arrives at your customer, the sooner you're likely to be paid. Attorneys, doctors, and accountants are particularly poor about invoicing quickly. Our procedure is to type up all orders received on one day by 11:00 a.m. the following day. All orders shipped that day are invoiced and mailed by 5:00 p.m. that day.

If you ship product to others, always include a packing slip that shows the number of boxes, total units, weight of each box, shipping carrier used, and date of shipment. It is also a good idea to show who picked the order and who packed it. Our packing slip says "proudly picked by _____," and "proudly packed by _____."

Who will process incoming orders? What approach will you use to handle these orders? For most companies, it's best to use a two-step approach. First you create a picking slip. The carbon copy of this is a packing slip. This goes out to production or warehousing. After the order is shipped, the warehouse copy comes back to bookkeeping, who can then create the invoice and any back order if appropriate.

TERMS AND CONDITIONS OF SALE

When you offer your customers open account (they purchase goods from you now and pay you later) you need to establish when and under what conditions they will pay you. If you ship merchandise to others, you'll have to decide who pays the freight bill and who is at risk while the goods are in transit.

Your decisions on these issues are important from the standpoint of marketing, cash flow, and bottom line. You want to make the terms attractive enough to entice your customer to make the purchase. But, if you give away too much in this area you may quickly run out of cash or end up without profit.

You may wish to be fairly aggressive when you first start out. By this I mean you may wish to be quick to extend open account, allow larger cash discounts, and ship freight prepaid on small amounts. These concessions would all give you a competitive advantage.

Later, as you start hitting your sales goals, you might slowly tighten up these terms. Your eventual goal might be to equal the terms of your competition. This strategy is not for everyone, but has, in my experience, worked well.

Commonly used terms and conditions are as follows (with their definitions).

CIA. Cash in advance. This is most appropriate where the order is for custom products or services. You may also want to use CIA where the creditworthiness of the customer cannot be ascertained before shipment or delivery of service.

L/C. The next best thing to cash in advance is a letter of credit. This is a document provided by the customer's bank, which confirms that the security of the bank is behind the customer. There are many variations of L/Cs. They are most commonly used for international transactions and very large domestic sales. They are expensive and complicated. We avoid their use whenever possible.

If you find that you must use L/Cs due to a requirement by your bank, your customer, or to ensure payment, consult with a knowledgeable export attorney to determine what requirements to insist on. Be prepared to follow the dictates of the L/C in every specific, as each discrepancy that you create will cost you in time and money.

COD. Cash on delivery. This is a well-known term, but there are a few problems that can occur when using this supposedly safe method of payment.

On a custom order, the customer may go out of business or not actually have the cash when the product or service is delivered. To ensure against this, get all or most of your money CIA for custom orders.

The order is shipped, but the check is no good. If you do much COD shipping, you should ask for bank and credit references to reduce this risk. You may also send your COD on the basis of cash or certified check only.

Problems can occur when merchandise is shipped in several cartons. To save the customer money, you put a COD tag on one package for the entire amount. An unscrupulous customer may elect, though, to keep all the packages except the one with the COD tag, which is returned. To avoid this, divide the amount of the invoice by the number of boxes and send out each box with its own COD amount.

DP or sight draft. These are generally used in international situations, but can be used in larger domestic shipments. DP (documents on presentation) or sight draft uses your bank and the customer's bank as the collecting agent for the shipment. After your truck or shipping line provides you with a bill of lading, this document is sent by your bank to your customer's bank along with a document demanding payment. When the payment is made, the customer's bank gives him the bill of lading so that he can claim the freight.

Net terms. If you decide to offer your customer an open account (which provides product or services now for payment later) you'll need to establish what "later" means. The number of days after invoice that you require payment in full is the net date. You may require payment in ten days. Your terms would read "net ten days." Common net terms include ten days, thirty days, sixty days, and ninety days. Extension of credit costs you the use of your money. Therefore you'll want to limit your net terms to the fewest days possible, given competitive pressures.

Cash discounts. You may wish to encourage your customers to whom you extend payment terms to pay you sooner rather than later. This has many advantages, not the least of which is the common maxim that the sooner you are paid the more likely you are to get paid.

The use of cash discounts can substantially speed up payment. For companies offering net thirty it is very common to offer a 1, 2, or 3 percent discount for payment within ten days. This would read in the case of a 1 percent discount, "1 percent ten net thirty." A 1 percent discount for ten days versus net thirty will usually induce the most creditworthy and liquid companies to pay in ten days. Three percent ten net thirty terms will potentially result in a large percentage of your customers paying early.

Dating and anticipation. As a wholesaler or manufacturer, you may want to induce your customers to stock up in their off season. They, of course, are reluctant to purchase more than a bare minimum during a time when their sales are low.

Possibly you have a close-out or special purchase situation. You have been able to buy a very large stock of an item at a heavily discounted price. Now it is important that you sell and ship these items because of space or cash considerations.

These and other opportunities may result in the offering of dating terms. Generally, payment is set for more than ninety days and noted by the due date. For example, you might want to sell product for Christmas in July and offer net January 5 terms.

You may need to offer these terms for many reasons, but the extension of this cash deprives you of its use. Therefore, you may want to use anticipation discounts. This means that if your customer pays earlier than the net date he will pay less. Generally these terms are stated in one of two ways.

Net January 5, 2% anticipation. This would mean that the customer can take off 2 percent for each thirty days before January 5 that he pays. Sometimes you will want to write out these terms longhand: "Net January 5, 2% December 5, 4% November 5," and so on. To encourage early payment, spell out the customer's opportunity in the body of the invoice: "Deduct $74.00 if paid by December 5. Deduct $148.00 if paid by November 5," and so forth.

10th prox. The term "10th prox" means the invoice is due on the next tenth of the month. A 2 percent 10th prox, sometimes shown as just "2% 10th" (very close to and can be confused with "2% 10"), means that a 2 percent discount can be taken if paid on the next tenth. To add further confusion to this method, it is common to see "2% 10th net 30." This then would mean that if you were invoiced on the eleventh of January, you could take a 2 percent discount if you pay by February 10, but the invoice is due in full anyway on February 11. The good news with this concept is that you generally can plan for substantial cash around the tenth. The bad news is that nobody wants their product shipped between the first and the tenth.

You can also mix and match the above terms. You might end up with 30 percent cash in advance, 30 percent on delivery, 40 percent net thirty. Or you can make up your own terms. For instance, I once made an arrangement with a toolmaker to pay a thousand dollars per week during production of the tool.

Consignment or flooring. In this situation, you are maintaining ownership of the product while it is at your customer's place of business until it is sold by him. This use is most common when a new product is having a hard time getting placed or when the item being sold is a very big ticket (pianos and organs, for example). After the product is sold, the customer has an agreed-upon number of days to pay for that item.

The following are some commonly used freight terms you should be familiar with.

FOB. This stands for "free on board" and legally means that the shipper transfers the risk of the freight to the customer as soon as he puts it on board a common carrier. Many, if not most, businesses misuse this term to mean that the customer will pay the freight, not the shipper.

Freight prepaid. The shipper is responsible for the freight bill. Generally it also means that he doesn't pass the freight charge along to the customer. A variation is "freight prepaid and add." This usage is common with UPS shipments and situations where the customer has no way to pay the freight company on arrival. Therefore the shipper pays the freight bill, but adds the amount to the invoice.

Most companies require that their customer buy a certain quantity at one time to qualify for freight prepaid. For example, this might be expressed as freight prepaid on orders over $1,500, freight prepaid on five hundred units, or freight prepaid on truck-load quantities.

CIF. International shipments and some domestic transactions might be arranged CIF, which means the selling price includes the Cost of goods, Insurance, and Freight. In this arrangement, the shipper is paying all costs of shipping, handling, and insurance to the customer's port.

Freight allowance. In this situation the shipper offers to pay some of the freight. You can show this as a percentage discount, an amount per pound, or merely a negotiated amount.

Freight collect. Here, the customer pays the entire freight bill. Generally, the customer also picks the carrier.

Freight allowed. I've left this one until last because it is rarely used. However, it is my favorite, and the one we have used at AC International. This means we ship the merchandise freight collect (or prepaid and add in the case of UPS), but the customer may subtract this charge if she pays this invoice within the net credit terms. The advantage here is that we do not end up with the additional handling of freight bills to pay, and it encourages our customers to pay their bill on time.

Generally, freight-allowed terms will have limitations similar to freight prepaid terms, such as minimum-order quantities.

Your terms do not have to apply to everyone equally, although there are some fair-trade regulations concerning equal pricing and terms to customers that would be judged equal. We use almost every term shown above to cover individual situations.

WARRANTIES AND GUARANTEES

You have been open a few days when a customer calls or comes in. He is hopping mad! His aluminum siding is sliding. Her buttons have popped. The braces are broke. The permanent wasn't.

You need to have a clear policy as to what you will do when your product or service doesn't perform as promised. You also need some idea what your policy will be when you and the customer don't agree on whether the product is the problem or what service was intended.

For many of you there are probably industry standards that will help you with this. However, you need to find out what these are. Call an industry association to see if they can help. If not, see if your suppliers have some ideas. Finally, you may want to ask people in the same business as you who don't see you as a competitor.

Write down your policies and put them where your employees can see them clearly. In many instances, you may want to put them where the customer can also see them clearly.

In establishing your return policy consider the law of two hundred. On average, a bad experience with your company will be repeated until it is heard by two hundred potential customers.

RETURN AUTHORIZATIONS

You will not want your customers just returning product to you indiscriminately. It is all too common that a customer will change his mind while your merchandise is in transit. You want to be the one to decide whether or not you will accept a return.

You need to have an RA (return authorization) system. Generally, you will agree to accept returns of defective material, over-shipments, or incorrect shipments. There will even be times when you will accept a return of product that the customer decided to return on a whim. Your order desk should be prepared to give the customer a return authorization number (an RA number) for situations such as these.

Of course, you would prefer not to have merchandise come back. Train your staff in methods of persuading customers to keep the mistakes. You may want to offer discounts, longer payment terms, or consignment.

Many customers are now asking permission to destroy or dispose of small amounts of defective material rather than create the expense of shipping and handling. You may wish to authorize this where you are aware of the defect. It may also be appropriate where the amount of money involved is small. However, it may well be worth the extra expense if you need to monitor these defects or if you believe the customer is throwing away perfectly good items.

BOOKKEEPING PROCEDURES

The management system that should have your highest priority after sales is bookkeeping.

Your sales may be excellent, but if you don't invoice them correctly or collect what you've invoiced, you're headed out of business. You buy product at the right price, but if you don't make certain that your supplier invoices you correctly, watch out. Many times each month I catch errors in the amount we are going to pay.

The checking account. It is *critical* that every effort be taken to keep this account up-to-date and accurate. The first step in this process is the use of numbered checks. You may even wish to use checks with two copies. The first copy will be kept in a numerical sequence file after it has been entered (posted) to the disbursements account or checkbook. Attach the second copy to the invoice it is paying or file it under a noninvoiced category such as rent.

You can also achieve most of the above by using a system known as "One-Write." This system is available through Safeguard Business Systems. Find them on the Internet or call their 800 number. Many companies now do most or all of their check writing electronically, through banking services or private systems.

Use a calculator or computer to check your math. Double-check your results by taking an adding-machine-tape total of the numerical copies and comparing that result to the one in the checkbook (or disbursements journal).

Reconcile your checkbook with the bank statement as soon as you receive it. Even the best bookkeeper makes an occasional mistake, and all banks do. Catch them quickly before they cause you serious grief.

You will need to decide who has access to the checkbook, who may sign checks, and how many people must sign a check for it to be valid. Golden nugget: *Only owners should sign checks.* If there is more than one owner, it is much better if only one owner signs most of them.

There are at least three good reasons why only an owner should have check-signing authority. One is very obvious. The easiest way for someone to rip you off in a big way is to allow them to sign checks. If you must sign, and therefore see, every check that goes out the door, you can be reasonably sure that they are all going to legitimate vendors, government agencies, or employees.

Furthermore, you have a last chance to check the accuracy of the bill to be paid, and the payment. You might recall that you've already paid it. You might notice that the cost figure is not what you negotiated. You might catch an incorrect extension.

Finally, it is actually better for your bookkeeper or controller. If they do not have the authority, they avoid the appearance of impropriety if something goes wrong. I trust my controller totally, but she does not have check-signing authority.

FILING

My partner claims that he is the best filer in the world. He also maintains that his biggest problem is "unfiling." If you maintain a properly designed filing system, and you insist that those who have access to it file things where they belong, you should not have any problems "unfiling."

You'll use your filing system every day. You'll need to look up an invoice to prove something was shipped. You'll need a copy of a purchase order to show your supplier how you were overcharged. You'll need to find a copy of a contract, letter, or quotation. You'll want the information now, and you'll want to be able to read it.

Buy a decent filing cabinet. It's better to buy a sturdy used one than a flimsy new one. Set up as much of the filing system in advance as possible. Most types of businesses will begin with an alphabetic file for invoices by customer. You may also like to keep a numerical invoice file as a backup in case the one in the alphabetic file is lost.

You'll want three payables files. One contains receivers (document showing receipt of merchandise by your receiving clerk) attached to purchase orders. This is a temporary file for after you have received merchandise, but before receiving the invoice.

The second payable file is those "to be paid." Generally you will keep these alphabetically by vendor. You may wish to keep a separate file by date to remind you that a bill needs to be paid. Some companies keep the invoices to be paid in a date file.

The third payable file is "paid." These are generally filed by supplier name in alphabetical order. Most paid payable files have four critical documents attached together: purchase order, receiver, invoice, and check copy.

Every company should have a correspondence file. The computer has caused many folks to stop keeping hard-copy correspondence files, relying instead on the computer memory. Important letters should be kept in hard copy, too.

A new file is the fax file. We keep ours by the month for general correspondence divided by incoming and outgoing in date order. We also keep separate files for those with whom we have a large amount of fax correspondence. Always file a copy of the fax instead of the original if it is on special fax paper. The images on some fax paper will fade over time.

You'll need a file for legal documents. The more important ones should also be kept off premises in a safety deposit box. Copies of these plus the less important ones need to be kept close at hand.

This is by no means an exhaustive list of every possible file you may need. Hopefully it will stimulate you to carefully consider the kinds of files you'll need to keep. Again, additional information may be available by calling someone in a similar business.

CREDIT CARDS

For the retailer or Web-based business, credit cards are a necessity. For business-to-business companies such as wholesale, manufacturing, or business services, the credit card is now part of the marketing strategy for most such concerns.

In order to have your own credit card account, so that you can process your customer's credit card, you actually have to have good credit yourself. Be prepared for a rigorous assessment of your credit standing prior to being signed up. If your credit is not very good, or if you are new in business, you will have to pay a premium in charges for processing. There are processing companies who take the riskier accounts and charge for that risk. Your bank may be able to help you find one.

You can also sometimes get a better rate if you go through an industry association or through the National Association of Small Businesses. You can also go through a Web-hosting service. This can be very expensive.

Compare the prices of the various services just like you would the charges for a cell phone or insurance carrier. There can be very considerable savings by doing some research.

Part 3
Last-Minute Attitude Check

"We're alive, partner!" This exclamation is the theme of a movie called *One Good Cop*. It was Michael Keaton's victory cry each time he and one of his partners would narrowly avoid death or worse. During the next three to five years, maybe even longer, you may want to keep that phrase in mind as your business experiences its own close calls.

Keaton's character had the right attitude. Every time he was knocked down, he got up and kept going. Your attitude will have more to do with your ultimate success than any other single thing. I believe you should develop the following attitudes.

1. You must expect success. You can't be satisfied with merely hoping for it. You must set aside your doubts. You haven't elected to take this journey with the idea that if it's too hard, or takes too long, or isn't quite what you'd expected, you'll just toss in the towel. You need to make a personal commitment to see this enterprise through to success.

2. You must be prepared for failure. *"What?!"* you say. "How do you square that with your last comment?" You will fail. Hopefully the failure will only be temporary and won't bring about the failure of the entire business. Through failure we learn. Success teaches us little. To the extent that you are mentally and emotionally prepared to fail, you'll be able to take failure, large and small, in stride. If you aren't, your inability to handle failure may result in the total loss of your enterprise.

3. You must conquer fear. If it weren't for fear, every one of us would have already achieved every goal we could ever have imagined. Fear holds us back. For instance, you may really think hot air ballooning would be fun. However, your fear keeps you from trying it.

In business, your fear will keep you from calling on that major account that could put you in the black. Maybe you've called on the account and made your presentation, but now fear is keeping you from calling to see if a decision has been made.

Fear will keep you from taking advantage of opportunities that cross your desk. A little fear might be a good thing to the extent that it keeps one from chasing every opportunity in sight. However, many businesspeople become paralyzed by such fears as adding to their line, computerizing their accounting, or selling overseas.

4. You must quash negative emotions. No one wants to buy from a negative person. No one wants to work for one. Negative people don't even really want to be around themselves. Negativism gets in the way of getting things done. Does this mean that we should all walk around with a Pollyanna attitude? Not necessarily, although it surely would be preferable to its opposite. Realism is important. Negativism is not realism.

5. You must make goals. Daily, monthly, yearly sales goals are critical. Cash goals and purchasing goals are essential. If you run out of cash or product, what benefit are the sales? Business improvement goals should be laid out daily, maybe even hourly, as you see flaws that need mending or opportunities that need exploiting.

6. Prepare yourself *every day* to meet the challenges of that day with enthusiasm and decisiveness. If you don't start the day that way, events will control you rather than be controlled by you. At the end of the day, in the evening at home, or first thing in the morning, write lists of the things you need to deal with today along with sober thoughts on how you will do so. Then hit the ground running.

The days that I arrive at the office with less than total excitement usually end the same way. But, on those days when I'm ready for bear, by the end of the day I've usually bagged my trophy.

Part 4
The Dress Rehearsal

This section is for those companies who will be meeting the public and have more than one employee, such as retailers, restaurants, service providers, doctors, and wholesalers offering counter service.

It's very important that you appear to know what you're doing from the very first day. To help produce that result, you may wish to schedule a dress rehearsal. It will cost you an extra day's pay for your employees, but it will almost surely be worth it.

Prepare everything as if you were ready to open on rehearsal day. Invite your spouse, neighbors, friends, supplier salespersons to come in and play the role of customer.

Ask them to really put you to the test. Some should be demanding. Others totally passive. Try one customer at a time, and a houseful. Pay special attention to whether everything is clear to your "customers." How were they treated by your people? Did the person writing up the bill know what he was doing? How about credit card handling?

Have someone bring back a damaged product. Have people call the store to see how your people handle the phones. Run through your opening and closing procedures.

You may believe that you can do this just as well with real customers, but your mind will be going a million directions at once during the business day. By acting as a director at a dress rehearsal, you can fine-tune your business operations while focusing on just this aspect of your operation.

Part 5
The First Day

As you approach the building on day one, your first balloon is popped. People are not lined up waiting to get in. On entering, you find there is no voice mail, and two hours later the only call you receive is from your spouse asking how it's going. As the first day ends your revenues are just under ten bucks. A quick glance at your budget shows that your expenses for that day were closer to a hundred.

Now is not the time to question what went right or wrong. The fact that anybody bought anything from you today may be a great sign. The question you should be looking at is, "What did I do today? How did I spend my time?"

If you spent a great deal of the time watching the traffic go by, doing useless paperwork, or watching soap operas, you should probably get a copy of the employment section of the want ads for tomorrow.

During this start-up period, every minute of time that is not being devoted to a project essential to keeping the doors open must be spent selling, promoting, and planning promotion. Only one of those things you may be planning as a promotion is a grand opening. Many businesses have no need of such an event or cannot gain from it. Others such as ad agencies or beauty shops may want to hold an open house where potential clients enjoy a few snacks and admire your new facility.

If you're in retail, take ten-minute breaks (with a note on the window "back in ten minutes") to pass out brochures in the neighborhood. Don't stand in your doorway and look sadly at the passersby. Be bold, forget fear. Invite them in for a cup of coffee. Give them a coupon for a 10 percent discount next time they come.

Rent a clown outfit and stand in front of your place of business to attract attention. Hire a mariachi band to play in your front window.

When should you start taking all these drastic actions? *From the first day*. You have expenses. Those expenses don't stop and wait for sales. Each day you don't sell enough to pay those expenses puts you one day closer to an unacceptable result of all your hard work and money: going broke!

How should you spend your first day if you are a wholesaler, broker, manufacturer, or sales rep? On the phone, in your car, or on an airplane. You have to be in front of the decision makers. You can spend all your time fine-tuning your equipment, counting your inventory, or meeting with vendors and principals, but none of those activities is going to result in a sale. You need sales! *Now!*

How about service providers such as doctors, lawyers, and CPAs? It is the rare professional who isn't uncomfortable about "selling" his services. It hasn't been so long since such action was considered unethical or even illegal.

Such is not the case today. The day-to-day overhead expenses of most professionals are among the highest of very small businesses. Besides, each hour that a lawyer or doctor isn't practicing, the lost opportunity cost of doing so as an employee is very high.

First contact every other member of your profession in your area to offer your services to them. Doctors can commonly benefit from referrals of other doctors who have too large a caseload or who don't practice in your specialty. Ad agencies may be able to pick up small clients from other agencies. What is unprofitable business to one company may be life and death to a start-up.

Restaurateurs, go out and visit every owner and manager of a business anywhere nearby. Give them a free lunch coupon or two. If your food is good, they will pay for that free lunch many times when they return with employees, customers, and suppliers.

Join local service and professional clubs, the chamber of commerce, charities, or the boosters for the high school. Meet people. Hand out cards.

Visit or call companies with which you have potential synergy. Contractors should leave their cards at the local lumberyards and hardware stores so that a do-it-yourselfer can get a lead for the times he is over his head.

If you are opening a family counseling center, you'll want to leave your card with area pastors, doctors, school nurses and counselors, and social service providers.

If you're renting cars, you should be contacting insurance agents, claims adjusters, body shops, auto repair facilities, and hotels.

The negative guys are piping up: "I sell manufactured products to wholesalers. After I've called every one twice in the same week, what is left for me to do to help my sales?"

1. Go out and call on the retailers that they service. Do this on your own or with one of their salesmen if possible. Sell product direct to these retailers if you don't already have distribution in that area or take their order and give it to your customer to ship.

2. Set up a meeting with a group of end users of your product. Find out what you can do to make the product more appealing. Ask them to use the product and come back to you with testimonials. Offer to give them free product in exchange for their help.

3. Offer one or more of your customers a discount on product if they will send out your brochure in one of their mailings. The fastest turnaround would be in a packing slip or invoice.

4. Offer free product to your wholesaler if she will include the free one in each shipment she makes to a customer.

5. Send out the craziest low-cost advertising piece you can think of. We have seen brochures rolled up in tubes, mailed in a bottle, or delivered by FedEx. Do anything to get noticed.

Let me throw out one more example. Then you should be able to devise a similar list for your business. Let's say you are a photographer.

1. Look in the paper each night and write down the names of the couples who are announcing their engagement. Call the bride and offer your services. Get your first few weddings at any cost. If you do a good job, the referrals are great. The same is true for birth announcements and major wedding anniversaries.

2. While looking in the newspaper you might even take a look at the photos of executives in the business section. If some don't look too attractive, call and offer a free sitting to create a professional head shot that will improve their image. This contact may lead to photos for brochures and advertisements.

3. Leave your card with the best four-by-six color picture of a baby you have ever taken at the local baby furniture store, each toy store, and with every OB/GYN in town. Offer the manager or owner a 10 percent commission for anybody he sends your way. If you don't get anything in a week, offer a 20 percent commission.

4. Go talk to the manager of the fanciest restaurant in your area. Suggest that she let you take pictures of the patrons. By the time they finish eating you would provide them with a five-by-six color photo encased in a folder with the restaurant's logo on the front. Keep the price reasonable, but get the couple's name and address. Follow up with a brochure that tells of all your services.

5. Go to local advertising agencies and offer to do their next photo shoot for free. (They pay only for materials, not your time.) You risk one day in exchange for the potential for much future business.

Sell ▪ Promote ▪ Sell ▪ Promote ▪ Sell ▪ Promote ▪ Sell

That is your job and virtually your only job during business hours until you are covering your nut (expenses). Clearly, if you are the one who provides the service, or you must create the product, ship it, and so on, you will have to take care of these things as well. As much as is humanly possible however, do these things at night during this critical time. Sell during the day, run your machinery at night. Sell during the day, type invoices at night, box and ship before eight o'clock in the morning.

Some of you may be able to reverse the process. For instance, doctors, lawyers, printers, travel agents, and other service providers must generally perform their professional services during business hours. However, they should use dead time, lunch hours, evenings, and Saturdays to find folks to sell.

Evenings also provide time for creating brochures, sending follow-up letters, and planning sales calls. Your family is going to scream that you work all the time. Explain to them that if you work very, very hard now, you should be able to slack off later. If you ease up now, you may be fighting for your business life for years.

Part 6
Surviving the First Week

Are we having fun yet!? Did you hit your sales goal for the week? Have you screwed something up real good yet? Have you had enough nos to last a lifetime? Is your family still basically support-ive of your decision to get out on your own? The correct answers to the above should be: "Not quite," "almost," "yes," "I'll get over it," and "hanging in there." Those answers would mean that you have what it takes to make this work.

The first week is tough. Unless your business is very special, you already need a vacation. What those questions were designed to elicit is:

A. Do you still have a positive mental attitude?

B. Did you set your sales goals unrealistically low or high, or did you set them at all?

C. Have you been actively going after business, trying things, taking risks? There is no truer statement than "If you're not screwing up, you're not doing anything."

D. If you haven't faced rejection this week, you either haven't asked for the order or you're seriously underpricing your product. In most cases the incorrect answer here means you haven't even called on any customers.

E. If your family is already nervous, anxious, angry, or all three, you haven't properly prepared them. Sit down today and have a heart-to-heart talk. Be totally and completely honest about your feelings at this time, and about the sacrifices they are facing.

It is now Sunday night. Tomorrow starts a new week. Don't be alarmed or concerned if you don't sleep well tonight. Your adrena-line will keep you going. This next idea took me over twenty-five years of sleepless nights to develop. You may already know about it, but if not, it could be the extra 1 percent advantage you'll need to succeed.

Get out your legal pad, notebook, computer, or whatever you use to write notes, scribble down ideas, or doodle while on the phone. Get a clean sheet and write the next day's day and date in big letters at the top. Start from the first line on the page and write down as many things as you can think of that you need to do, could do, or should do tomorrow . . . or soon.

Here is an example of one of my to-do sheets.

Monday, May 6

1. Follow up with Paul regarding his call at Schwinn.
2. Rent must be paid today.
3. Call Tony about his new product: Price, minimum quantity, terms.
4. Make sales calls on Fisher, Nike, and C & G.
5. Call Jim at Bill's wholesale to see how he liked the samples.
6. Make sure the samples went out to Custom House and Denver Sales.
7. Check inventory on neon orange water bottles. Also white.
8. Where is that promised order from Midwest Distributors?
9. Do we have everything we need to start the Kmart order?
10. Get Mr. Tuffy brochure printed.
11. Redo May's sales goal based on shipments last week and orders in house.
12. Promise Kodak their shipment by Tuesday.
13. Need two extra temporaries from the service tomorrow.
14. See when bookkeeper will have April profit-and-loss.

Here is what the list is going to do for you.

1. Compiling the list during a quiet time on Sunday night—or any night for that matter—provides a chance to let the great computer between your ears digest information and foster creativity. You'll think of things in this environment that you won't come up with any other way. New products, approaches, and solutions will just pop into your mind.

2. You now have a list to go by. It'll allow you to work very rapidly on the things that are most important. Some specialists in the science of lists believe that you should go back over the list and create priorities. That may work for you. I prefer to scan the list several times per day and select those items that seem most appropriate for that moment.

3. As you complete an item on the list, scratch it out. There is a terrific psychological uplift to that action. As the page gets darker and darker with lines crossed out, your satisfaction level goes up and up.

4. There is something about writing it down. When you write down these activities, there is more of a feeling that they must be done. Therefore, the less appealing items, once written down on a to-do list, are more likely to get done, and sooner.

5. Finally, having written all of this down clears and settles your mind. This will go a long way toward helping you sleep, even when you are faced with enormous pressure.

CHAPTER
5

The First Month

BELIEVE IT OR NOT, the bruises will heal, it will get worse before it gets better, and you will see your children again. If these are not some of the things you are currently thinking about, you aren't working hard enough to make it. During this period of your business's development, you need to be as devoted to it as you were to your spouse on your honeymoon . . . as devoted as a mother is to a newborn . . . *and for all the same reasons.*

If you're not coming very close to your goals yet, now might be a great time for you to write down your daily schedule—where you go on a particular day and whom you talk to. By engaging in that exercise, you may be able to see where you are poorly allocating time. Wise use of your time in these early days will greatly improve your company's fortunes.

Part 1
Training, Training,
and Retraining

The comparison of your month-old business to a newborn doesn't stop with their common need for massive doses of time, energy, and emotion. Both also need constant training and retraining. In fact, a baby may be easier in this regard. One writer claims that infants rarely have to learn the same lesson more than once. This won't be true for your employees. Maybe not even for you.

One aspect of starting a new company that makes training difficult is that you haven't done it before. Thus, as you learn, you need to untrain your employees of the bad habits you had earlier trained them in.

Training should be a daily enterprise. Some management experts suggest a daily meeting for this task. Some suggest you can accomplish great results a minute at a time. My personal preference is to write a short memo that treats the issue, make copies, and disperse them to those who will be affected an hour or so before a meeting announced with the memo. If I believe the meeting will take five minutes or less, I conduct it standing. If longer, sitting. However, the critical issue for me is to keep the meeting on the subject at hand and as brief as possible. I invite questions and comments, but I am not interested in providing grandstanding opportunities for those in the group. There will be plenty of opportunity for that in the looser format of a brainstorming session.

Part 2
Decision Making

One of the most formidable new skills you'll have to learn in the first thirty days or so is how to make a decision. Most who haven't led before haven't had the opportunity, or the burden, of making critical decisions—especially ones where timing is essential. Hence, it's easy to second-guess the decisions you do make. My advice is: **Don't.** Rather, just charge ahead, and do your best to make it work. If it doesn't, park your ego at the door and make another decision: how to solve the new situation.

How *does* one go about making good decisions in a timely manner? The only skill harder to teach is creativity, and they operate similarly. Here is a step-by-step approach that *can* be used by anyone.

STEP ONE

Determine the specific problem or opportunity that needs to be addressed. At least half of decision making is knowing what the problem is, and the problem frequently isn't what it appears to be.

You have an employee who doesn't seem to be cutting it. He appears lazy and disinterested. You have encouraged, admonished, trained, and threatened. Nothing is working. You need to decide whether or not to fire this person.

The problem seems to be that you've made a poor hire. You feel bad about letting the person go. You aren't sure how quickly you can replace him. Right now, he's better than nothing. Take the situation and stand it on its head, shake it around, and turn it inside out. Here are just a few of the possible problems that aren't so obvious that might provide an easy solution.

- During your attempts at motivation, etc., you never really explained to this person what you expected and/or what he could expect long term.

- You've been doing a great deal of talking. Have you done any listening? Maybe your employee is going through a difficult time, or has a tendency to say yes to you during training even when he doesn't understand.

- Is he really better than nothing? Could the rest of your staff fill in until you could find a replacement?

- Does he have enough specific direction? Some employees need a detailed list of things to do.

- He hates the work and is staying only because he feels bad about letting you down.

- There really isn't enough to keep him busy.
- He finishes tasks very quickly and therefore appears to be lazy when he doesn't know what to do next.

Do you see that each of these possible problems practically screams its solution? So, step number one is to evaluate the situation from every perspective you can think of and make certain that you have correctly identified the problem.

Many times you'll identify what you believe to be the problem and you'll still be faced with several valid options. In this case, you'll move to step two.

STEP TWO

Gather as much information as you possibly can in the time available. Ask questions of those who are likely to be affected. Give a call to someone who you believe has faced a similar dilemma. Go to the library and bookstore or search the Internet to see what may have been written on the subject. Call your CPA, attorney, or other professional who may have insight into the situation.

A few years ago, our product liability insurance policy was canceled. This was during one of those times when the commercial insurance companies were losing their shirts. The company who had written our policy decided to get out of commercial insurance altogether. The obvious first call was to an insurance agent, and then another, and another. It soon became clear that the normal method of securing new insurance was not going to work. No one thought we had a chance of getting a policy.

We didn't consider it an intelligent option to remain uninsured. Moreover, many of our customers required that we carry insurance if they were to continue carrying our product. In this case the problem was clearly defined, so step number one in this exercise wasn't going to be any help.

I began seeking information. The problem was nationwide and across all industries. As a result, there were many articles on the subject. I read them all. Any lead that came out of these stories, I followed up.

I called other friends in business. Many still had their coverage. I asked for the names of their insurer and/or agent. I called my CPA and my lawyer for ideas on where to look or how to get around the problem. Sometimes the call resulted in a lead. Sometimes that lead pointed to another source, which yielded yet another possible person who might be able to help. We called suppliers and some customers to ask who insured them.

We researched any potential information that we could think of. One of those calls may have resulted in our finding insurance. It didn't. Thus we went to step three.

STEP THREE

As you do your research, you will, from time to time, want to put your creative juices to work in hopes of turning the information you have gathered into a solution.

There are many ways to do this, but all of them require one thing: allowing your brain to do all the work by itself. Some call it right-brain activity. Others call it alpha. A lightbulb going on is the symbol of success in this approach. Prayer or meditation is often quite helpful. Sleeping on it works quite well. In my opinion each works about the same way: After you gather all this information, you tell your brain what you need. Then you forget about it. Think about nothing, as in some forms of meditation. Think about something else entirely, as is commonly the case in an alpha state. But stop searching for an answer, so that your brain can be free to come up with the solutions on its own.

When the ideas start to flow, let them. Don't reject anything at this point. It is very likely that you will get these ideas in the middle of the night, just before you doze off, or right after awakening in the morning. Try to stay in a dreamy state for a while and let the ideas develop. Edison used to hold a glass tumbler in his hand off the edge of the bed. If he dozed off, the glass would fall and wake him up. Then he could continue his idea session.

When you feel that you have everything you are going to get, find a pad and pencil and write your ideas down. As the day progresses some of these thoughts may seem ridiculous, but you will very likely have one or two real gems.

We considered buying out a company that still had insurance. We talked about dropping some of our more obvious insurance problem products. (We were carrying bicycle helmets for infants.) We discussed the only offer we had. The amount would have eliminated any hope for profit that year, but we would have had coverage until the insurance climate changed.

We suggested to some underwriters that we would agree to a large deductible. We called all the vendors who supplied us with raw materials and finished goods. We figured that if every one of them had insurance and could provide us with a certificate of insurance, this might satisfy our customers. We even considered starting a nationwide political movement to change the way product liability was being handled.

We considered becoming a foreign corporation. Consumers rarely sue foreign manufacturers. It is easier to go after the importer, wholesaler, or retailer to whom the foreign manufacturer sells.

We finally made a decision, which in this case was very expensive. We accepted the only offer to cover us that was available. For the next two years we paid 2 percent of all sales to maintain only five hundred thousand dollars in coverage.

STEP FOUR

Now that you have come up with a list of approaches, it is time to pick one. Get as much input as possible from those you trust. Then go for it. By this time you should have a real good gut feeling of which approach is best. Repeatedly I have heard famous leaders talk about the importance of following their gut instincts. But of course those instincts have been honed by first following steps one, two, and three outlined above.

Typically, you are dealing with an issue that has a limited window of opportunity in which to make a decision. I still go through these steps as completely as possible in the time allowed.

If this process seems foreign to you, you may need to go through it very deliberately the first few times you're faced with a major decision. Others will recognize the process as something they do subconsciously all the time.

CHAPTER

6

Months Two Through Six

GONE ARE THE OPENING-DAY JITTERS. You've fumbled your way through the first few weeks. By the end of the month you almost feel as though you and your staff can handle the routine aspects of running the business.

Don't become discouraged by the fact that there are times each day when the unexpected causes a minicrisis, or even a major one. As long as you are in business, you'll be faced with events you have no control over or which you've had no experience with. Through the use of three-track thinking and the decision-making approaches just discussed, you should be able to deal with each of these without needless anxiety.

Now it's time to incorporate some practices that you as the manager will use to help run the business from now until you retire. We'll begin with the most important daily activity you should perform.

Part 1
The Daily Numbers

Business is about people. The better your people, the better you'll do. Business is about selling. Nothing happens until something is sold. Business is about managing. Organization is critical to maximizing profitability. The scorecard for business is numbers.

Golden nugget: *Each day you will want to have a set of statistics that will tell you how your employees are doing and how you are doing as a team.* You will compare some of your employees to each other. You may evaluate some of your company numbers to other similar firms. Most important, you'll want to make evaluations about past numbers, your plan or budget, and your future.

Every business will have some numbers that are unique to them, but there are many that are universal. If you're adept at using a spreadsheet program, you may want to program these daily numbers into your computer so that you can manipulate them.

SALES

This item should be at the top of every list. What were your total sales for the day? What is the total so far this month? How does that MTD (month-to-date) figure compare with your plan for this month?

With these three pieces of information you can start to manage your business. Why were sales today less than you hoped for? Why is the month-to-date figure less than the plan? If these numbers were substantially higher than the plan, should you reevaluate your plan, or are there reasons why you expect the remaining portion of the month to balance the fast start?

Do today's numbers suggest a need for action? Are you out of a critical material or part? Do you need more people? If yes, should they be permanent or temporary? Should you cut back on your ordering or increase it?

Some companies may benefit from breaking their sales numbers into two categories: orders and shipments. This would be true if you generally have a backlog or back-order situation.

Using this approach, your new orders for the day would help you make decisions about advertising, promotion, selling time, discounts, and effectiveness of your sales force. Shipments give you the data you need to properly manage your manufacturing and shipping departments.

A variation on this theme occurs in service industries where appointments are made, such as doctors, plumbers, and beauty salons. You may want a daily number that would indicate the number of hours of appointments that were booked each day. This would affect your planning concerning hours of operation, advertising and other promotion, and need for additional personnel.

PROFIT

The daily profit number becomes more important when your product mix has a wide variety of margins. In a retail store, you might have some items that you buy for a dime and sell for a dollar. Other products might cost you $300 and you sell them for $330 (I hope not, but I've seen it). In this type of situation a daily gross profit number will allow you to fine-tune your sales effort toward either more gross sales or a higher average margin. Let's consider an example.

You may know that you really need to create more total gross profit per day. You are now producing $150. You need $240. You also know you wouldn't have to hire more salesclerks to sell three more video recorders at $330 each. It is unlikely that you'd ever sell one hundred more bottles of head cleaner at $1 each to reach the same $90 in additional profit. Thus, even though your profit margin on the one is only 10 percent versus 90 percent on the other, you need to aim your sales, advertising, and promotion efforts at the 10 percent item.

DAILY CASH RECEIPTS

Your daily cash receipts number will tell you whether you're going to have enough cash to pay today's bills (and maybe whether you're going to have anything to take home to your family today). If those receipts aren't what you hoped for, you'll be able to take some kinds of actions to improve them, both short- and long-term.

You may wish to change your terms. If you usually allow net sixty days, you may want to send out a letter informing all or certain customers that as of June 1, your terms will be net thirty.

You may want to prioritize those shipments that will be delivered COD. Another option is to start calling certain customers and offering a discount for faster payment. Or you may want to intensify your collection effort.

ACCOUNTS RECEIVABLE BALANCE

That brings us to the second part of this number, the accounts receivable balance. You'll want to see this number in conjunction with the day's shipments, cash receipts, and the beginning accounts receivable (A/R) balance for the month. It might look something like this:

Beginning A/R-6/1	$15,682.00
Shipments 6/7	$ 1,345.00
Cash receipts 6/7	$ 990.00
Shipments MTD	$ 5,431.00
Cash receipts MTD	$ 3,806.00
A/R balance-6/7	$ 17,307.00

If I were to see these numbers on my daily report, I'd want to immediately check my accounts receivable detail. Who owes me what, and is it past due? We'll deal with methods for collection in section 3, but for now the important thing is recognizing that these daily numbers will help you pinpoint the things you need to do. In this case you'd check your A/R detail to see whether a collection effort might improve your daily receipts.

It may turn out that your credit customers are paying you just fine, but your sales in the first seven days of last month were low compared to the last twenty-three days. Therefore your collections should improve as those invoices mailed in the latter part of the month become due.

CHECKING ACCOUNT BALANCE/DISBURSEMENTS

This part of your daily report might look like this:

Beginning cash 6/7	$6,555.00
Payroll 6/7	
Payments to vendors 6/7	$4,352.00
Tax payment 6/7	
CODs paid	$ 533.00
Other _____	
Other _____	
Cash receipts 6/7	$ 990.00
Ending cash 6/7	$2,660.00

You may also want to prepare a similar report that shows these totals on a month-to-date basis. This will allow you to evaluate your expenditures against a monthly plan or budget.

OTHER

Depending on the business you are in you may also want to see such numbers as:

- Sales calls made
- Calls received by order desk
- Daily payroll expense
- Inventory—total or by certain items
- Purchase orders placed—total value of open POs
- New payables—total outstanding payables
- Production—by machine—total value of production
- Backlog—by item—by total value—by days to produce
- Back orders—by item—by total value
- Total presentations made—total converted to orders
- Loan balance—loan available
- A/R over sixty days
- Downtime—by machine
- Capacity utilization—by percent
- Capacity available—by value of lost opportunity

There is a fair amount of time and energy required to compile some of these numbers. You may not have the personnel to do as many as might be useful. Start with sales and, if appropriate, orders. Checking account balance would be second. A/R and disbursement would generally be important where applicable. Most of the rest is very specific to your type of enterprise. Do as many as you can that help you run the business.

Here is an example of a very complete daily report.

Preparation Date 7/12
Transaction Date 7/11

	Today	This Week	This Month	Budget
Beginning cash	1,450.98	3,553.76	1,212.78	
Cash receipts	1,700.00	1,895.77	13,375.60	35,000.00
Payroll & tax			1,255.00	5,000.00
CODs	55.00	290.00	1,775.56	5,000.00
Overhead	294.52	294.52	1,350.55	1,500.00
Payables	355.00	1,576.90	5,883.66	15,000.00
Commissions			877.00	2,500.00
Notes paid				1,500.00
Other	870.73	1,712.38	1,870.88	2,000.00
Total disbursed	1,575.25	3,873.80	13,012.65	32,500.00
Ending cash	1,575.73	1,575.73	1,575.73	
Beginning A/R	40,786.97	38,709.24	41,295.00	
Beginning backlog	7,559.90	8,670.55	4,220.55	
New orders	1,456.50	2,619.35	15,963.42	38,000.00
Shipped	2,202.37	4,475.87	13,369.94	37,000.00
Ending backlog	6,814.03	6,814.03	6,814.03	8,000.00
Cash receipts	1,700.00	1,895.77	13,375.60	35,000.00
Ending A/R	41,289.34	41,289.34	41,289.34	
Beginning A/P	35,689.96	33,379.90	29,930.83	
New A/P		3,531.96	11,287.79	16,000.00
Paid A/P	355.00	1,576.90	5,883.66	15,000.00
Ending A/P	35,334.96	35,334.96	35,334.96	

Sales/Salesperson	Backlog	New Orders	New Orders MTD	Shipped MTD
Bob	1,250.97	312.75	4,554.11	4,002.92
Diane	3,378.36	790.98	8,510.65	7,979.22
Art	1,665.56	100.35	1,995.55	1,225.99
Cindy	1,265.01	252.42	903.11	161.81

A quick glance through this daily report would offer insights and trigger a few questions:

A. Cash receipts are doing fairly well for nine business days. (There would be one weekend by the eleventh.)

B. You have practically spent your whole budget for overhead. You would want to go back and see what was spent. Then evaluate what is left that you must buy during the balance of this month.

C. New orders were a bit off yesterday, although you are doing close to projection for the month. It still might not hurt to have a talk with one or more of your salespeople.

D. A/R seems in reasonably good shape with cash receipts almost equal to shipments for the month.

E. New A/P is running way ahead. Did you have to purchase this amount of inventory so early in the month? What will you need to purchase during the balance of the month?

F. Your salespeople seem typical in that the four include one star, two solid players, and one laggard. It appears that your laggard is going downhill fast. In addition, she seems to be selling the things you least like to ship. As a result, her backlog is very high compared to her sales. It is probably time to make a switch, especially if Cindy is on payroll and not commission.

Part 2
The Monthly Statements

Income statement. You'll want to produce one every month. Your business can be in big trouble for a long time and you won't even know it without an income statement. We have fully detailed the income statement in section 2, chapter 2, part 6.

Inventory. This is the value of all merchandise that you carry for resale. It does not include office furniture, production equipment, or other items that aren't being offered for sale. As mentioned earlier, there are some very sophisticated aspects to placing a value on that inventory.

In addition to the question of how much direct and indirect overhead to include in the value, there are other issues such as LIFO and FIFO. FIFO means first in, first out. If you use the FIFO method you make the assumption that the inventory of items you continuously purchase that are now in your warehouse are those you have most recently purchased. If you use LIFO (last in, first out), you assume that your current inventory is made up of items purchased earlier, and that the items you have recently purchased are sold.

In an inflationary environment the use of FIFO would result in a higher valuation for your inventory. Good for the balance sheet; bad for income tax. LIFO would have the opposite effect.

These and other questions have profit and tax ramifications, and should be discussed in detail with your accountant. All that aside, in evaluating your inventory for the purpose of determining whether you are profitable, you must be consistent. If you change the method of valuation from period to period, you will not have any idea what your profit is.

You may find it costly in terms of time and energy to take a physical inventory each month, but it's usually worth it. You should almost certainly set up a perpetual inventory (in which each sale or receipt of product is recorded and changes your inventory balance immediately). You will achieve excellent advantages from doing one or the other. Your month-end inventory report might look like this.

Item	On Hand	Value	Purchases	Sales	Average YTD
B52	522	570.55	80	120	110
XKE	6	9.00	30	50	30
711	140	280.00	65	70	60
R2D2	50	500.00	0	2	10

The last column, average YTD, means the average monthly sales you have experienced so far this year. There are many other meaningful averages you may like to look at such as average last twelve months or last four months. The first would give you long-term experience with the product. The other might show a trend.

As you look at the information above, the first thing that sticks out is that you are over inventoried in R2D2s, especially considering how much they cost. The second thing is almost as obvious. You should probably be buying way more XKEs. Your B52s are a little heavy, maybe a sale is in order, but your sales of this item are good, so you don't want to give them away. Product 711 shows an almost perfect example of purchases and inventory in relation to sales.

Gross-profit-margin method of determining profit and loss. You probably shouldn't take an inventory every month. You may not even find the time to take a proper inventory every quarter. However, you'll still want to have a P & L (profit and loss) prepared monthly. You can do this by establishing a normal gross margin for your business. It may take three or four actual inventories to begin to get a handle on this normal amount. Each time you take an inventory, you'll arrive at a gross-margin percentage. Soon you'll be able to determine an average for your operation. If you show 45 percent for one period, 52 percent for another, and 46 percent for another, you can just add them and divide by 3.

With this number you can now determine the dollar amount of your cost of sales and your gross profit without taking an inventory. However, it is easy to become deluded when using this method, especially if you don't take an actual—the term is "physical"—inventory for a long time. Maybe you have had to discount more heavily during the period you are using the gross-margin method than you did when you took an actual inventory. Over time, you may begin to add overhead, because according to your P & L you are quite profitable. Then you take an actual inventory only to find out you've been losing money all along.

Another way to avoid this problem is to maintain a perpetual inventory. This means that either by using a computer or a manual method you account for every item sold or bought during the period. In this case you would know the value of your "book" inventory without actually counting it. The reason I refer to this inventory as a book inventory is to differentiate it from a physical inventory. You see, you could still be way off base. Through bookkeeping errors, short shipments by your suppliers, invoicing errors, over-shipments by your staff, or outright theft, your actual inventory may be substantially different from your book inventory.

In order of preference you will want to use physical inventory, perpetual inventory, and, only as a last resort, gross-profit method.

Accounts receivable aging. If you allow your customers to purchase from you on account you will find that not all of them pay you according to terms. In fact, you will likely end up having some customers who take quite a while to pay . . . if not forever.

To track the quality of your customers' payments and as an aid to your collection effort you must produce an aging report of your A/R. Generally, it will look like this:

Customer	Current	30–60 days	61–90 days	91 days or over	
ACME	380.55	57.95			
B-One			195.49		
Century	549.90				
Dave's				775.90	
E-Plus		88.80			
Falcon	50.50				
Total	980.95	146.75	195.49	775.90	2099.09
Percentage	47%	7%	9%	37%	100%

By spreading your receivables in this way, you get a picture of your situation with outstanding accounts. ACME, Century, and Falcon are probably okay. B-One needs some attention, but Dave's is serious. E-Plus is a bit past due, but it is a small amount. The situation with Dave's has even caused your entire aging to be skewed. It is very serious indeed to have 37 percent of your outstanding balances in the ninety-day column.

We will come back to this area in section 3 as we talk about how to collect receivables.

Accounts payable aging. This is done in exactly the same way as accounts receivable aging. With this report, however, you are getting a picture of how well you are paying your suppliers. Use the same chart as above, but change the "customer" heading to "supplier." If Dave's is one of your important suppliers you may be in danger of his cutting you off from open account or even not shipping you at all. By preparing this aging on a monthly basis, you may begin to see trends that indicate you are getting further and further behind in your bills. You will also find it easier to make decisions of whom to pay when you have less than enough to pay everyone.

Sales analysis. With this report you will take a look at how your customers are doing with you. You can divide this by salesperson. You will be looking for trends and opportunities. This report can be formatted in many different ways. This is my particular favorite:

SALESPERSON #556

Customer	Sales	YTD	Same Month Last Year	YTD Last Year	Total Last Year
Falcon	532.25	1,045.90	135.55	388.50	947.95
ACME	165.47	644.12	676.90	949.88	1,778.33
Dave's		549.24	70.70	510.76	887.32
Century	98.50	220.11			
E-Plus	40.65	40.65	489.44	838.91	2,772.98
B-One		10.50		21.00.	42.00
Total	836.87	2,510.52	1,372.59	2,709.05	6,428.58

You can probably already see how helpful this report would be. This particular salesperson is down in her sales year to date versus last year. She was also off this month compared with the same month last year. In fact, she is down more for the month than she was year to date. It may be that she just had a bad month, but it bears careful evaluation next month.

You will note that this format lists the accounts in order of best customer by sales, YTD. This allows me to see who my best customers are. In this case clearly Falcon is coming on strong, but E-Plus has fallen way off. Why didn't Dave's order this month? Better to check now than to find out two or three months from now that he has switched to the competition. It may affect ordering patterns and it is easier to get him back if you call him soon after the decision was made to switch.

Other sales reports that could be valuable include item sales by customer, order frequency by customer, or profit margin by customer.

There are many other reports that are useful to certain industries. Restaurants may want to keep track of the number of times they turn their tables per day or per meal. They might also track waste percentage. Job shops should be interested in machine utilization analysis both by number of hours of production and value of production. Lawyers and accountants may want to know the percentage of billable to nonbillable hours worked by each partner and associate. Consider what information would be important for you to monitor monthly. Check with consultants or trade associations in your business category to see what others do.

Part 3
Dealing with Crisis

The balance of section 2 is devoted to the most likely emergencies and near emergencies that may develop in the first weeks and months after you open. Each will be followed by a variety of solutions.

As you look through these or refer back to them, please see them first as a source of inspiration for specific ideas on how to handle specific problems. Then begin to develop a sense of how to solve all problems with creativity and a can-do attitude.

1. Tomorrow is Friday. For your company that means payday. Time to pass out paychecks to your employees. Time to take home the bacon for you.

Unfortunately, sales have been soft for a full week, or your largest customer is behind in paying you, or you made a substantial error in your checkbook, or you had to put out a large amount of cash to fix a piece of equipment or . . . any one or two of many things that could happen, and now, you can't make payroll tomorrow.

> **A.** Get on the phone and start calling accounts that owe you money. First call those that are due or past due and attempt to collect. You'll want to get a firm commitment for a check to go out that day. Second, call those that are almost due and ask if they can send the payment now as a favor. If this hasn't created the results you need, call those that are far from due and offer a special discount for early payment.
>
> If some of these accounts are local, you should ask if it would be okay for you to pick up the check. And don't be embarrassed to state your actual need. Don't just say that you can't cover payroll, but give the whole story. "Hi, Bob? I could really use a favor. My receivables have been way off this week, and I'm a bit short to make payroll tomorrow. You have this one item for $535.50 that would just about solve it for me. If you are in a position to help me I could give you my FedEx number so you could send it overnight." After his agreement: "Bob, I really appreciate this. Let me know when I can return the favor in some way."

B. Find a customer to take something early. Years ago, it seemed as if our business had a tight cash situation about every other month. One of our customers used to receive a great benefit from this situation. We would call, tell them how much we needed, negotiate a big discount, and deliver the merchandise that day or the next in exchange for a check. In each case this customer probably would have needed the product a month later than we sold it to them. It cost us a pretty penny to get this money, but we needed it, and the customer was more than happy to help out.

C. Call a supplier to whom you've just mailed a check. See if they have already banked the check. If not, use almost the identical approach as above to persuade them to hold the check for one week.

D. Start calling anyone you can think of who might be willing to lend you the money for a week or a month, depending on your situation. Let them set the interest rate.

E. Talk to your employees, starting with managers, to see if they can hold their checks for a few days or take half now and half later. You'll be surprised how often an employee will help in this way and be practically "happy to help." This is another one of those areas where you don't want to ask too often. Happy to help can turn to "this is getting old."

2. One of your primary suppliers is out of product, and can't supply you for six weeks. Sounds far-fetched? I opened a retail bike shop two days before a bicoastal dock strike. Dealers who had been in business for years couldn't get bicycles. I opened on the first of July. I received my first new bike on December 10.

A. Ask your supplier for ideas. Not just the salesman; go to the production manager, sales manager, marketing manager, vice presidents, and even the president of the supplier. Is there anything they can do to speed the supply?

Is there a substitute available from them? Do they have a foreign subsidiary that makes the same item? Do they have a customer who might be overloaded with that product at this time? Can they recommend a supplier who can solve the problem? You will of course want to assure them that their help in finding you material through another supplier will strengthen your relationship, not cause them to lose a customer.

B. Hit the Web. You may be able to find one or one hundred additional resources within an hour or two of research. Of course, the more options you find, the greater the chance that one will be available at the right time, right price, right terms. Don't correspond with the suppliers found on the Web using e-mail contact information on their "contact us" page.

Or if you do, only do so after trying by phone. The e-mails on these sites are notorious for being dead ends. Even where they are addressed to a real person and not "sales@" or "info@," the recipients commonly have a "not my job" attitude and pass over these unsolicited requests from unknown parties to get to known needs.

If there is no phone number on their Web page, you might have to use one of the few remaining benefits of "Yellow Pages." But of course it will be the Web-based "Yellow Pages." Or if you're rich, call information.

C. Call the appropriate trade association to see if there is a buyer's guide for that industry. Have it sent by overnight courier. If there is no buyer's guide, ask the association if they have ideas of who might be able to help—not necessarily just vendor's names, but others who might know who to call.

D. As mentioned before, start calling competitors. Generally, start by calling those that are far enough away not to consider you a threat. You may find someone who has too much. You may just learn of another source or substitute.

E. You can stay in business by dealing with used, reprocessed, or off-spec material (not exactly up to the specifications normally associated with that product).

F. Redirect your attention to a product that can fill the gap. This could either be another product you're already carrying, or it could be a new item.

G. Reduce your overhead to an absolute minimum until the product is available again. Call your landlord and ask for a rent concession. Lay off employees. Cut back your hours of operation. Call suppliers who are due to be paid and ask for an extra thirty days.

Be certain that this experience results in a lesson. If this supplier is the only one carrying this product and it represents an important part of your income, you need to find a way to substantially improve the consistency of supply or change the emphasis of your company.

3. A critical employee quits or can't work.

A. Immediately learn the task yourself, if possible. You'll save money, increase the depth of your company, and give yourself more information about who you should hire.

B. Call a temp service. There are companies offering temporary workers for almost every occupation. You also end up with two additional benefits. If you don't like this person's work, you just call the temp agency and ask them to send someone else. This isn't nearly as emotional as telling someone he's fired.

Furthermore, if the temp turns out to be well qualified and is looking for full-time, permanent work, you can hire him. Some temp agencies have rules regarding some form of compensation for your having hired away their worker, but if the temp is good enough, it's well worth it.

C. Call your supplier salespeople. They may know of someone in the industry who is looking for an opportunity.

D. Think of friends or associates who may be able to fill the gap for a short time. If your spouse is not already working with you, he or she may be able to handle the task until you can find a permanent replacement.

E. Of course you should use the usual hiring approaches such as running ads or calling the state employment agency. However, the above approaches are designed to deal with an emergency where the loss of the employee's talents for even a few days could result in serious problems.

4. You lose your location. You can insure your building against destruction through fire, flood, or earthquake. You can also purchase business-interruption insurance that is supposed to give you enough staying power to reopen in a new place. What if you don't have that insurance? Or you have a month-to-month rental, and your landlord gives you notice? Maybe you miss a lease payment, and the building's owner holds you to the letter of the lease and kicks you out?

For many businesses, this type of disaster in the early going is all but insurmountable. This is especially so where there has been a large investment in build-outs, signage, or fixtures that can't be easily transferred to a new location. Here are some approaches that might save your bacon.

A. If you have enough capital left for the first and last months' rent on a new location, and believe that you will still have the staying power to save your business, start a dawn-to-dusk search for a new facility. You will probably be far less particular this time. Use two or three real estate agents, but don't count on them alone. Go out and canvass the neighborhood yourself. Some builders and owners don't use an agent, and therefore the property doesn't show up on the listings.

B. If you are really strapped for cash, try to find a building that has been vacant for a long, long time. There will undoubtedly be a reason for this, but you aren't in a very strong position to hold out for prime rental space.

Approach the landlord with a plan that allows you to conserve as much capital as possible while giving up as little as possible. You might be able to move in for free and get one or more months of free rent. If your situation is particularly dire, you might ask for your rent to be a percentage of sales or profit instead of any fixed amount. You might use a combination of fixed plus a percentage.

You could have a fast escalator clause. Maybe you pay nothing the first two months, one hundred dollars the next two, two hundred dollars the next two, and so forth until you are at or slightly above the market rate for this type of location.

C. Can you move the business into your home, garage, a friend's home, garage, or business? Can you sublet a small area in another business? Maybe there is a vendor or customer who has a substantial vested interest in your staying in business. He might be able to provide you with the necessary space until you can afford and find a new location.

D. Consider merging with another similar business. Of course, this means that you'll have all the benefits and detriments of a partnership. However, it might be just the solution.

E. If your cash position is strong, but your chances of finding the right kind of location are weak, consider buying out a competitor.

F. One of the least expensive locations is a ministorage. If all you need is a warehouse, light assembly, or packaging this may be perfect for you. I have known several business owners who have survived in a ministorage for several years.

5. You become temporarily disabled by illness or accident, and are unable to work, or must severely curtail your hours or activity. Once again there is insurance available for this type of situation. Disability insurance is fairly inexpensive and highly recommended by most agents. You may want to carry it during the early phase of your business.

A. Go back and look at the approaches that were suggested for replacing a critical employee. After all, that is what you are. B, C, and D are very appropriate for this situation.

B. Check with your suppliers to see if they know of anyone who has retired from the business who might be able to run yours for a while. You might also contact the chamber of commerce and the Small Business Administration for names of individuals who are retired, but who would have the skills necessary to keep you in business until you can get back on your feet.

C. If you'll be out for only two or three months, would it be possible to simply try to reduce overhead to the lowest possible level, and close up your operation until you can return? Your landlord might be willing to forgo rent for that period or defer it until much later. You can lay off employees, and notify suppliers that you'll be unable to pay them until you return.

6. You are a manufacturer, dentist, restaurateur, or other who depends on equipment for your livelihood. A critical piece of this equipment goes on the blink. The manufacturer tells you the necessary part will not be available for three weeks. How about six weeks? Just for fun, let's say that the three or six weeks pass, and you are now told it will be three or six more, because they sent the wrong part. This is not at all far-fetched.

A. Your first move should be to work your way up the chain of command of the machine supplier. You will want to let each person in that hierarchy know that you want the necessary part and/or technician at your place of business by the next morning. It is the rare situation indeed that such a part would be so scarce that it would not be able to be found somewhere in the system, such as a reseller of that machine or the parts for it, an end user who has a backup piece of equipment or part, a machine that isn't currently in use, a makeshift part that will work until the right one is ready.

Don't take no for an answer. Insist that your very survival is at stake. Talk to everyone and anyone you can. Somewhere there will be a sympathetic or inventive ear who will find you a solution.

B. If you are a manufacturer, you may have to have your product made for you at a job shop until your machine is back in operation.

C. If you are in the situation of a dentist or similar practitioner, see if any of your friendly competitors has underutilized facilities they would be willing to rent for a time.

D. Again, you may be able to get help by contacting other suppliers. Start with suppliers who are most closely related to that equipment, such as those who provide you with the raw materials you use in that machine.

E. If you get this far without a solution, call the competitive makers of the disabled equipment. They may either help you with a solution in hopes of supplying you with the next machine, or they may be willing to sell you one of theirs with an exchange for the one you now have. This will be especially true if the equipment uses supplies provided by this same vendor.

The six emergency situations cited here are just about the worst things that could happen to you in the early stages of your business. In each case, however, there are numerous solutions available. A can-do attitude mixed with creativity can conquer almost any business problem.

The First
Three Years

1

Why Businesses Succeed

To the uninitiated, business looks pretty easy. Maybe that's why so many try it. Those who have taken the leap know that there is much more to this game than a good idea and some seed money. Henry Ford bankrupted two car companies before his third effort clicked. He is far from alone.

Fortunately, through this book and others like it, you can improve your chances for success. What follows are six very specific ingredients. I believe that if you keep these six elements at the forefront of your thinking, you will succeed. Prior to listing the six ingredients to business success, though, allow me to define the "success" that I'm referring to.

The least that a business can do to be considered successful is survive and pay its owners a living wage. Beyond that, a moderately successful business might pay its owners a wage equal to what they could earn by providing the same services working for someone else. A very successful business will do all the above and repay its investors for their risk at a level commensurate with that risk. The highest level of financial success would include all of these at a very high rate, plus create wealth (value of the enterprise if sold).

Financial success is not the only goal. Many owners would want the business to provide them with a satisfying and challenging career. They might also be looking for certain nonfinancial benefits such as travel, vacation time, or a thirty-hour work week.

In a very small business, the definition of success can become quite wrapped up with the needs of the owner. As mentioned earlier, there should be a separation of these in many instances, but sometimes it is very hard to see the lines of distinction.

Ingredients to Business Success
1. Desire
2. Sales
3. Marketing
4. Luck
5. Accounting
6. Planning

DESIRE

You've got to know what you want and want it *bad!* You must *focus!* You know what you want to accomplish. You knew there would be short-term sacrifices. Maybe you didn't know it would be this hard or take this long. You read section 1, but only believed half of it. You thought you were different . . . better, somehow.

Well, this is the time that separates the champions from the also-rans. Building a successful business is a long race, to be sure, and you are nowhere near the finish line. However, it is your strength and endurance now that will determine if you are even in the race for the second lap. You may not even be as strong as some of the others, but you must want to win more than they do.

Desire includes having a survivor mentality. There must be an underlying feeling in those running the business that failure is not an option. Now this is tricky, because failure *is* a valid option. There is a time and a place where packing it in is the best thing to do. Until that time comes, however, everyone in the organization must believe that folding the tent isn't up for consideration. Such an attitude alone may keep a business right side up for months after others without a survivor mentality have gone broke.

SALES

An associate of mine started a business. Within a year the company had enough sales to break even, but not enough to pay him. At the end of two years his sales were still the same. The overhead was pretty well fixed, so even a small sales increase would have resulted in good profits. From time to time as we discussed his undertaking, I would ask: "If you reached your current sales level in twelve months, why haven't you been able to sell more than that in your second year?"

The answer was simple. He had stopped selling. He was now only servicing his existing accounts. A very small business must maintain a constant sales effort. Selling must be very high on the list of priorities for use of time, energy, and dollars.

MARKETING

You must provide products or services that people need at a price they can afford. If you pass those two hurdles, you must then come up with an effective method of telling your potential customers that you have a great product at a reasonable price. Our business has experienced its greatest growth in product lines from buying out companies who managed to achieve a good product at a right price, but had no idea of how to get the word out.

Finally, you must also establish a method to deliver your product or service to interested customers. Should you sell it direct to the user, or through a series of middlemen? How do you package it? How many distribution centers do you need? Successful businesses understand the options in marketing and use that knowledge as a tool.

LUCK

I list luck fourth. Others I have read would list it first. I believe that most luck is made by the lucky. Nothing irritates me more than hearing someone who hasn't known me long exclaim: "Boy, is he lucky!" This is usually from the lips of someone who has never even walked across a college campus, complains about a forty-hour work week, and spends every evening in front of the tube with a beer in his mitt.

But there is luck (or providence) in the equation. Does the recession hit at a time when you have cash in the bank or when you've just borrowed all the bank will allow? Does the city decide to do roadwork in front of your new restaurant the second week you are open?

One must take the bad with the good. Is it luck when an inventor calls you with a new idea and you end up with a $100 million company? You could say so. However, how did he happen to call you? It could have been your advertising, your reputation, or any number of things you can justifiably feel proud of.

ACCOUNTING

Good accounting can help you in every phase of your business. It's easier to keep your desire intact on even the worst days if you feel that you're in control of your destiny. It's hard to feel in control of any part of your business if you're uncertain about your inventory levels, sales levels, collection effort, cash on hand, production capability, profitability, or even your solvency.

Your sales effort will be vastly improved by supplying those in your sales department with information about how their accounts are doing.

Your marketing will improve if you can accurately determine what you can afford in advertising, promotion, and trade show expense.

Clearly, your planning will be enhanced if you have historical numbers from which to derive your projections.

PLANNING

Planning can move you along your path more quickly. It can help you to miss some of the potholes in the path. It provides you with a mile marker to see how far you've come, and how far there is yet to go. It's a very useful skill and important to the overall success effort.

2

Why Businesses Fail

YOUR FIRST THOUGHT might be that "why businesses fail" would just be the flip side of "why businesses succeed." While there are some similarities, there are also some significant differences.

Ingredients to Business Failure

1. Inadequate capital
2. Product or service not needed
3. Underpricing
4. Excessive overhead
5. Insufficient time commitment from owner
6. Bad luck and/or timing
7. Poor understanding of business
8. Problem location
9. Poor accounting controls
10. Internal theft

As you can see, the reasons for business success are all positive attributes and skills. The reasons for failure are primarily very specific mistakes. In fact, many of these business killers take their toll on businesses that do quite well on the six success attributes.

INADEQUATE CAPITAL

You can start many types of very small businesses on a shoestring. I know; I have. However, you start with a major handicap. A few minor missteps, or one big one, and you're history before you start.

For a retailer, undercapitalization means starting with inadequate inventory. A consumer will come into your store and you won't have what they want. Because this happens frequently, sales aren't enough to cover overhead. Now you can't even buy enough product to maintain your opening inventory levels, much less add the items your customers are asking for. Later customers are even more likely to be disappointed.

Maybe you're a wholesaler. Because you haven't enough capital, you have to sell everyone COD. Because you have desire, and you are a great salesperson, you overcome this problem. In three months you build up a little reserve, so you offer an open account to the biggest customer in town in order to get her business (she won't buy COD). You didn't know it at the time, but she got to be the biggest player in town by paying her suppliers very, very slowly. Without the cash from that sale, you aren't able to pay your supplier, and you are virtually out of goods. With no product to sell, your business can't last.

In each of these cases even a little cash buffer would have helped—maybe as little as one thousand dollars to five thousand dollars. If you're in this situation, start now to arrange backup financing through your bank, friends and relatives, or outside investors. You may not ever need the help. But it is better to arrange for it now, and never need it, than to try to raise it when the wolf is at the door.

PRODUCT OR SERVICE NOT NEEDED

Fewer than 50 percent of all products make it in the marketplace. When I feel I have already seen every bozo idea there ever was, someone will bring me another one. Amazingly, even the best marketers in the country, such as Procter & Gamble or Coca-Cola, misjudge consumer tastes.

It doesn't cost a fortune to research your market to see if what you want to sell is of interest to anyone. However, don't think that just because your neighbor and your tennis partner think your idea is real neat that you can start planning how to spend your fortune. Ask everyone you can think of about your plan. Show it to your banker, your accountant, and the head of your local chamber of commerce.

Possibly the public wants your product or service, but there are already plenty of quality providers in your territory. Are there too many dermatologists, Italian restaurants, or craft stores in the neighborhood? Consider a variation, a special niche, or a different neighborhood. If not, what do you plan to do to overcome established competition: advertising, promotion, discounting, hustle?

Have you already made the mistake of offering a product or service that nobody wants? There may be time to save the farm. Quickly evaluate the assets you are left with. A good location? A Yellow Pages ad? An investment in equipment or fixtures? How can you use these assets to provide a different product? Even simpler, can you change what you are offering in some way to make it successful?

UNDERPRICING

An excellent method for taking a bite out of market share is to underprice the competition. It is a very common approach for a new business to offer a big price advantage to get new customers.

These discounts need to be seen as a cost of doing business. If you do $5,000 in business and give a 10 percent discount to get it, you have a real cost of $500. If you have figured your overhead for all other costs at $2,000, but you don't count that $500, you may think you made money or lost only a little. Keep up this personal deception for a few months and you could easily run out of cash and never understand why.

The obvious answer to the problem of low prices is higher prices. You may be surprised to discover that you can raise prices quite a bit before you see a significant loss in sales. It's smart to create a story for your increase. Be honest. "Gosh, Barbara, after analyzing my statement, I realized that if I kept selling to you at those prices, you'd need to find a new supplier next month. I would have been out of business." This approach carries the ring of truth and will generally work quite well.

EXCESSIVE OVERHEAD

I'm sure most of us would like to start our new business with all the luxuries. I've seen plenty who've tried. Start with a very nice location (and very nice rent to go with it), big payments on the first-class furniture and fixtures, and plenty of talented staffers. With all this in place, if you do everything else right, you'll need only one hundred thousand dollars per month in sales to break even.

Ask yourself these three questions every time you want to add to overhead. Will this expense add to sales? Is this expense absolutely necessary to maintain long-term quality and service? Do I take a substantially greater risk by adding this overhead than I do by going without a while longer?

Items like advertising are much harder to quantify by these three questions, but at least it will keep your focus on the reason for advertising; adding to sales. Other expenses, like a newer truck or a second accounting clerk, should be easier to figure using just those questions.

INSUFFICIENT TIME COMMITMENT FROM OWNER

I've already emphasized the dedication new owners must make to their fledgling enterprises. There's another slightly different aspect of commitment, though, that needs to be addressed.

Many new owners, especially those who've purchased certain kinds of franchises or an ongoing business, have convinced themselves that their new business can be run by a manager with just part-time oversight from the owner.

While there are certain types of business (such as an ice cream shop) that may lend themselves more to this approach than do others (such as a law practice), the decision to be a part-time owner will handicap any new company's chances for survival, much less success.

I tried to operate my car rental business that way. I hired two managers. One was a salesman, the other a mechanic. How difficult could it be to keep sixteen of twenty-two cars operational and rented? As it turned out, that was the least of my problems. Qualifying drivers, making appropriate repair decisions, one of the managers not showing up . . . now, those are problems.

I could have hired better managers, but how much can a start-up afford? I could have provided better training, but training is an ongoing proposition. The decision to close that operation had nothing to do with the managers. It had to do with the owner.

At least until the business is up and running very well, and you have had a chance to thoroughly train your managers, run the business yourself.

BAD LUCK AND/OR TIMING

In the previous chapter, we talked about good luck playing a part in a business's success. Bad luck, most commonly in the form of bad timing, can be a significant contributor to success or failure.

You spend years and years in professional training. You get out of school, put in a few years working for someone else. You scrape up every nickel, give your notice, and hang out your shingle. Before you have had your first profitable month there is a radical change in your area that buries you. How about an example or two:

1. You open a law practice specializing in the lucrative area of personal injury law. Your state passes a no-fault insurance program.

2. Obstetrics is your area. It seems likely that people will continue to have babies. Shortly after you open, malpractice insurance rates go out of sight. The minimum payment per month is twice your rent.

3. What could possibly go wrong for a CPA? Congress passes a new tax law that really is simple to understand by a layman. (Okay. That was a little far-fetched.)

These kinds of company-killer timing problems can occur with manufacturers, plumbers, ladies' shoe stores, or any other kind of business. What can you do to guard against such occurrences?

Become as informed as you possibly can about the industry you are entering, the economic climate of the geographic area you intend to serve, and the specific pitfalls that could confront you from the standpoint of luck and timing.

If you're aware of certain risks, plan your backup strategy in advance. The lawyer could be prepared to provide legal services for product liability cases instead. The doctor might have a plan to switch to pediatrics. It might even be a good idea to open the business with both offerings, and only narrow the scope later as the risk subsides.

POOR UNDERSTANDING OF BUSINESS

Many enthusiastic entrepreneurs lack a basic understanding of the way business works. They don't have basic sales skills. They don't understand how to collect money owed. They aren't knowledgeable about purchasing and negotiating. They fail to comprehend marketing strategies. They have no experience in hiring and motivating good people. The finer points of securing financing are beyond their grasp. And the day-to-day business of operating a company isn't a part of their experience.

If you are currently lacking in any of the skills mentioned above, you will shortly receive a basic education in each of them.

PROBLEM LOCATION

Problem locations can include those that are good but have too high a rent or those that are too far away from customers or that lack convenient parking.

If it seems clear that your business is in trouble primarily because of location, and that a change might save it, don't feel that because of your lease or the expense of moving you're without solutions. The last thing you should do when confronted with such a dilemma is to merely hope things will get better. You need to move into action.

POOR ACCOUNTING CONTROLS

Accounts receivable. The A/R ledger has to be reconciled with the sales journal and the cash receipts journal. If not, it *is* possible to lose an invoice, have the customer never pay, and never realize it. It's also a good idea to add up the totals of your numerical invoice file and compare the results with your sales journal.

Accounts payable. Make certain that your A/P ledger agrees with your purchase journal and your disbursement journal. If you don't do this exercise, you could double-pay an invoice, or lose an invoice and not pay it. The next time you need product from the supplier you will be past due on the account. This may result in your having to pay the old bill (which you weren't expecting) and pay for the next order COD because you lost your credit standing with this supplier.

Cash register tape. Every day you need to be certain that your cash balances with your tape. This is a perfect opportunity for an employee to steal from you if he or she knows you aren't balancing the cash drawer daily.

In addition to all the profit-and-loss reasons for properly accounting for this information, there is also the IRS, not to mention the state taxing authorities. If they do the balancing of these items for you, they'll always do so to their own advantage.

INTERNAL THEFT

Employee theft and embezzlement are common company killers. When they hit, the results are usually fast and irreversible. Fortunately, there are steps you can take to protect your business.

You as the owner should sign every check. When signing the check, scrutinize the invoice or voucher. If you have any question about its propriety, question it now, not later.

There may be times when you'll be out of town and unavailable to sign checks. Try to anticipate the needs of the company while you're gone and fill out and sign as many checks as possible.

You'll generally need to leave a few checks signed in blank. Unless it is your wife, partner, trusted relative, or associate of many years who'll fill in the payee and dollar figure, you may want to put limits at the top of each check: "Not to exceed $500.00," for example.

Theft of inventory is another big problem. If you sell a product that has a value "on the streets," you are very likely to become a target of internal theft. It's a well-known fact that retailers suffer far more loss out the back door due to employees' light fingers than they do out the front door via shoplifting.

The most important step in preventing all types of losses due to employee dishonesty is to make certain your employees understand that you won't tolerate stealing. They should understand that you will fire and prosecute anyone caught stealing.

You may also be the victim of another type of employee theft. This would be the one-time major heist, either by an outsider or an employee who has inside information and access. Examples might include a situation where an individual responsible for closing up at night purposely fails to lock a door or turn on the alarm. They return later with a truck and clean you out.

About the only thing you can do to protect yourself against this kind of loss is the use of insurance. Be careful here, because your standard theft policy may not cover some kinds of insider-created losses. Consider special coverage such as employee bonds.

CHAPTER
3

Almighty Cash

THE LIST OF PROBLEMS associated with having too little capital is a long one: Broken equipment stays broken or, if essential, gets patched together; advertising is cut back or eliminated; staffing can be cut to the bone or beyond. Loans aren't repaid. Opportunities are missed. Tension increases with each approaching payroll. Suppliers are calling to collect. Your precious selling and management time is used for fending off creditors and your banker.

Because the importance of cash in the early going is magnified by the precariousness of your status on every other front, you must be looking for every opportunity to conserve precious dollars. Following are some basic approaches for maximizing your cash utilization.

Part 1
Bookkeeping Concepts

A consultant I've worked with makes the claim that most companies that get into trouble do so as a result of determining their budget based on an overly optimistic sales forecast. The better approach is to set a budget the owner knows he can live with and then try to sell more than the plan, adding expenses only as the sales allow.

Using this rule of thumb, the first step in creating a business budget should be a determination of a sales level that you feel you'd meet even if everything went wrong. An excellent method for arriving at that number is to create three projections.

The first is your optimistic sales goal. This is a makable figure if everything goes right and you get a few lucky breaks. Therefore, before going any further, produce your expected sales for the next twelve months, by month.

To further refine these estimates you may wish to divide them by geographic area, sales territory, product or product group, or industry served. You may want to break them down by all the above or add some more of your own. For our example, we'll show the three projections by sales territory.

OPTIMISTIC

	Sales 1	Sales 2	Sales 3	Total
January	1,000	1,000	500	2,500
February	1,000	1,500	500	3,000
March	2,000	3,000	1,000	6,000
April	3,000	3,000	1,000	7,000
May	3,000	4,000	2,000	9,000
June	4,000	4,000	2,000	10,000
July	4,000	3,500	1,500	9,000
August	3,000	3,000	1,500	7,500
September	2,000	3,000	1,000	6,000
October	2,000	3,000	500	5,500
November	1,000	1,500	500	3,000
December	2,000	3,000	1,000	6,000
Total	**28,000**	**33,500**	**13,000**	**74,500**

Once having prepared the optimistic sales budget, you'll next prepare your realistic estimate. Spend the most time with this one. You may decide to use it all year as the measuring stick of your success. A guideline for establishing these numbers might be that you'd be disappointed if you couldn't attain these levels. Again, you'll gain more from reading this section if you stop and prepare this budget before moving on.

REALISTIC

	Sales 1	Sales 2	Sales 3	Total
January	1,000	1,000	500	2,500
February	1,000	1,000	500	2,500
March	1,500	2,000	500	4,000
April	2,000	2,500	1,000	5,500
May	2,000	3,000	1,500	6,500
June	3,000	4,000	1,500	8,500
July	4,000	3,000	1,000	8,000
August	2,500	3,000	1,000	6,500
September	1,500	2,000	500	4,000
October	1,500	2,500	500	4,500
November	1,000	1,500	500	3,000
December	2,000	2,500	1,000	5,500
Total	**23,000**	**28,000**	**10,000**	**61,000**

Finally you'll want to produce the pessimistic projection. I refer to it as the drop-dead number. These are the sales numbers you could attain even if everything went wrong. In fact, you can't conceive of any way possible that you won't sell at least this much. Prepare such a projection now.

DROP DEAD

	Sales 1	Sales 2	Sales 3	Total
January	500	1,000	500	2,000
February	500	1,000	0	1,500
March	1,000	1,500	500	3,000
April	1,500	2,000	1,000	4,500
May	1,500	2,500	1,000	5,000
June	2,000	2,500	1,500	6,000
July	2,000	3,000	1,000	6,000
August	1,500	2,500	500	4,500
September	1,000	1,500	500	3,000
October	1,000	1,500	500	3,000
November	1,000	1,500	0	2,500
December	1,500	2,000	1,000	4,500
Total	**15,000**	**22,500**	**8,000**	**45,500**

After you've completed this exercise, take your drop-dead number and subtract another 10 percent. You'll now have created a sales budget that you can really count on. Therefore, our example budget will be based on sales over the next twelve months of $45,500 minus 10 percent, or $4,550, which equals $40,950.

The next step is to establish what expenses you can afford, given those sales. You should begin by determining the expenses that are the least avoidable. The first of these is cost of sales.

For the purposes of this exercise we'll assume that you sell only one item. It doesn't matter how many you buy, your cost will be the same. You also sell everyone at the same price. You buy each one for $1.75 and sell them for $3.50. Your margin is 50 percent.

Your incoming freight is prepaid. There is no other direct cost of sales other than a commission you pay to independent salespeople of 5 percent.

You also offer terms of 2 percent ten days net thirty, and about half of your customers take the discount. Thus your average cost is 1 percent of sales. You have no outgoing freight cost since your customers either come to you or pay their own freight.

The next least avoidable expense is rent. You're renting month-to-month and pay $300 per month.

You have a basic phone bill of $35 and rarely make long-distance calls. However, you have a Yellow Pages advertisement for which you pay an additional $135 per month. The $135 should be counted as advertising.

There is only a single employee other than yourself. This person works half time and takes care of all the shipping and receiving. You pay this person $10.00 per hour, which at 20 hours per week and 4.3 weeks per month would give this person a gross paycheck of $860. In most cases, a small business will want to add 10 percent to this as an estimate for Social Security, disability, and other mandated payroll-related expenses. Call this $86 "payroll tax."

You've leased some furniture and office equipment for which you have a payment each month of $70. You estimate that your tax accountant will fill out the forms for $150. You also figure you'll spend $100 per month on stationery, invoices, and other office supplies.

Let's take a look at the budget so far.

Gross sales		$40,950
Discounts	$ 409	
Net sales		40,541
Cost of sales	20,475	
Commissions	2,047	
Gross profit		$18,019
Overhead expenses		
Office salaries	$10,320	
Payroll tax	1,032	
Rent	3,600	
Telephone	420	
Utilities	0	

Legal	0	
Accounting	150	
Lease payment	840	
Advertising	1,620	
Auto expense	0	
Interest	0	
Office expense	1,200	
Travel	0	
Total overhead		$19,182
Net profit		$–1,163
Provision for tax		0
After-tax profit		$–1,163

Having completed this budget and recognized that it has no provision for any unexpected expenses, you must now ask yourself whether you're willing to spend an entire year of your life to lose a thousand bucks while not paying yourself anything. Personally, that idea seems revolting. With the understanding that you can't add to the sales number, what can you do to pay yourself, turn a profit, or both?

A. Use the process of elimination. It's almost impossible to have a business without telephone expense. You've already contracted for the office equipment lease and the Yellow Pages advertising. It seems unlikely that you could save an appreciable amount in the office expense area. The accounting fee is hard to escape unless you're a tax expert.

B. The first possibility would be to increase your margin by charging everyone more. You'll recall that before all we said was that you sold everyone at the same price, not that you couldn't raise the price. I don't intend this as a trick answer, but only to indicate how important it is that you turn every category on its head in an effort to find the hidden profit.

Many start-ups price their product too low because they believe that others in the business are trying to cut a fat hog. Others charge too little because they're unaware of how to set prices. These are the types of situations that are most likely to be fixed with a price increase.

Raising the price is not a guaranteed method to produce the extra gross margin you need. You can't be certain what effect raising the price will have on unit sales. Most products only have so much elasticity in their pricing. It's possible that a direct competitor with the exact item will take your business. A similar item that competes with your product for the customer's time or budget in that category might reduce demand for your item. Conceivably, the higher price may cause marginally interested consumers to back away.

Special exceptions would be luxury items that sometimes have more perceived value as they become more expensive, patented items for which there is a need and absolutely no available substitute, and products to which you add substantial service or other added value. (All of these characteristics are true of services as well.) If you believe that your product fits one of the special exceptions above, you may find that you actually sell more at a higher price.

For the most part, though, you'd expect your sales to follow one of the oldest economic principles known to man, the supply/demand curve. This theory postulates that the lower the price the more you'll sell, and vice versa. The relationship between the two is typically plotted on a curve. There is a certain optimum point where you'll sell the most dollars at the highest price. It's the point where supply and demand cross.

Unless you have experience with this product in the market you are entering, or have substantial amounts of money to invest in market research, you're not in a very good position to determine this precise point. Amazingly, even those who have bundles of money are not that good at figuring it out. My general rule is to charge whatever the market will bear. Start high, since it is easier to come down. Try to add value or services to commodities so you can charge more than your competition. Put the product in a beautiful package to increase perceived value. There are many products for which the package costs more than the content.

C. You could eliminate the early-payment discount. This item is not costing very much, and is undoubtedly resulting in a faster turnover of cash than if it was not offered. However, as sales increase, it will become a larger number, and you may want to compare this cost to the cost of borrowing the money.

D. You could eliminate commissions by doing all the selling yourself. In many cases this might be appropriate in the early going. The savings would be enough at least to turn the loss in our example into a profit. Plus, notice that if the sales actually ended up 10 percent or 20 percent higher, you'd end up with some take-home pay for yourself.

E. The most likely expense for meaningful savings is the employee. In fact, unless this business has an absentee owner, one has to question what the owner will be doing all the time. It's possible he has to spend all of his time billing and paying the bills, but it hardly seems likely for this amount of business. Surely he has time to do the shipping and receiving himself.

The flip side of that coin is that his services should be worth far more than the ten dollars per hour he is paying the employee. The reality, though, is that unless sales are higher the company can't afford this position. At least not at this hourly rate or this many hours.

This certainly isn't the end of the evaluation. There are many more possibilities in this simple budget. Here are just a few more to get your own ideas pumping:

- Do a little research into other suppliers of your major lines of product or services. See if you can either purchase the same or equivalent products for less, or use the leverage of potentially moving your business elsewhere to convince current vendors to drop their prices.

- Raise your prices, but give a freight allowance not offered by any of your competitors. Make certain that the price increase far more than offsets the cost of your freight policy.

- Increase your advertising, either through the Yellow Pages or other methods. For every dollar you spend, however, you should have a high degree of confidence that it will generate three dollars in additional sales.

- Appoint more commissioned salespeople and devote all of your energies to sales management. This would be among my favorite solutions. People generally make the most money from supervising others.

- Manufacture the product yourself to lower your cost.

- Hire one excellent salesperson and get rid of your commissioned agents. Even under your optimistic scenario, they didn't seem to be producing much. You may be able to do much better with someone who is dedicated full-time to your company.

Now you have established a budget that you're confident will produce the income you want at a sales level that you're absolutely convinced you can achieve. This may be easy, compared to the second step in budgeting: staying within it.

As discussed in section 2, you need a reporting system that gives you important numbers daily, weekly, and monthly. Every item on your budget should be evaluated at least monthly. Where are you over? Where are you under? Why? What can you do to bring your spending into compliance? If nothing, how must you change the budget to continue to reach your goals?

Keep in mind that your sales number and your cost of sales are both part of your budget. You may be such a great money manager that you're within a percentage point or so of your fixed overhead items every month. That won't help you much if your sales aren't high enough to generate the gross profit necessary to cover your expenses.

If this is the case, the first thing you'd better do is determine how it's possible that you're not reaching a level of sales 10 percent below your lowest expectation. Did you set your sights too high to begin with? If so, should you completely rethink your sales budget and your whole business plan with it?

If your projections were reasonable and you aren't hitting the numbers, is your sales force at fault, your product quality not acceptable, or are your prices too high? Dig deep for this answer. This is the real make-or-break question for your business. Maybe your sales are terrific and you're well within your plan on the overhead items. Unfortunately, you planned for 55 percent margins and they're actually coming in at 45 percent. If your sales are one hundred thousand dollars, this will result in missing your budget by ten thousand dollars. This situation can destroy your plan real fast.

Your options would include:

1. Raising your price.

2. Changing your sourcing to secure a lower cost.

3. Checking your payables invoicing and receiving records to make certain you're not being shorted in shipments or incorrectly billed.

4. Evaluating your inventory figures to see if there's any chance you have a theft problem.

5. Double-checking your sales invoices to be certain that what you're charging is averaging the amount necessary to reach 55 percent margins if all the other aspects check out. Also checking for mistakes in invoicing or in the posting of those invoices. You may be understating sales due to accounting errors.

6. Going over your shipping records to see if there's any chance you've been shipping more weight than would be expected for the invoiced amount. Possibly a mistake is being made in the shipping department.

7. A common place for an error in the cost of sales area is freight-in. When you figured your margins, did you take the delivery cost of the product into account? Can you reduce or eliminate this cost by negotiating with your suppliers or buying more at one time?

Next, you'll want to look at those items that are budgeted as a percentage of sales to see if they're holding to the planned percent. For example, your overall commissions may be higher than expected. Here are some options for dealing with that situation.

1. Replace the salesperson who doesn't hit the numbers projected.

2. Decrease the commission rates. This would take substantial amounts of evaluation as you try to decide how it might affect sales.

3. Raise prices for those sales with higher commission rates. The possible effects of this decision have been dealt with above and will be dealt with again, in later pages.

4. Eliminate one of the salespeople, and bring those sales inhouse. You'll want to consider what the likelihood is that you can keep those sales, and what it might cost you in time and direct sales expense (such as travel).

Other budget categories that may have percentage estimates rather than dollar projections include discounts, franchise fees, royalties, freight-out, product liability insurance, and others.

With each of the items that are projected as percentages rather than dollars, you'll have options to consider if you're not meeting those percentage goals.

1. If your freight-out is not in line with your plan you may want to: (a) change your freight policy, (b) work out better discounts with your trucking lines, (c) check to see if a packaging change would affect your cost of freight, or (d) consider using your own trucks.

2. Are you consistently over budget on royalty percentage? You could renegotiate your royalty rate, change your advertising or sales emphasis to items with lower or no royalties, or raise prices on items with royalties.

3. Early-payment discounts can be difficult to predict. When the economy is strong and you least need the money, your customers will take their discounts and hurt your profits. When times are tough, and your cash is at its tightest, your customers will be in the same pickle and the percentage of your profit going to discounts will drop.

The balance of the items on your budget are predicted by dollar amount rather than percentage. My experience has been that estimates on cost of goods, commissions, and total sales are more likely to break your budget than the so-called fixed overhead items. However, it's very easy to spend more than you plan to for salaries, advertising, travel and entertainment, or professional services.

At least once per month you're going to want to compare what you really spent in each and every category. For even tighter controls, you can create a declining balance ledger for each budget item.

That you're spending more than expected for some things doesn't automatically mean that you need to cut. If you've done a thorough evaluation of your expenses, and you feel you have cut as much fat as you can without getting into meat, you may have to make an adjustment. This adjustment might mean that you can't make a profit at current sales and margin levels, which could leave you with some important questions to answer. Questions like: "Can *I* ever make money in *this* business?"

The two important words in that sentence are "I" and "this." Does the business you've chosen have terrible margins for all practitioners? Maybe it's just too overcrowded in your territory. Could it be that this is a declining industry? Possibly you're not particularly good at this business, but you would be very successful in *another* business.

For now, though, we'll assume that you still have a chance to make it in this enterprise. For the rest of this chapter we'll focus on how you can get your expenses down, even when it seems impossible.

Salaries. Even in the smallest business this is usually the largest fixed expense. However, most owners take a look at the salary line on their P & L and feel there's nothing they can do. Even when the company is losing money, many owners feel they should have more staff, not less.

- You'd probably be amazed at how much slack you and the rest of your staff can pick up if you eliminate your least important position. One year we cut 35 percent of our white-collar staff and never missed them at all. Incredibly, we enjoyed a 40 percent increase in sales in the six months immediately following the layoff, and still felt no need to replace them.

- Consider converting a current full-time position into a part-time position.

- Consider hiring temporary help from an agency when you have busy times. It's much easier to call the agency and tell them you no longer need the temp helper than it is to lay off someone you've hired.

- Is there equipment or some system you could use to increase efficiency, thereby eliminating a position?

- Is it possible that you have one or more employees who aren't paying their way? Either they're overpaid or underqualified? Worse, maybe they're not working as hard or effectively as they should?

The real lesson here is that no matter how much you may like your current staffing situation, it's very likely that you could improve your bottom line by making changes. We'll discuss personnel in greater detail in a later chapter in this section.

Interest expense. This is another area that can get a company into trouble fast. We have seen historically low interest rates for companies who can qualify, but very small businesses and start-ups often use their personal credit cards for credit at rates approaching or above 20 percent. Use debt sparingly and try to reserve it for capital purchases, not operating expenses.

Several years ago I became good friends with a fellow who'd just sold his business for $30 million, and that was when $30 million

was a great deal of money. One day I asked him the secret of his success. His words strike home for many of the fast-track businesses
that lost it all because of debt. He said, **"We kept our growth at
twenty percent per year, and never borrowed one red cent."**

Let's take a look at that proposition. We'll assume that you sell
a hundred thousand dollars your first year. How will that grow at
20 percent per year?

Year	Sales	10% Profit	Year	Sales	10% Profit
2005	100,000	10,000	2025	3,833,760	383,376
2006	120,000	12,000	2026	4,600,512	460,051
2007	144,000	14,400	2027	5,520,614	552,061
2008	172,800	17,280	2028	6,624,737	662,474
2009	207,360	20,736	2029	7,949,685	794,968
2010	248,832	24,883	2030	9,539,622	953,962
2011	298,598	29,860	2031	11,447,546	1,144,755
2012	358,318	35,832	2032	13,737,055	1,373,706
2013	429,982	42,998	2033	16,484,466	1,648,447
2014	515,978	51,598	2034	19,781,359	1,978,136
2015	619,174	61,917	2035	23,737,631	2,373,763
2016	743,008	74,301	2036	28,485,158	2,848,516
2017	891,610	89,161	2037	34,182,189	3,418,219
2018	1,069,932	106,993	2038	41,018,627	4,101,863
2019	1,283,918	128,392	2039	49,222,352	4,922,235
2020	1,540,702	154,070	2040	59,066,823	5,906,682
2021	1,848,843	184,884	2041	70,880,187	7,088,019
2022	2,218,611	221,861	2042	85,056,225	8,505,622
2023	2,662,333	266,233	2043	102,067,470	10,206,747
2024	3,194,800	319,480	2044	122,480,964	12,248,096

Isn't compounding wonderful? To make matters even better,
unless you make some very serious errors in the overhead department, almost any business should be able to grow 20 percent per
year without borrowing at all.

Travel and entertainment. For many businesses this is a very large expense. Sometimes this is because the company needs to travel quite a bit to see clients or oversee production. Other times the reason has more to do with this category's being one of the last bastions of tax-free benefits.

If you have a large travel budget because you and/or your spouse are taking every tax-free vacation/business trip possible, then you aren't really looking for any help in fixing this expense line. If, on the other hand, you have what you believe is substantial *necessary* travel, and you're having a hard time keeping it within an acceptable percentage of sales, there are ways you may be able to manage it.

Much of what lies ahead involves keeping your costs in line, but for now, let's leave the business of budgeting and begin a short lesson in collections. *As for the 50 percent or so of you who plan to skip this topic, you're probably the ones who need it most.* So please read on.

Part 2
Collection Procedures

In 1980 I owned and operated a wholesale company with approximately one thousand retailers as my customers. I was completely computerized and sent statements to my customers every month in addition to their invoices.

We offered a 3 percent cash discount for payments received within ten days of invoice date. We charged 1.5 percent per month interest on accounts that were not paid within the standard thirty-day terms. The U.S. economy had enjoyed two very prosperous years. For all of these reasons, the company was collecting its accounts in an average of thirty days.

In addition, we had needed to write off only 0.5 percent of our total sales because of the bankruptcies or liquidations of our customers. This was excellent, given the number and quality of our customers.

Because of our excellent results in this area, we paid little attention to collections. Then it happened. The recession of 1981. Within ninety days our average days to collect went from thirty to seventy-five. In other words, we collected almost nothing during that period while continuing to ship to accounts that were falling further and further behind. We almost went broke. *It can happen that fast!*

Here are the steps you need to take to establish a disciplined approach to collections.

1. You'll reduce the amount of time and effort in collecting money if you spend time in the beginning by checking the credit-worthiness of your customers. There are some standard practices, and then there are some secrets. The standard practices will rarely provide much insight, but the secret approaches can and do.

> **A.** The most standard thing to do is send your new customer a credit application, such as the one that follows:
>
> Company name in full:
>
> Is this a division or subsidiary of any other company? If so, please provide the name of the parent company in full:
>
> If the company is a sole proprietorship, please indicate the name, home address, and home phone number of the owner:
>
> If the company is a partnership, please indicate the name, home address, and home phone number of all partners holding at least a 25 percent share. Please indicate the percentage ownership of each:
>
> If the company is a corporation, please indicate the state of incorporation, and the name, home address, and home phone number of the president and the secretary of the corporation:

Please provide the name of any banks where you have checking, savings, or lines of credit along with address and phone number. Also provide the account numbers, the name identifying the account if different from the company name above, and any contact person at the bank who is familiar with the account. Also send a copy of your most recent checking account statement [Secret #1. If they will provide this—and many will balk at the idea—you'll learn far more about their cash flow than anything that the bank can tell you in the standard credit check.]:

Please provide five references. [Secret #2. Everybody asks for three, so every deadbeat company always has three prepared references. By asking for five, you greatly reduce the likelihood of getting friendly instead of honest references.] Include the addresses, phone numbers, fax numbers, and any contact person familiar with your account. Also send a copy of your most recent statement from that supplier. [Secret #3. The statement will point up the reality of the payment history with that supplier, where the phone call may not.]:

Are you delinquent in any tax payments including payroll withholding? [Secret #4. Nobody ever asks this, but a company in trouble will commonly start missing one or more payroll tax payments.]:

Please send a copy of your most recent financial statement. Is this a compilation, review, or audited statement? If internally prepared or a compilation, please also provide a signed copy of your most recent federal tax return. [Secret #5. Banks, leasing companies, and landlords always ask for reviewed or audited statements. If none is available, then they require signed tax returns. *No one* asks for this information on a credit application to establish an open account, even though the amount of money "loaned out" by you to your customer may be much greater than the amounts involved in a lease. You will learn more from these documents than from most of the rest of the above.]:

Are the principals named above willing to sign a personal guarantee for amounts above $5,000? [Secret #6. The amount shown may be higher or lower, but many of your customers will be intimidated into signing a personal guarantee. It is unlikely that you will ever enforce this guarantee, but it gives you substantial leverage in collection. They are far more likely to pay *you* on time than another supplier who has no guarantee, and when they are in trouble, they will pay you first for sure.]:

Finish the application with a requirement that the president or majority owner sign and date the document, acknowledging that the above is true to the best of their knowledge under penalty of perjury.

B. Call the references. It is so common for companies to go to the trouble to compile this application and then not make any calls.

When you call, have a prepared form ready to fill in the information that you receive:

Date:	Name of supplier called:
Phone:	Person contacted:
Length of relationship:	
High credit: $	Current balance: $
Amount past due: $	Average days to pay:

What does this customer do when he's in trouble: [Secret #7. Nobody asks this, but it is extremely revealing. First, if the vendor has been prepared by the customer to give a good reference, this direct question may catch the contact person off guard. Furthermore, you want to know how this person handles a cash problem. Does she run and hide? Or is she candid, available, and truthful about how the situation is going to be resolved? Guess which kind of customer deserves a higher credit line?]

Each of the completed reference forms should be attached to the credit application to become a part of the customer's permanent file. If a pattern of slow pay begins to develop, you may want to call back some of these references for an update on the account's status.

From all the above data, you will assign the customer a credit limit. It is a very good idea to send them a letter congratulating them on being granted open account status and informing them of their credit limit. You may want to suggest that if their account is paid promptly, you will be happy to evaluate the situation later for possible increases in the credit line.

If you feel you must turn down any extension of credit at this time, it is also imperative that you send a letter so stating along with some reasons for your decision. You may wish to keep open the possibility of a later loosening in your policy based on X dollars of sales paid COD or other criteria. Your letter should be very diplomatic since, usually, you will not want to chase them away as a customer.

C. The credit limit should be shown at the top of the customer card, or included in the customer master file in your computer. Many computers will provide a signal to the operator before printing the order or invoice if that order would put the customer over their limit.

2. Invoicing is the next step in the collection procedure. As stated above, send out your invoices the same day you ship. Many companies put the invoice in an envelope on the outside of the

shipping box. Sending your invoice this way presents too many opportunities for it to be lost. Mail the invoice.

Make certain that your terms are clear and concise. One of the credit card statements I receive from a major national retailer has no indication anywhere of a due date. Don't make that mistake. Clearly show the invoice date, the ship date if different (it shouldn't be), and the terms of sale. You may wish to go so far as to show the due date and the amount saved if paid by an earlier date where applicable.

3. Send out a statement at the end of the month. Consider using your invoice and statement mailings as a place to advertise other products or services you sell, or to communicate things that are happening at your company.

4. Begin your collection procedure on the third day after the due date. You or your collection clerk should have a standard operating procedure for calling and writing to past due accounts. Here is my suggestion along with scripts for phone calls and suggested faxes or letters.

> **A.** First phone call on third day: "Hi, my name is, Rob. May I speak to whoever is in charge of paying the bills?" (This assumes that you don't know. You want to speak to someone with authority to pay. The accounts payable clerk may not be the one who decides who to pay and when.)
>
> "Hi, my name is Rob. I'm with Acme Printing. Are you responsible for paying the bills?" If the answer is no, you will want to ask who is. If yes: "I was going over our accounts receivable, and I noticed that you had this one little item that has just gone a few days past due. Since it was my recollection that you generally pay right on time, I was worried that you might not have received this item."
>
> What you are doing here is putting the person at ease. You compliment them by saying they usually pay on time. They might have been slow before, but you cover yourself by saying it is your "recollection" that they pay

on time. You have also given them an out if they need it. "You're right," they respond, "I don't show that item on my payables ledger."

All of this may seem excessively polite when you are trying to collect from someone. However, my experience has shown that a small business will gain a great deal from this type of approach.

If they indicate that they do not have the invoice, offer to fax it right over. If they don't have a fax machine, mail a copy of the invoice with a brief cover letter asking for payment by return mail. Or, if the company accepts e-mail attachments, send the invoice electronically.

Whether by fax, by e-mail, or by mail, call again when you figure they have received it. For the fax, wait an hour. For mail, two to five days, depending on what part of the country you are mailing to. For e-mail, ask for an electronic receipt (usually an option in the e-mail program). When you call, ask for the person by name. Then ask if they have received the invoice copy. If yes, ask them when you can expect payment. If they respond in any way other than that they will send it right out, ask them why it cannot be taken care of immediately.

If they say they will mail it right out, mark the date that you both agree it should reach you on their file. Keep a record of each phone call by time, date, contact person, and details of discussion. Also keep a copy of all correspondence in the file.

B. Responses to wrong answers: Many times you will be told that they did not receive your copy by mail. Immediately send out a copy of the letter and invoice by certified mail, return receipt requested. If the amount is large enough or important enough you may want to use an overnight service. The key is to use a system that requires a signature. This will quickly eliminate this excuse. Follow up again with a phone call on the day you figure the item has arrived to confirm with your contact that they now have the invoice copy.

Another favorite and well-known response is "The check is in the mail." A possible variation would be "The check has been cut and is in for signature." Again, you need to press for a date by which you both agree the check should arrive. If it doesn't arrive by the day after the agreed-upon date, it is time to call again. Do not press for check numbers at this juncture as you should still be in the trusting phase at this point.

You may hear that "cash flow is terrible right now," along with varying degrees of elaboration designed to make you feel sorry for them and confident in their eventual payment. Within reason you will want to listen to and work with your customer as long as they appear to be giving you an honest evaluation of their situation and a workable plan. However, anything over sixty days is unacceptable, and you should make this abundantly clear.

Another perfect response to the cash flow excuse is to be prepared to offer your own sad tale. You just don't know how you can make payroll if their check doesn't arrive by Friday. Your banker will require you to put them on COD if you haven't received their check by the cutoff date for the month.

One of my favorites is to be very sympathetic. "You know, Cheryl, I can really relate to what you're going through. I have been there myself. I want to help you any way that I can, but there are limits. Can you assure me that you will get me a check by the twenty-second? Don't tell me you can if you aren't totally sure. Please, if for any reason you aren't able to follow through on this promise, you call me before I have to call you. I will respect you more for calling me and telling me that you will be five days late, than for not calling me and being three days late."

By providing the above information, you've set up a complete system of guidelines for your customer to work within. Now if they don't comply, you have every justification to turn the heat way up.

C. The fifteenth day: By now, you should have determined whether your customer is being honest with you about their cash problems, or whether they are the type that keeps giving you excuses.

For the first group, you will want to start offering some alternatives. Request a partial payment, along with a payment schedule for the balance. Offer to have them return merchandise with a 20 percent restocking charge.

For the second group you will now want to ask if you can pick up the check. This will be practical only for some. However, if you have an account with any of the overnight services, you can order a pickup. Ask your account if you can have DHL or FedEx pick up the check that afternoon.

Commonly this idea will be met by a new assurance that the check was mailed yesterday or earlier this morning. Now is the time to ask for a check number. You will also want to check the postmark date when the check arrives to see where the truth lies.

D. Thirty days past due is time for action. If you have been using a clerk to make the calls until this time, it is now time for you to call. You will want to attempt to reach the owner (for smaller companies) or controller (for larger businesses).

Your conversation might proceed something like this: "Hello, Mrs. Stevens, this is Bob Barnette, president of Acme Printing. I wanted to take this opportunity to call you personally on a matter that is creating a potential problem between our companies. It is my understanding that your company has an excellent reputation for paying its bills on time. It was on that basis that our firm extended credit to yours.

"I don't want to harm anyone's career, but I feel as though Cheryl in accounts payable is not being straight with me. We are very willing to work with companies if they have cash shortages from time to time. However, it is critical that we get information that we can count on during those times. This doesn't seem to be happening with Cheryl. Can you help me on this?"

This approach will usually result in an answer within twenty-four hours. Use the same techniques as above to confirm the new arrangement: agreed-upon date, FedEx pickup, partial payment, and so on.

E. At forty-five days after due date it is time to send another certified letter. Go to the trouble to get a "proof of delivery" from your shipper if the product was shipped. Send a copy of the proof of delivery, any previous correspondence, the invoice, and any other documentation you can provide to eliminate another delay because they "need more information."

Enclose a cover letter to the president (or controller, whoever it was that you contacted at thirty days). Make certain that you indicate that you have mailed a second copy of all the information to the payables clerk, as well.

F. Offer other ways to pay. Suggest they pay by credit card. If you don't have credit card services, see if you have a business friend who might let you process the card through their service.

If they have insisted that the check is in the mail a couple of times, suggest that they fax over a copy of a new check they are writing to replace it. If you haven't received the original in a few days, see if your bank will process the faxed copy. You may have to establish this option in advance. You can also do check by phone if you have a bank that offers it. This can also cut down on the excuses.

Final thoughts on collections: It is not as important what you say in your collection effort as it is that you make a collection effort. It should be consistent and systematic. If you are having the work done by a clerk, make certain that he knows your philosophy, method, and the importance you place on this part of his job.

The older an invoice gets, the harder it is to collect.

Slow-pay accounts tend to pay first the suppliers who are bugging them the most for payment.

People tend to pay the following businesses last if they are short of funds: lawyers, doctors of all types, accountants, travel agents, advertising agents, and other service providers. Interestingly, some of these folks are also the worst collectors.

G. Collection agencies and lawyers: If you are not very good at collections or your industry has a serious problem with slow pay, you may want to use a collection agency or a law firm specializing in collections.

This is a very expensive method of collection. Small amounts may cost you as much as 50 percent of the invoice total. Larger invoices may still cost 25 percent to 33 percent. The better agencies send out the first letter or two for a flat fee and begin to charge the larger amounts only as they begin to use more expensive collection methods.

In addition to the expense of using this collection method, you will also be likely to end forever the relationship with the customer whom you turn over for collection.

The least expensive and best method of collection is a properly trained specialist employed by your company, with personal backup from you.

Part 3
Payables Approaches

Your approach to payment of your accounts may have almost as much impact on the performance of your company as does the collection of your receivables.

In a perfect world, we would all enter into small business with plenty of cash. We would make money from the first day, never outgrow our financial resources, and never have a crisis interrupt our ability to pay. I have actually known a couple of small business owners for whom this has been true.

Even if it's true for you, your bookkeeper will need to be alerted to take every discount possible, including some that aren't that evident. Since many discounts are based on payment within ten days, it will mean that your system for ordering and taking receipt of goods—proper filling out of purchase orders, logging in of inventory, etc.—will need to be well oiled.

Some companies do not offer an early-pay discount. However, you may find that if you call their accounting department and propose to them that you would be happy to send the money early for a 2 percent discount, they may decide they could use the money. If you were to average a 2 percent discount on all your purchases during the year, it can add up to a great deal of money. A company doing $1 million in sales at 50 percent margins buys $500,000 worth of goods. Two percent of that is $10,000.

What can all this credit worthiness do for you?

1. Provide more credit. For instance, you may currently have a credit line of $10,000 with a particular vendor. You may need or want to increase your line to $20,000 or more. If you have been discounting, you are almost certain to get an increase in your credit limit.

2. There may be a product line that you currently don't carry because the supplier limits distribution by area or by size or type of customer. As you seek to be added as a customer your credit standing may be a deciding factor between you and a competitor. (My experience has shown that other factors such as proven ability to sell, promises of time and energy devoted to that line, and plain old salesmanship can be more decisive. But in a close battle, credit may win the day.)

3. Even the best-run companies sometimes have a bad year. This may result in cash tightening up. But your supplier's accounts receivable (A/R) clerk who is looking over the aging and deciding who to call first is unlikely to even think of calling the account who always pays by discount. This will be true at least until the item is sixty days or more. At that point, since you are known to normally pay by discount, you have maximum credibility in explaining your circumstances and your plan for dealing with the payment.

4. Creditworthiness can provide a springboard for very rapid expansion. A company that has maximized all of its credit lines and is constantly paying late will find the going tough when they want to expand rapidly. This is because there is nowhere to go for supplier credit, the best and least expensive form of capital.

However, the company that has been paying within ten to thirty days can ask for and get one or both of the following: a larger line of credit, or an extension of terms beyond the norm. For instance, if normal terms are net thirty, they will have a good chance of asking for and getting net sixty or even ninety.

Once in a while, cash might really get tight. If it happens more than occasionally you may want to seek advice from your CPA or other adviser about why this is true and how to correct it. For those occasions when you need a few ideas of how to get through a dark time, consider the following:

Call your creditors before they call you. If you are going to be over thirty days past due, or if the account is one that you know will call at three days or fifteen, call them a couple of days before you would expect their call. Your script goes something like this:

"Hello, Chris. I wanted to give you a call about my account. Did you hear about our flood?" At this point you will want to give far more detail than the A/R clerk wants to hear. Explain exactly how the situation has affected your ability to pay. Tell her your plan for payment. Ask her for a continuation of shipments on open account according to a formula you propose.

For instance, you might suggest that as you need product, you will call her and you will both agree to how much you will pay to get your merchandise shipped. A common approach is the amount of the new shipment plus 10 percent of the old balance.

Be just as humble as you can be on the one hand, and as reassuring as possible on the other. "This will only be a temporary problem. We would expect to be back to paying within terms by March or so. Will you work with me, Chris?"

Other extremely effective statements include: "I'll always give you the straight scoop. I won't tell you I can send the money on a certain day unless I know I can. If I think I can, but am not certain, I'll say it that way. I won't tell you the check's in the mail unless it is.

"You'll always be able to reach me personally. If you're told that I'm not in, it's because I really am out. I'll call you back the same day if at all possible.

"If you're ever dissatisfied with anything that my accounts payable [A/P] clerk says or does, don't hesitate to call me, personally."

In a nutshell, you want to be honest, humble, assuring, available, and persuasive. Then you must do what you said you would do. If the supplier's A/R clerk or controller is going out on a limb for you, you must follow through on every promise. If, for any reason, you can't, pick up the phone before the time you will miss your promise and eat humble pie again.

A few last thoughts on payables.

If you should ever bounce a check, call the supplier before they receive the notice from the bank. Explain the circumstances and ask that they redeposit it. If your situation is not going to clear up by the time the check would hit your bank the second time, ask that they hold the check for a few days. You will call them when it is "good." Again, end the conversation with: "If you don't hear from me within a couple of days, don't hesitate to give me a call."

Don't ever say you've lost the invoice unless you have. Don't ever say the check is in the mail unless it is. Don't ever send a check unsigned to buy a few days. These are old, tired tricks that every A/R clerk knows. They will work against you.

4

The Personnel Process

You can build an excellent business with a total payroll of one . . . yourself. I have seen several such companies, especially those centered around service providers such as lawyers, consultants, and CPAs. For most businesses however, you'll eventually need to hire some people to help your business grow and prosper.

The personnel task can be looked at as a process. The steps are:

1. Evaluating the need
2. Establishing the task and pay range
3. Conducting the search
4. Screening the applicants
5. Training the new hire
6. Managing people
7. Handling terminations
8. Producing the employee handbook

EVALUATING THE NEED

You're in business, after all, to earn a living and to make a fair return on your and your investors' money. If a new employee will not contribute to that result, at least in the near-to-medium term, you may be wise to stick with the personnel you have.

One way to determine whether an additional body will provide a return on your investment is to listen to the sage advice my grandfather used to give. "If I can hire someone to do it cheaper than I can do it myself, then I'll hire it done."

There are times, though, when failing to add a staff member can badly damage your business. It is fairly common to find start-ups in which the owner is adequate at a certain task. However, as the company starts to build, the owner is soon in over his head. At this point a decision must be made to gain the needed proficiency or hire someone who has the proficiency.

When I started my bicycle retail store, I was adequate enough at repairing bicycles that my small group of clients rarely noticed my limitations. As the business grew, however, I was constantly faced with repairs that I couldn't handle, and I had to send some customers to a competitor. Since I was well aware of my limited abilities as a mechanic, I eventually had to decide whether to hire a qualified individual to do this work or risk losing all customers with sophisticated equipment.

An additional reason for hiring a new person is the customer following he or she has. Many examples come to mind. Manicurists usually have loyal customers who will follow them from shop to shop. This is also true for accountants, hairdressers, and others.

ESTABLISHING THE TASK AND PAY RANGE

Once you've determined to bring another body on board, it's time to decide exactly what you'll want that person to do. In the most formal sense, you'll need to produce a "job description." This is important for many reasons. First it will further establish your need for this position. As you write out the list of things you want this person to accomplish, it will become evident whether the individual will add to the company's efficiency, range of services, or customer base.

Second, the job description will help you determine the pay scale. Without thorough consideration of the task you have in mind it will be difficult to determine what the job is worth.

Third, the employee, once hired, will benefit from being able to see a crystal-clear statement of what you expect. Most people want direction and are much happier with a job that has been clearly stated.

Additionally, you'll be able to evaluate employee performance more easily if you can look back at what you wanted from that position. You may be able to make some intuitive judgments about the performance of your staff, but it's always useful to have hard data to confirm your intuition.

Having completed the job description, you can now attempt to figure the pay necessary to hire someone with these skills. You may want to ask your CPA for advice. You can also look through the want ads and read the descriptions there. Some will show the pay offered. Try to establish an affordable range that will allow you to hire a person with the skills you need.

CONDUCTING THE SEARCH

My company has been quite successful hiring through networking. When a position is opening or we're planning to add staff, we first call family, friends, associates, or anyone else who might have a lead on an exceptional candidate.

Once we've made the opening known to everyone, we'll ask our own employees for any ideas they may have. Your current employees aren't likely to recommend a friend or family member whom they believe will make them look bad or hurt the company.

If we strike out using the above approaches and want to fill the opening quickly, we'll advertise in the local paper. We've also had some success using entry-level people provided through a city program that places workers who are members of "disadvantaged" groups.

High school and college placement centers can often produce good people for part-time or summer jobs requiring little experience.

I've used an employer-paid agency only once. This was for a highly paid executive. The candidates suggested by the agency were well qualified for the position. I'm not confident that the expense (the fee is generally three months' wages) was worth it.

Our current practice is to look to friends, acquaintances, known individuals in the industry first. Failing that we immediately proceed to "temp-to-hire." There are hundreds of temporary placement services both nationally and locally.

The advantage of this approach is that there is little or no interview process. The agency sends individuals who are qualified for the position. If the agency knows your company well enough, they will also know some of the personality traits that might be a good match.

You can send home a temp after four hours if they are clearly not the right person for the task. You may want to evaluate them for a day, a week, a month, or even longer depending upon the requirements of the position. If you eventually feel that they would make a valuable addition to your company, you put them on your payroll.

There are at least two disadvantages to this approach. One is that you may have to spend the time and money to train several folks before you find the right one. Of course, since they are temps, they might decide to grab a permanent job while you are still evaluating them. By keeping communications open, you should be able to let them know if they have a good chance of being hired and thus reduce that likelihood.

The other disadvantage is that there may be a cost of hiring them. Generally I find that unskilled workers are usually free to hire after thirty to ninety days. The greater the pay range, however, the longer you have to keep them as temps before they become "free" to hire.

For some positions, such as comptroller and general manager, temp agencies may seek a fee no matter how long the individual worked for you as a temp.

When writing an advertisement for a job opening in your company, take the same care you would in writing any ad. What kind of person do you want? How can you show your company in the best way to attract that kind of person? If you're planning to offer a pay rate higher than the market, talk about it. If you hope to find someone who is willing to work under the market rate, don't mention the budgeted figure in the ad.

We usually state that we have a friendly office. We want to attract people who like people.

Don't waste your money boasting that you're "an equal opportunity employer." It's illegal to be anything else. For exactly that reason you should be careful not to include language that appears discriminatory (the exception, of course, is if you're part of a religious organization).

SCREENING THE APPLICANTS

Unless you have loads of time on your hands, you aren't going to want to personally interview every person who responds. Have a prepared list of questions and comments about the position ready for each phone call. Whoever answers the phone should have this list and understand the reasons for the questions in order to make a judgment whether or not to encourage the person to come in.

It's generally not a good idea to get into the money issue over the phone. This is because you'll be in a better position to persuade an excellent candidate to accept your proposed salary level face-to-face.

The next opportunity to screen job seekers is by having them fill out an application when they reach your office. There are many application forms available online, at the stationery store, or in countless books on employee management. I offer no special advice in this regard. We use a standard form that we purchase from the stationery store.

The first interview should be conducted by the person most directly responsible for overseeing this position. Limit your personal interviews to the top two or three candidates. Discuss these with the supervisor so as to make a joint decision.

Additional hiring guidelines:

1. Ask applicants why they left each employment listed on their résumé.

2. Call all references and verify their reasons for leaving and all other information they provide. Ask about specific work habits like on-time arrival, attendance, chattiness, and ability to get along with coworkers and supervisors. Check whether they're a leader or follower.

3. Ask them about their reasons for wanting this position and how it fits into their career plan.

4. Ask them what their income was at their last job, and their desire for this one. (In most negotiations it's better to let the other party make the first offer.)

5. If they need to possess certain testable skills, do as many tests as possible to determine their capability.

6. Ask for personal references and call these as the last step in the process. Ask applicants to help you with resolving any problems you've run into during your investigation.

7. Conduct a second interview with the top two or three choices if you think it will help to make the decision. Ask others in the organization to interview as well if you think they can add insight.

8. Establish a probationary period of ninety days. Establish the hourly pay rate $.50 per hour less than you are planning for the position. Let them know that there is an automatic pay increase if they successfully complete probation.

9. Use your intuition.

TRAINING THE NEW HIRE

The indoctrination process begins with the final interview. You want the employee to understand your philosophies and approaches to business since these will affect the job he or she is about to undertake. You'll never have this person's attention again as totally as you do in the interview.

Once you offer the job and agree on pay, duties, and hours, resist the temptation to continue too long with the indoctrination. The new hire has his head in the clouds and will remember little that happens in the next few hours. He is primarily interested in telling spouse, parents, brother, sister, and friends that he has a new job.

Encourage him to give proper notice with his current employer. This will indicate that you expect the same should the occasion ever arise. If you need him right away, suggest that he request the earliest possible leave from his current employer.

I like to spend about one hour with each new person after he's had a day or so to meet his fellow employees and get the lay of the land. I use this meeting to again emphasize my personal philosophies. It is also a time for the newcomer to ask questions that may have come up. Above all, I try to emphasize that my door is always open for problems, suggestions, or questions.

MANAGING PEOPLE

Personnel management is generally the most time-consuming task of the small business owner. You must ensure that the work is getting done correctly and on time. You must give people a sense of fulfillment and belonging. Additionally, there are the issues of evaluation, compensation, discipline, and benefits. Finally, the government has a long list of rules, regulations, and requirements concerning employer/employee issues.

For the most part, managing others comes down to communication. It's critical to convey the following elements:

1. Your vision. To communicate a vision, you must have one. If you don't know which way you want your business to go, how will your employees be able to make proper decisions? Once you're clear on your direction, don't expect your people to figure it out on their own. Tell them where you are headed, and how they fit into the plan.

2. Your expectations. What do you expect from each employee? In order for people to have a sense of self-worth, they need to know what they must do to be acceptable. They can then decide whether they want to work hard enough to merely get by, get ahead, or be a superstar.

3. Your evaluation and reward system. What can they expect from you? If people who merely get by are getting rewarded at the same level or better than those who are putting out a big effort, the results are fairly predictable. Similarly, it is hard to maintain discipline if those who act contrary to company policy are not dealt with in a clear and fair manner.

These are three simple ideas, but not simple in the implementation. Think about how difficult it is to maintain harmony in your own home among those whom you love and hold dear. It can be much more difficult to manage people who do not have the kinds of ties that are felt in a family. You can do it, but it takes hard work.

HANDLING TERMINATIONS

From time to time people are going to leave your employ. You will fire some, lay some off, and ease some out. They will find better jobs, move to a new location because of a spouse's job, or go home to raise a family or retire. It is all a part of the process that started with the recognition of a need for that position.

The most important part of any separation of an employee from your business is the opportunity that such an event provides. No matter how well that individual performed her duties you are in a position to *increase* your capabilities in that position. You also have the potential to lower your costs. Maybe best of all, you have the chance to start over. All that you've learned through your relationship with the departing employee does not have to be learned again with the new hire. You have a golden opportunity to train this new person in a way that will bring you benefits for years.

Your chances for achieving that goal increase in direct proportion to the time and energy you devote to three aspects of the transition. The first step is the separation interview. This is the conversation you have with the employee that confirms your decision to let him go or his decision to leave.

Use this conversation to learn about that employee's perception of what is right and wrong with the position, the company, his supervisor, and your leadership. These conversations can be very emotional and difficult, but they can also pay big dividends.

If the leave-taking is amicable, ask the departing employee to create a new job description for the position. This may merely be a picture of how the job is currently done, or better yet, it can be a suggestion as to how it *should* be done.

You'll next want to reevaluate the need. *It is common practice to use the departure of an employee as an opportunity to cut overhead.* However, you shouldn't either automatically replace or cut. Begin at the beginning. Do we need this position? What are the effects on the business, the other employees, the profits, and your own goals?

PRODUCING THE EMPLOYEE HANDBOOK

I used to think that an employee handbook was another one of those things that only big companies needed. In each of my enterprises there has been no consideration given to vacation, sick leave, work rules, or government strictures until there were at least five or six on staff.

Nothing was committed to writing until there were nine or ten faces under our roof, and the company was three or so years along. The one- or two-page memo that I produced was generally a compilation of ideas the top managers and I produced when we started hearing complaints that none of it was written down.

Producing a handbook provides important benefits such as:

1. Offering legal protection to the owners and fulfilling legal requirements.
2. Indicating management's commitment to its employees.
3. Assisting in new-employee orientation.
4. Enhancing the professional image of the company.
5. Communicating benefits, and clearing up misunderstandings about benefits.
6. Eliminating questions about fairness.

Compiling a handbook doesn't have to be complicated. It should begin with the company's mission statement and then clearly and concisely specify the working hours for each category of employee; the dress code, if there is one; information about benefits such as vacation, holidays, and health insurance; and the timing of salary reviews. You should also include the general rules regarding theft, relations with coworkers, and relations with customers.

Part 1
Bloated Payrolls,
the Business Killer

In my experience I can't recall more than one or two instances where employee overhead was the ultimate cause of a company's demise. Most owners faced with an excess of personnel jettison people in time to save their business. On the other hand, I've seen countless examples of bloated payrolls resulting in serious damage to an otherwise healthy enterprise.

It is really quite easy to justify each new position. Once an individual is hired, it's equally easy to see that she's making a real contribution. This is partly due to that individual's instinct for survival. She'll find things to do in order to appear valuable.

The difficult part of this process is to take a hard look at each position and determine what is need, what is want, and what is pure luxury. To add an element of additional complexity to this issue, everything changes as your business changes.

My company once had a production supervisor whom we believed was the ultimate indispensable employee. We lived in dread of the day that he'd quit or die. We considered a key-man insurance policy to help us get through such a crisis. Then, of course, he left.

If he'd left two or three years earlier, we may have just gotten out of manufacturing altogether since my partner and I are not familiar with machinery. However, by the time this employee left we'd trained other employees who were able to perform 90 percent of his function. We were able to farm out the last 10 percent to outside consultants at a fraction of the cost of a full-time supervisor.

The point of this lesson is twofold. First, there are no indispensable employees. There are others who can do the work. The work can be farmed out. Sometimes there isn't a need for that job to be done at all.

Furthermore, you may have two or three employees doing what could be done by one or two. Can the work be consolidated? Do you have too many employees assigned to a certain task because some are incompetent or not pulling their own weight?

Two likely times for payroll costs to get out of hand are during expansion and during contraction. Rapidly growing companies commonly lose control of their staff requirements. This is due to an inability to properly evaluate the need for each position when so many other aspects of running the business are tugging on the owner's time.

During slow times, there is a hesitancy to let anyone go. The business side of your brain says that it will be difficult and expensive to replace good people when sales pick up again. The heart side says that you feel bad about sending people home to an uncertain future—people whom you've come to know and like.

There is a simple answer to this kind of thinking. No matter how difficult and expensive it may be to replace good workers, it will be much more difficult to recover from the financial difficulties you'll face by not taking the action. One of those possible difficulties is loss of the business, and *everyone* in the company losing their jobs.

Part 2
Final Thoughts on Personnel

1. Keep a file on each employee. There are standard forms available. You'll want to keep track of the starting date, the pay, the benefit schedule, attendance, and so on.

2. Keep a copy of all written information about the employee. This would include letters or memos the employee has written to you or that you've written to the employee about any job-related subject. Keep copies of evaluations or memos produced by others about that person's performance.

3. Have employees sign a statement that they've read and understood the handbook and/or any other work rules that you may impose or change from time to time. Also have them confirm by signature that they've read and understood any reprimand you've placed in their file.

4. Praise often and in public. Criticize carefully and in private.

5. Expect a lot and you'll get a lot; expect little and you'll surely get it.

5

Building Sales

I WANT TO PAINT A PICTURE in your mind. Please sit back, relax, and imagine that the next sentence in this paragraph is written in letters ten feet high; the letters are covered with velvet and trimmed in diamonds and are stretched across a football field where you are viewing them from the Goodyear blimp.

NOTHING WILL MORE SIGNIFICANTLY AFFECT THE FUTURE FINANCIAL SUCCESS OF YOUR BUSINESS THAN YOUR ABILITY TO SELL!

You can sell your way out of bad management for a long time, but you can't manage your way out of no sales for even one day. Every day that your sales fall below the absolute minimum necessary for you to pay the rent and lights puts you one day closer to losing it all.

This chapter covers seven aspects to building your sales:

1. Personal salesmanship
2. Sales management of others
3. Advertising

4. Promotion
5. Trade shows
6. Using e-mail and the Web
7. Pursuing new territories

Part 1
Personal Salesmanship

The owner's title should be "president of sales." The only situation where the owner of the company does not need to be a master salesperson is when there is a full partner who is. If you're just about to go into business or have already taken the plunge, or if you're not a master salesperson, and you don't have a full partner who is a master sales rep, you need to memorize the next twenty-five pages of this book. It is not difficult to become a master salesperson. It takes only a willingness to accept and practice five basic principles.

When Moses stepped down from Mount Sinai, he brought with him two tablets containing ten irrefutable laws burned into stone by God. To date, I've yet to come across any other set of principles that have stood the test of time like those ten—except the five that follow for selling.

Don't believe any system for selling that doesn't include these five. As you read books on selling you'll notice that almost all of them dwell on these five principles. Other writers may call them by different names, but they eventually arrive at the same five.

SALES PRINCIPLE #1—ENTHUSIASM: LIGHTING THE FIRE

As sales are to business success, so then is enthusiasm to sales success. If you never get the hang of the rest of selling, you can get a long way by just exhibiting excitement about your company, your product, and yourself.

If you don't think that your business is fantastic, a value to the community, and a work of art, why would you expect your customers to rate it more highly than you do?

If you're not brimming over with enthusiasm for your product and the benefits it can bring to your customer, why would you expect your customers to hand over their hard-earned dollars for it?

If you don't believe you can add value to the product or service you offer, and that you are the best resource your customers can find for what you sell, why, pray tell, should they think better of you than you do?

Unfortunately, there are plenty of people in positions of sales responsibility who think the products they sell aren't a good value. They believe that their company rips off the public. Some barely have enough self-esteem to get them past the mirror in the morning. You don't want anybody like that working in your sales department, *including yourself.*

My dictionary defines enthusiasm, as "intense, high-wrought emotion that compels to action." Every word in that definition deserves a look. Salespeople should be intense. They should believe in what they do with an almost religious fervor. This doesn't suggest that there isn't room for constructive criticism of product, company, or self. It does mean that when the time for criticism is over and the time to sell has arrived, a good salesperson leaves his or her doubts at the door and goes into the selling situation believing wholeheartedly in the endeavor.

High-wrought is not a word I would have thought of myself, but I'm glad Webster put it there. The super salesperson creates an environment that compels the attention of her customer. Through eye contact, voice patterns, body movements, even theatrics, the buyer should be grabbed by the presentation. Here are a few attention-grabbing approaches:

1. Surprise is probably the best way to keep your presentation exciting. I had a teacher once who, during his first lecture to each class, jumped on top of a table to punctuate a point. That was thirty years ago, and it is vividly implanted in my mind along with the point he made. In selling encyclopedias door-to-door there was a point in the canned pitch I learned where I would slam the book down on a coffee table or the floor. This was partly designed to show how tough the binding was, but mostly to increase the intensity of the presentation.

2. Magic is one of my favorite methods. Like a magician, I like to keep product hidden in my briefcase or sample bag until the last minute. I may even reach in to get it, and leave my hand with the product out of sight for a minute or so while continuing to build suspense.

Amway creates demonstrations of their products that are quite amazing. The best I observed was one for a shoeshine spray. After wiping the dust off the customer's shoe, and spraying this product onto the shoe, the resultant shine was absolutely magic.

3. Action is another intensity builder. I always encourage bicycle dealers to show how the parts work while showing a bicycle. Pick up the rear wheel and turn the cranks. Apply the brakes. Shift through the gears.

One part of action is involvement. The more that you ask your customer to actively participate with you in the presentation, the more likely you are to cause the intensity to be contagious. Give your prospect something to hold. Have him use your product. Let him turn the pages of your written material while you look over his shoulder or read it upside down.

4. Drama leaves a lasting impression. The more dramatic your presentation, the more you can control the emotion of the moment. For some this will mean lots of action, exuberance, and lighthearted fun. For others such as insurance salespeople, plastic surgeons, and undertakers it means being solemn, sensitive, and serious.

Use one of these ideas, all of them, or make up some of your own, but don't let the customer set the tone of the meeting. You want upbeat, exciting, and positive, and it is up to you to create those moods.

There may come a day when you don't feel particularly upbeat, exciting, or positive. What can you do on such a day? You need to develop the ability to be enthusiastic even when you don't feel that way. Maybe you've just had a spat with your mate or one of the kids. Possibly your sales are off and you're worried about your financial situation. There are many negative things in this world that will keep our enthusiasm in check—if we let them.

With all of that in mind, allow me to introduce you to (or remind you of) one of the most famous lines in sales. It's so oft repeated that I'm no longer certain who was the original author: "To be enthusiastic, act enthusiastic."

This truth has many corollaries. If you're in the dumps, the simple act of smiling will make you feel better. If you're sick, watching the Three Stooges will help to cure you. Stressed out? Close your eyes and visualize your favorite vacation retreat.

Emotionally healthy people use these techniques and many others all the time to overcome negative emotions. Before you face a customer, you need to create a positive emotion—enthusiasm.

Greet your prospect with a warm smile and a handshake. When you're dealing with a new customer, introduce yourself and ask for her name. Ask about family or business. As you create positive emotions, they are likely to be returned in kind. As you receive encouragement, you will feel better and better. Thus your original effort to act enthusiastic will begin to make you feel enthusiastic.

Why is it important that you feel genuinely enthusiastic? Because honest enthusiasm creates believability. Superior poker players can hide their true feelings. Most of the rest of us aren't good at that trick at all. Thus, if we are not truly excited about what we are proposing, it will generally show right through.

People who are enthusiastic are more likable. Customers are much more prone to buy from someone they like. They feel compelled to buy from you to reward you for a good job of selling and to encourage you to like them.

SALES PRINCIPLE #2—FIND THE NEED AND FILL IT

The following is a true story. Only the names have been changed to protect the foolish.

A retailer stood talking with a sales rep. They were discussing how slow business was. A young man walked in the front door and approached the two. While still out of earshot, the store owner said to the rep: "See that lawn mower over there. It's been gathering dust for a long time. I'm going to sell this fellow that mower."

Our hero, the retailer, moved into combat in full battle dress. He shook his victim's hand, complimented him on his shirt, and moved gracefully and enthusiastically into his presentation. He used every sales weapon in the book as he wore down the target with features, benefits, and great offers of current discounts and future service.

The sales rep was practically moved to tears by this amazing performance. Finally, the dealer moved in for the close. The customer, who had not been able to say a word since the first minute, finally had the floor. With a dazed look in his eyes he responded: "Gee, mister! That was sure a wonderful presentation. And I'm certain that your offer on that mower can't be equaled, but I actually came in here to see if I could use your restroom."

The dealer had failed to establish the need before launching into his presentation. Unless you're a "hit-and-run artist," and therefore interested only in selling to a person one time, you don't want to sell him the wrong thing. More important, even if you're not looking for repeat business, you'll have a much higher rate of success if you establish what it is folks need. You do this, quite simply, by *asking questions*.

The Opening

When you begin the selling situation with a customer, patient, or client, you can create the right environment quickly by doing one or more of the following:

1. Make your opening original.
2. Provide an opportunity for exchanging handshakes, names, and/or cards.
3. Immediately begin talking about or asking questions of the customer.

Retailers: Don't ask, "May I help you?" First, a good salesperson never asks a question that can be answered no. Second, that opening is tired and lacking in charm. How about one of these:

"Good afternoon. My name is June. I'd be happy to help you in any way I can to make your selections today. May I ask your name?"

"Hi! What kind of perfume are you looking for today? For yourself or as a gift?"

"Hello. Those doggy bones are one of our most popular. What size dog are you shopping for?"

Phone salesmen: Don't lie and tell the customer you talked with him three months ago. Catch his interest with an intriguing fact. "Did you know that the average fluorescent bulb only lasts six hundred fifty hours? Would you be interested in learning about a new bulb that's guaranteed to last two thousand hours?"

Another possibility is to go right to the frustration of the buyer. "Hi, Mrs. Strong. My name is Joey, and I am that most awful creature, a telephone solicitor. I believe that my company is offering a product that could be of use and value to your firm. Are you responsible for the purchase of fluorescent lightbulbs?"

Restaurateurs: Have each of your employees introduce himself to your patrons. Your host should ask for the name of the party before asking about the size of the party. Asking for the size first sounds as if you're interested only in how much money you'll make and the technical difficulties of seating them. Asking for the name first suggests you're interested in them!

Pass the name of the party along to your servers. These, in turn, should address the party by name and offer their name: "Good evening, Mr. and Mrs. Albright. We're glad you decided to visit Mario's tonight. My name is Albert. Please let me know if there is any way I can make your evening more enjoyable."

How do we apply this technique to the rep who is calling on a customer for the first time? Well, the rep should be prepared to include in her opening remarks a compliment about the store, the office, or the buyer. Through prior preparation, or by quick appraisal between the time she arrives and the time she begins her presentation, she should find something she can remark positively about to the buyer. Naturally, the more sincere the compliment, the more effective it will be.

While extending a hand to prompt a handshake, the rep might say: "I really have to compliment you. I've called on hundreds of jewelry stores and this is the first time I've seen someone smart enough to put their repair department up front." The rep should let the customer respond to this comment for as long as the customer likes.

When the customer comes up for air, the rep should offer her card and her name. Then ask for the customer's name.

Another approach a rep might take is to do something that forces the buyer to ask him the first question. I sold a four-pound lock and chain to the bicycle trade when dealers were used to those little, lightweight dog chains. I created attention by walking into stores with this huge lock hung around my neck. It took a real dullard not to ask, "What in the heck is that?"

"Why, it's the best bicycle lock money can buy," I'd respond.

This was generally followed by laughter and comments such as, "I'm sure it is, but who's gonna buy a super lightweight bike and then lug that thing around to lock it up?" At this point I exchanged names and headed into the pitch. My audience was totally intrigued.

Once you've made the first call on an account and maybe the second, third, and fourth, what can you do to make the fifth call just as alluring? Bring him a copy of an article on something he's interested in. Ask how his kid did in that T-ball championship you discussed during the last visit. Tell him some industry scuttlebutt you've just heard.

Establishing the Need

If you've done it right, the opening will have established the buyer's name and his general intentions, and created an atmosphere of care and concern. At this point you should begin to ask questions and listen carefully to the answers.

I am frequently asked whether or not to probe into the issue of affordability. After all, an important customer need is to receive value in exchange for the dollars she'll hand over.

The answer from my perspective is this: Don't bring up the subject of cost during the time you're asking about the need, unless the customer does. If you have only a single price point for the product or service under discussion, you may want to ask leading questions (often called qualifiers) to see if you are wasting your time with this prospect.

If, however, you have a range of items and prices that can fulfill this person's requirement, my approach is to suggest the highest-priced item that will truly fit the situation. After making the recommendation, the subject of price is bound to come up. If the customer goes into a dead faint, you can gracefully move down a notch while explaining how little he'll give up in the less expensive model.

As you read the body language of each reaction to pricing, you'll eventually see the comfort level reached. If you believe that you've moved to a level that won't be truly satisfactory to your client, don't hesitate to say so. Then try to move the customer back up to the lowest level you believe will be appropriate for the individual's use.

SALES PRINCIPLE #3—THE OBJECTION: A SALESMAN'S BEST FRIEND

Enthusiasm will turn the worst salesperson into a successful mover of product. Finding the need and filling it creates professionalism, repeat customers, and higher tickets. The understanding of objections and the proper method of handling them adds a measure of depth and confidence that will help you enjoy selling and reduce the anxiety surrounding the sales situation.

Only interested customers raise objections—disinterested ones will agree with everything you say . . . until it's time to hand over the credit card.

Many are the occasions where I've made a flawless presentation to a potential buyer who said "uh-huh" fifty or so times as I entranced him with my story. The order seemed to be in the bag, since no objection was raised at any point, not even about the price. When it seemed like a good time to ask for the order, my request would be met with "No. I don't need any today. I'm really not interested."

After a few last efforts to turn the situation around, this wounded warrior headed out the door, and tried to figure out what went wrong. No real genius was required. The customer had told me in three different ways why there was no order.

"Uh-huh" repeated over and over means "I'm bored."

He specifically stated: "I'm really not interested."

He raised not one objection, not even about price.

Give me a buyer who says: "Isn't that too _____." Fill in the blank with: heavy, small, bright, old-fashioned, fragile, expensive, red, or you name it. What he is saying is, "I might buy one of those if it was: lighter, bigger, duller, more modern, tougher, cheaper, or blue."

You are now faced with providing an alternative that answers the objection. Failing that, you need to ask more questions to better determine the need. Through asking questions you will be able to find out if the objection is a deal killer or merely a preference . . . a "want" as opposed to a "need."

> You: Really, George? Why do you feel it is too small?
> George: A. I'm just not sure it will work with my unit.
> B. All the ones I've seen before were bigger.
> C. It doesn't seem worth the money.

As you can see, the first objection can be a very serious one unless you have other sizes to offer. The second should be able to be answered with features and benefits of the smaller size. The last protest may require a more technical description of the cost/benefits of miniaturization.

The important thing is that objections—and answers to your follow-up questions—prove you're talking to an interested buyer.

Sometimes objections are thrown out merely to offer token resistance or to set up a request for a discount. This is particularly true of the most common of all objections: "The price is too high."

It's amazing, but true. Sales reps who are quite capable of handling objections relating to product quality, availability, or terms turn to absolute mush-heads when confronted with the question of price.

Unfortunately for persons with this handicap, consumers and hardened professional buyers alike raise the price issue almost automatically. They commonly ask for a better price even when they feel fairly confident that there is no better price. The fact that they are questioning the price means: "I want one [or twenty gross] as long as we can agree on the price."

My first reaction to the "price is too high" objection is to ask: "Compared to what? Is there a similar product you feel offers more value?"

In some situations you may wish to ask: "What would you feel is a fair price for a glow-in-the-dark harmonica?" This line of attack is particularly useful when you're in an industry where haggling is commonplace. Don't ask this question if your price is firm.

Other ideas for handling the "price is too high" objection:

"Why do you say that?"

"Would you like to see a similar item with fewer features?"

"We truly believe that we offer the lowest price in town on this item. Have you seen it elsewhere for less?"

"That is the best I can do in tens. However, there is a pretty good discount at one hundred. Are you in a position to take that many?"

"You know, John, you get what you pay for. Our company just won't compromise on quality. As a result, we do charge more than some others. Is quality important to you in this application?"

"It's our policy to make an honest profit. If our competition sells it for less, I'd question whether they will be around next time you need a part or some service. Are you interested in making a hot deal today and possibly sacrificing future service?"

As with the handling of other objections, the principle is the same. Use questions to probe more deeply into the buyer's needs. The more information about those needs you can determine, the more likely you are to provide the right product for your customer, and the more likely you are to list the most appropriate features and benefits that will result in a sale.

SALES PRINCIPLE #4—LESS TALK
MEANS MORE SALES

There is a strange notion among folks who don't make their living in the field of professional sales that good talkers make the best salespeople. Forget that idea. Replace it with this one: *The best salespeople are those who are the best listeners.*

First, as stated above, you should be interested in determining your prospect's needs. This can't be done if you're doing all the talking. The more you can get the customer to talk about herself, her interests, and the nature of what she'd like to purchase, the more likely you are to gain the sale.

In addition, your client will sense that you care more about her and her needs since she sees that you're listening intently to her requests, ideas, and objections. It's easier to buy from an individual who "really cares."

Furthermore, time is money. If you waste time with unnecessarily long presentations, you'll have less time to sell this prospect on other items, and/or less time to sell to others. Remember too that your customer may be short of time. In a retail setting a customer who is shopping on a lunch hour may have to leave before you can finish the sale. Keep in mind: Customers almost never come back to hear the same sales pitch—between your business and their destination are hundreds of opportunities for them to spend their money on something else!

When selling business-to-business the owner or buyer has plenty to do besides listen to you dazzle him with your knowledge. You may find the interview cut short with a polite "I've got another appointment, but we can talk more about it on your next visit." How many opportunities will that buyer have to purchase a similar product or service from a competitor between now and your next appointment (assuming you can get one)?

Another major problem with runaway mouth is the increased opportunity for error. There are no perfect products or perfect companies. For every item sold there is some kind of potential substitute. In every selling situation there is a potential deal-killing objection. Each word you utter over the minimum could be the very one that upsets the applecart.

Last, but by no means least, you *will* bore and *may* confuse your listener with too much information. Boredom is obvious, but confusion is more subtle and quite common.

SALES PRINCIPLE #5—THE CLOSE: AN ABSOLUTE NECESSITY

If you do a splendid job with the first four sales principles, you'll still lose a large percentage of your potential sales . . . if you fail to close.

Why do otherwise talented salespeople find it difficult to close? First, there is the fear of rejection. After all, every one of us likes to feel that others will respond positively to what we propose. It's the rare individual who will not have an ego attack of some type when told, "No, not today."

The second area of concern is the fear of being seen as pushy. Most of us have been on the customer side of the table in auto dealerships, appliance stores, or in our own homes with a water-softener dealer. We know that we don't appreciate the high-pressure close. Therefore, we're concerned about leaving our customers with that image.

Another golden nugget for your immediate profit . . . *reliable approaches to bring about the low-pressure close:*

"Would you like the red one or the blue one?"

"Will that be cash or charge?"

"Can you wait while we alter it, or do you wish to pick it up later?"

"Will there be anything else?"

"Now, with your new DVD player, I'd recommend a service contract!"

"Would you like us to begin the work Monday or Wednesday?"

"I think you're going to love your new computer!"

Look over the above list. Think about saying each of them at
the end of your presentation. Do they seem pushy to you? Haven't
you heard salesclerks in all types of nonpressure selling situations
use these same phrases and not felt offended?

Now read through them a second time. Notice how not one of
them can be answered with a "no." In order for the customer to
answer in a way that slows down or stops the sale, that individual
must take a bold stance against the purchase. It's very hard for
most people to be bold.

Indeed, it's this very lack of boldness that creates the need for a
close. That, and a feeling among many that if a person wants
something from another, there is a certain civility in asking for it.
This is why you may find it interesting to watch some sales presentations in action at your local retail store. The higher the ticket,
the more interesting it is to see what happens as the time for the
decision is coming nigh.

It is all too common to see the salesperson run out of things to
say. At that point he either correctly proceeds to a trial close (more
about that in a minute) or close, or he'll stand there waiting for
the customer to say something.

The customer, who has also run out of things to say, is inclined
to make the purchase, but is the type who doesn't really like to
make decisions. So she stands looking at the product or the wall
and mulls over what to do next. She just isn't very likely to say, "I'll
take it," until the clerk asks, "Would you like it?"

The clerk, who hasn't read this or any other book on closing,
thinks that the only way to complete this deal is to ask, "Would
you like it?" But sometimes when he says that, the customer says,

"*No.* I think I'll shop around some more." The clerk just can't stand the idea of more rejection today, so he says nothing.

As you stand and watch this development, think to yourself how many of the above standard closes would inoffensively and quickly seal the deal. This is what closing is all about.

In cases where the sale would amount to hundreds or thousands of dollars, you may wish to try a "trial close" before the close. The more money involved in the transaction, the more likely it is that your customer may become bold enough to say no . . . even in the face of one of the above closes. The idea of a trial close is to test the water and see if you think the customer is leaning toward buying.

Here are some examples of trial closes:

ROY (the customer, with last objection): Well, this sure isn't like the one my dad used to use.

YOU: Is that important to you? What features were a part of your dad's mower that you feel you'll miss?

ROY: No. It really isn't that. It's just all this newfangled stuff. And nothing is made out of steel anymore.

YOU (beginning the trial close): Gee, Roy, I agree with you one hundred percent. However, this model has the most steel of any on the market today, don't you agree?

ROY: That's true.

YOU: I understand what you mean about all the newfangled features, but does this model have all the features you want?

ROY: Sure. I was really impressed with the fact you don't have to pull a rope anymore to start it.

YOU: So this machine seems to offer everything you want.

ROY: Uh-huh.

YOU (now into the close): You know, Roy, this mower comes with a one-year, one hundred percent parts-and-labor warranty. For another thirty dollars you can extend that to three full years. Would you like me to include that in the total?

(For extra strength, move toward the counter where you'll write up the ticket as you ask this question.)

Another trial close might go like this:

You: Would you like to try it?

That is the whole trial close. If you can demonstrate the item, the customer who agrees to try it out is usually ready to be closed. This works well when selling automobiles, bicycles, sewing machines, musical instruments, table saws, vacuum cleaners, and the like.

Still another approach:

You: Sally, you mentioned you would only be using this for parties. Therefore it seems like the model seventeen-oh-five would be best for that. Okay?

Sally: It would seem so.

You: You also mentioned that you want it to hold sixty cups. Again, that seems to be the seventeen-oh-five.

Sally: Right.

You: Can you think of anything else that is important to you?

Sally: No, I really can't.

You (the close): Well, good. Is there anything else we can help you with today?

Sally: No. I think that will do it.

Through routine use of the trial close, you'll be able to determine in almost all cases whether or not the customer is ready to buy.

Have you begun to notice an interesting thing about the entire selling process? Most selling involves asking questions. You begin by asking about the person: his name, something about himself to create good feelings about you and your company.

Next ask about his need: how big, how many, and how much?

After you establish the need, it is your turn to talk. You tell the customer why you believe you have the solution to her needs. This should cover only three features and benefits. You then make a specific recommendation for purchase.

The customer returns to the spotlight as he raises objections. You again go into a questioning mode as you try to determine which objections are real. Then you use the real objections to help you further define the best product or service for the prospect.

The trial close is another time for questions as you probe the issue of whether or not the customer is close to a decision. Finally, if the climate seems right, you *ask* for the order with inoffensive questions that can't be answered no.

If you've done all the above correctly (and it doesn't take a mental giant to accomplish that), you should write up over 90 percent of the customers for whom you honestly have a product for which they clearly have a need. Your ratio will be smaller if: (a) you are trying to sell something that doesn't truly fit the need; (b) the customer is truly browsing and isn't ready to buy; or (c) you're cold-calling by phone or door-to-door and are in the position of having to create a need the customer didn't even know he had.

What about those who say no?

1. If you believe that they have made the wrong decision, step back to the objection phase and begin to probe again.

YOU: Is there something about the product that you are still uncertain of?

CINDY: I really just hate to buy at the first place I stop.

YOU: Well, can you imagine a feature you need that this microwave doesn't have?

CINDY: No, I'm sure it's full featured. But maybe someone else will have it on sale.

YOU: This unit sells for one hundred and seventy-nine dollars. Is it worth it to you to drive all over town in hope of saving, let's say, ten percent or eighteen dollars? If no one has it for less, you may end up back here after wasting all that time and gas.

CINDY: You're right, of course.

You: Did you like this stainless steel unit or would you prefer the white?

Through this approach you've moved through her objection, back to a trial close, and then on to your second attempt at a close. Most books on selling recommend that you try at least five closes before giving up. If the ticket is large enough, and the likelihood of losing the customer is high enough, you should definitely try five closes.

If you are selling a $49.95 blender, you may be better off to stop at two.

2. If you have failed to deal with an objection that is solvable, try several different approaches.

You: I know you want a red one. What if I gave you the better model in red for only ten dollars more than the other unit?

Ed: No can do. I was already beyond my budget as it was.

You: Ed, I can have the exact one you want here by Tuesday with just a twenty-dollar deposit. That will save you looking all over town for it.

Ed: I really wanted to use it this afternoon.

You: Listen. If you can give me a few minutes, maybe I can find one nearby that I can swap for. Would you like some coffee while you wait?

Ed: Sure, that'd be all right.

3. If you have the right product and the customer even agrees that it is, but can't be persuaded to make a decision now, try this approach.

You: Is there anything I could do that would convince you to say yes right now?

Pam: I don't think so. I just hate to make snap decisions.

You: If I understand you right, you like the item and feel that it is priced right?

PAM: Definitely. I have no argument with either.

YOU: What is it that you are concerned about?

PAM: My husband may object, or I may need the money for something else.

YOU: What if I were able to get you a thirty-day, unconditional, one hundred percent money-back guarantee? You could return it, even if your only reason was you needed the money for something else.

PAM: Sure! How could I pass up a deal like that?

4. When all else fails, you want to be able to withdraw from the effort . . . and do so gracefully. One way is to offer to put the item aside for a day or two. This can be done with or without a small deposit.

Another approach that is especially useful when you feel the customer is going to go out and buy a cheap, junky version, is to suggest where they can get it.

YOU: We just won't carry that brand in stock due to statements we have heard from our customers. I do know that Herald's Discount Center carries that model. You may want to try over there.

You have gained three things. First, you have given the customer additional help in filling his need. That may be remembered next time he needs something you sell. Second, you can direct him to a competitor who you doubt will be able to gain loyalty. Left on his own, your customer may end up with a serious competitor who may get all of this customer's future business. Third, you have established that the item he is going to buy may be of lesser quality. You have confirmed this by indicating that it is available at a lower-quality store. This opens the door for the customer to further scrutinize the purchase when he gets over to Herald's. He may decide, on further reflection, to come back and get the better product.

Part 2
Sales Management of Others

Manufacturers, wholesalers, business-to-business service providers, and job shops can all benefit from the use of outside sales representatives. Some companies who deal with the public have the same opportunity, such as travel agents, mortgage lenders, and apartment owners.

What is an independent sales rep? The term "independent representative" sounds exactly like what it is. This person works for himself. He or his company, generally referred to as a rep firm, will not be on your payroll, but will earn their money from three sources of services they may provide:

1. The most likely situation is that you'll pay them a percentage of every sale they make. This may range from as low as 1 percent to as high as 20 percent, although the average is probably between 5 percent and 10 percent.

2. The rep may require that the companies he represents (called principals) pay some kind of base or guarantee. A base means an amount of money that is paid to the rep in addition to all amounts made on commission. A guarantee is an amount paid as a minimum, even if the amount of sales would not justify that much commission.

3. The rep may provide other kinds of services at a charge. These could include mailings, mass fax communications, inclusion in some kinds of advertising, or trade show services. They may also ask for expense money for travel, customer shows, or association memberships.

What does a rep do for you? She represents your line of products or services to customers who are likely to buy from you. The rep will have already established relationships with customers. The idea is that she will be able to use these relationships to open the door for your products. You should expect your rep to thoroughly learn your product line, the strengths of your company such as delivery or quality, and policies concerning price, freight, and terms.

It's critical to communicate the vision you have for your company to your reps. If they don't see the big picture, it will be difficult for them to pass it along to the buyers.

Your reps should be able to help you with some aspects of marketing. They will give you feedback as to why your product is or is not selling, and what changes might help make improvements. They should also be able to make recommendations concerning who you should or shouldn't be selling. This could be for reasons of competition, pricing, or credit problems.

You may or may not even be able to get an appointment with some of the buyers you wish to sell. If you do manage to get in front of one of the snarling, growling beasts you will be at ground zero in terms of credibility, politics, and relationship. This will also be true of someone you hire for the job unless you hire an industry veteran at great expense.

The rep, on the other hand, has established himself with the buyers as someone who understands what will and will not work for that buyer's company. He has probably ingratiated himself with other members of the management and staff. If he's been around for a while, he may very likely know and play golf with the president or some of the VPs.

He's also done favors for this company and buyer before. He's gotten them out of messes. He may have helped to sell off a poorly performing product to some other customer who was better able to use it.

Most reps have one or two accounts where they can take almost any new item they think has possibilities and the customer will buy it automatically. They use these automatics to establish instant credibility with the principal after they're appointed. Be careful. These may be the only accounts the rep ever sells.

Another reason for using a rep is financial. You'll usually be able to find a rep who will do a good job for you on straight commission—in other words, no advance, no base, no guarantee, and no other fees. This means that you pay no sales fees unless the rep sells something and you ship it. Some companies don't pay their reps until they get paid for the shipment.

If you hire an inside salesperson, you have a fixed salary, taxes, benefits, office space, phone bill, fax expense, travel, entertainment, and possibly car expenses. It would be rare today to find a salesperson of any value who would not cost you at least five thousand dollars per month when all the above is taken into account. It could easily become ten thousand dollars.

Even if you handle these sales yourself, you'll have the expense of phone, fax, travel, and entertainment. You'll also have taken valuable time away from other possible duties, which may require you to hire help you wouldn't otherwise need.

Another benefit of hiring reps is your ability to reach into more selling territories without a huge overhead commitment. If you're a manufacturer and can afford only one inside salesperson, she'll be limited by time to one hundred to two hundred active accounts. For the same amount of money, you can hire a sales manager who can then appoint reps all over the country.

At one point in my career, I oversaw twenty-two rep firms. They called on sixteen different industries in eleven states. In some industries we sold directly to retailers, in others we used wholesalers, and in still others we sold to OEMs or end users. We did all of this with one sales manager.

Is there a downside to using reps? Sure. Successful reps may carry anywhere from ten to fifty lines of product. This means that your products have to fight for attention. If you aren't constantly motivating the rep to sell your line, some other company owner or sales manager will be moving his products to center stage.

A powerful rep can get your product in the door. He may also have the power to get your products thrown out if you terminate him. He may also "land" a better line that is competitive to yours, drop you, and move you out of his automatic accounts.

When you have your own dedicated sales force, you protect yourself from these risks. You also know that you have a staff that is spending 100 percent of its time trying to sell your product.

Even if you use reps you'll likely want to have some house accounts (customers where no rep or commission payment is involved). Sometimes, when you're between reps, you'll be able to establish a relationship with some customers. You might then decide to keep the account as a house account when you appoint the next rep. Obviously, the better reps aren't going to be interested in taking your line if you've snatched the best accounts for the house.

How do you find reps? Call the buyers you wish to sell. Tell them you're planning to introduce a new line into their area, and you wonder whom they might recommend as a rep. I have never had any problem getting one or more suggestions from every call.

After you've amassed a list of potential candidates, call each one and do a brief telephone interview. Give the rep some background on your company and product to see if she's interested. Determine if she has any conflicting lines (it's usually considered a conflict of interest for a rep to carry the same items from two factories).

Here are some of the things you'll want to inquire about:

1. Territory covered.
2. Types of industries serviced.
3. Major accounts called on.
4. Commission percentage expected.
5. Number of people employed as salespersons.
6. Other services offered and cost, if any.
7. Trade shows attended. Will he have a booth? Will he work yours?

8. How many lines does she carry, their names, and which are major and which are minor?

9. How much income must he generate from a line to stay "interested"? If your sales will generate five hundred dollars per month commission in a territory, this may be one rep's average principal and for another it may be below the minimum he'll accept.

10. How much notice does she expect before termination? How much notice will she give you if she wishes to drop the line?

During the interview you'll be trying to sell the rep on your company. At the same time you'll be deciding if you want to buy his services. Seldom will you be offering a line that will immediately become a top producer. Therefore you'll need to sell the rep on such things as quality, prestige, and future growth. Employ all the sales approaches mentioned previously, beginning with enthusiasm and need finding . . . right through to closing.

Don't despair if you can't find a rep. I've seen company owners sell the most bizarre products to major national mass marketers such as Sears, Kmart, and JCPenney. The same buyers have turned down our company's proven winners even though presented by well-established reps.

If it seems by this comment that I'm waffling in my otherwise obvious preference for using independent reps, it isn't so. I'm merely suggesting that if you're not able to find a rep in one or more territories that you believe will give you excellent representation, go after the accounts yourself.

Once you've entered into an agreement with a rep firm, you should draw up an appointment letter. This letter can be a massive legal document or a few short paragraphs. I've always opted for the few short paragraphs whether I was hiring a rep or acting as one. The letter should cover:

1. Territory to be covered by geographic area, industry, and placement in the distribution chain. Be very specific in order to avoid as many possible conflicts as possible.

2. The amount to be paid and when. In establishing the commission rate, consider: (a) what you can afford, (b) what you believe is necessary to motivate the sales rep, and (c) the long-term precedent you're establishing. (Once a commission is set, it's extremely difficult to lower it.)

As to when you pay commissions, I've seen this vary from the day of the sale to ninety days after payment. The most common approaches are: the fifteenth of the month following the month of the sale; the fifteenth of the month after the month of payment. Many companies will stretch this to two or even three months if the payment terms are long. When considering the "when" question, you'll want to take into consideration your own cash flow and the motivation of the sales rep.

3. Include a starting date and a termination clause. Most reps and principals feel that either one should be able to terminate with thirty days' notice. While this type of escape clause generally works to the reps' disadvantage, most will readily go along. There are plenty of times when their success with your minor line will open a door to a major opportunity for them to sell for your competitor. Thus, they'll rarely want to be bound to any longer term.

You *also* want a short term. You want to be able to make a fast change if the territory is not performing up to your expectations.

4. You may wish to conclude with a standard legal paragraph regarding the operative law (by what state law will you both be bound) and the method you'll use to resolve disputes. I generally prefer arbitration since it's cheaper and faster than a lawsuit.

How do you get the most out of independent reps? It's easy to spend hundreds of hours and thousands of dollars interviewing and appointing reps all over the state, country, or world, only to forget that they need to be managed. There are few people in business who feel greater pressure than reps. Every factory wants its rep to devote all of his time to their product line.

1. Reps say that the most important thing a principal can do for them is provide support materials: brochures; catalogs; price sheets with sizes, weights, specifications, and other needed information; samples; advertising slicks; discount policies; and anything else that will help them make the sale.

2. Managers maintain that their success with reps is directly proportional to the amount of time they spend "encouraging" them. Letters, phone calls, statistical analysis of their sales performance, field visits, sales meetings, and participation together in trade shows all provide opportunities to keep your company's needs first on their mind. There may be a fine line between encouragement and annoyance. In most instances you'll be better off erring on the side of annoyance.

3. Pay your reps on time. Most reps feel that their pay should be as important as your company payroll. They'll ask you whether your employees will keep working if they're not paid on time. Sometimes, if a rep feels aggrieved, he'll simply stop *working* for you, even if he hasn't technically *resigned*.

This is not to suggest that most reps will leave you high and dry over a missed commission during a financial crisis. It does suggest, however, that reps will spend their greatest effort working for the companies that will pay them in a timely fashion.

4. Find out what other things besides commissions will motivate reps. Contests sometimes stimulate extra sales. You may want to offer a trip or other prizes for new accounts, a percentage increase, or other goal.

5. New products, packaging, and promotions are always good motivators for sales reps. It's much easier for a rep to call back on a customer she has been to see only days or weeks ago when she has a clear-cut reason for the visit, such as a new product to show.

Part 3
Advertising

I wish I could offer you five principles of advertising that would be as likely to produce results as the sales principles I've offered. Unfortunately, the "science" of advertising is of much more recent origin, and is constantly evolving.

What I can list for you are the fundamental aspects of advertising—those factors that should always be considered before placing an ad:

FUNDAMENTALS OF AN AD

Purpose

In advance of any advertisement, promotion, or trade show involvement you should always determine what you want to accomplish with this resource.

1. To increase sales? By how much? In what territory or other target subgroup of your customer base? Over what period of time?
2. To increase awareness? Of your company? Your product? To what end? How will you measure results?
3. To communicate a philosophy or approach? To whom? How will you measure results?

Audience

The more you know about your audience, the more likely you'll be able to reach it through advertising. You must know who the typical customer for your product is and what forms of media he gravitates to.

Visibility

Your advertisement will be competing with thousands of messages for the attention of your audience. There are two well-respected ways to break through all this sensory noise and get your message heard.

1. Make the ad so unusual that people can't help taking notice. Use a professional to do the art and/or copywriting unless you have specific talent in these areas.

   This kind of ad can be fairly expensive. You need to spend the time and money to develop a unique idea. No matter how creative the ad is, you may lose the impact if it's not professionally prepared.

2. Create a simple ad with a straightforward message. Run it in the same medium in every issue for years. The idea here is to repeat the message so many times that the audience makes it a part of their subconscious.

   This approach is relatively inexpensive. It will usually take advantage of the smallest ad space the medium will allow. The ad will be inexpensive to produce. Since you'll be running it continuously for a long period, you'll earn the lowest rates.

Frequency

Never run any print advertisement less than three times in the same medium. For the "A" type of ad above, you'll have substantial diminishing returns after the fourth placement.

The first time readers see an ad, they generally give it the once-over-quickly routine. That assumes it's seen at all. Readers often assume that the claims are fabricated or stretched, and that there is no reason to switch from the product they're currently using.

The second time the reader sees the same ad, the credibility increases. This is probably due in part to our tendency to believe

what we read. Our brains seldom register that this is not a new recommendation for this product, just a repeat of the same ad we
saw before.

When your target consumer sees your ad for the third time, the
individual begins to figure you have some staying power. There's
also an inference drawn that you would not still be running the ad
if some folks weren't buying the product.

Measuring Effectiveness

Try to incorporate a measuring device into your ads to determine
how well they're doing. If you're looking for a mail response, change
the address slightly in each placement. You can do this by using a
department number: "Please send your check or MO to Bob's Neat
Stuff, 1522 Lincoln Avenue, Department 22, Wayne, IN 12345." In
the next ad or for a different medium, use Department 23.

If you use a phone number only, train your people to ask callers
how they heard about your company, product, or offer. Have each
employee keep a log of these callers.

Many trade publications offer a "bingo card" response service.
Your ad will contain a line at the bottom stating "For more information circle reader #123 on the reader response card." Somewhere in the magazine there will be a "bingo card" for the reader
to tear out and mail to the publisher. The publisher sends you the
leads as they are received.

Coupons, special offers, contests, and giveaways are other methods of gauging your response. While not all types of advertising
are geared to this type of analysis, you'll want to make every effort
to find a way to measure your ad's impact.

TYPES OF MEDIA

Direct Mail

Direct mail can be very effective, though you'll be fighting hard for attention in a medium that is saturated with highly sophisticated competition. What follows are some general rules for reaching a list of known customers, whether business-to-business or consumer:

1. Start with the envelope. Print something intriguing on the outside that will make your target curious about the contents. One mass mailer who sends our company at least two or three mailings per week puts "personal and confidential" on the envelope. It's amazing, but folks are actually more likely to open that envelope first.

   Another way to differentiate your mailing piece is to send it in anything except a standard white business envelope. How about hot pink? Maybe a nine-by-twelve with all of your ad material flat instead of folded? Mailing tubes really call for attention. We have had people mail our water bottles with their literature inside. We have had advertising pieces arrive by UPS or FedEx . . . an expensive—but effective—way to get attention.

2. Most mail gets opened eventually, with or without a clever envelope or method of delivery. The real test is whether your customer will read what you send and act on it. By far the most effective way to ensure a careful reading is a personal letter, but the recipient must *believe* it is personal.

   Most people recognize the ability of computers to create mass "personal letters." However, if the source of a letter might be expected to send a truly personal letter, then it's likely to be perceived as such. If recipients are active customers, for example, they'll be more likely to believe the letter is directed to them only.

The least sophisticated software can create letters that automatically merge the name and address of your customer, and sprinkle the name throughout the letter. This type of letter should be sent in a standard white business envelope with your company's logo on the outside.

If the "personal" approach is not appropriate for your mailing, the next most effective method is a "gotcha." The most outrageous gotcha our company ever sent was a brochure with a party theme accompanied by a sprinkling of confetti. This was strategically designed to sprinkle the recipient on opening the brochure. Some of the recipients appreciated the humor more than others, but we were remembered.

At the very least you must catch the attention of the reader with the headline of your brochure or the opening line of your letter. It's usually a good idea to use one of the "gotcha" words such as: free, save, guarantee, special, win, last chance, limited, new. Of course this line will almost always contain at least one "you." For example:

"This is your last chance to take advantage of our special offer to save 50 percent on one of our new, guaranteed, Harlenfitzers. If you respond by July 15 you'll also be entitled to a *free* tool kit, and a chance to win an all-expenses-paid two days and four nights in beautiful downtown Cleveland."

We used to have a company called National Sales Head-quarters. To get attention, we put out a newsletter called the *National Sales Enquirer*. We played off that name with outrageous headlines and stories that were purely designed to entertain. We used the names of well-known individuals in the industry (everybody likes to see their name in print), and used pictures and graphics to create a sharp look. Sprinkled in between the fun were serious articles about our products, special offers, and updates on our company's plans.

3. Make certain that you *ask for the order* in the ad. Make it easy for the customer to place the order with an order blank, 800 number, and complete information on prices, terms, and delivery.

Somewhere in the copy, usually near the end, include words to this effect: "Don't delay. Place your order for two dozen of our professional-quality hair dryers today, and you'll receive two free. Mail your check with the order form below and shipping is free. You can also call in your order to 1-800-123-5555 or fax us at 1-800-987-5555."

Just as with the personal sales call, you need to close the deal. Without a line such as the above, the average customer will read your information and think: "That company has some pretty nice things. I should order something from them sometime." This is not the effect you are after. You want them to make a decision to order before they put the ad aside. So ask them to place their order *now*, and then make it as easy as possible. In today's marketplace, you'll lose business if you don't offer an 800 number. They're not expensive, and they'll pay for themselves many times over.

Make it easy for your customer to place an order. Make it clear that they can order by fax, e-mail, or through your Web site. If you offer 24/7 phone ordering, say so. If you think your customer wants the 24/7 phone service, but you can't staff it, there are companies specifically set up to handle it for you.

Yellow Pages

While declining in importance, almost any business that is serving a local community will get its best return on the advertising dollar from the Yellow Pages. When I owned a retail store, I took the largest ad available, even though (or especially since) I had the smallest store in town. There was never a question that the ad was worth every penny. One day the phone started ringing off the hook. I finally asked a caller how he'd heard about my store. It turned out this was the day the phone books had been distributed.

Carefully investigate and evaluate the various Yellow Pages alternatives in your community. After asking around you'll probably be able to determine which Yellow Pages are working best for other businesses similar to yours. Take the largest display ad you can afford in the best phone book. Order smaller displays in the lesser books.

Provide your potential customers with a clear-cut reason for shopping with you, rather than competitors listed in the same directory. Create a headline that clearly spells out the difference: longer hours, more selection, easy access, better service, never undersold, exclusive brand name, unique services or offerings.

Only a few very small businesses have realized the potential of local 800 numbers. The cost for such service is quite reasonable. With all the changes in phone company tariffs over the years the average consumer has no idea whether a call to you will be a toll call or not. If this customer is trying to decide whether to call you or your competitor, the fact that you have a toll-free line could make all the difference. As an added benefit, you'll like the convenience of being able to call your store or office from anywhere using your 800 number rather than coins or a calling card.

You will be paying thousands of dollars per year for the space in Yellow Pages ads. Spend the five hundred dollars or so to have a good graphic artist help you prepare the ad. The Yellow Pages rep may be quite competent at laying out ads, but he's undoubtedly done it hundreds of times and may be in a rut. This will mean your ad will look like all the rest. *You want to stand out!*

Television

TV is still outside the reach of most very small businesses. Realistically, it wouldn't be an appropriate medium for most small companies, even if the costs were much lower.

For those who want to try television, cable has opened the door to a lower-cost opportunity. There are companies in most areas now who offer a complete package for putting you on TV. They'll help you write the script, tape the commercial, and buy the air time. Be careful. Thoroughly check their references with an eye to successful campaigns they've produced.

Radio

A very effective media for many very small businesses is radio, because it allows you to inexpensively target a specific demographic group in your local area. An upscale restaurant might find that a classical or jazz music station brings the highest return on its advertising investment. Business-to-business advertisers should consider drive-time, all-news, or talk-show programs. Companies hoping to reach full-time moms could look to a Christian radio station or one offering household tips.

Other Media

Some of the best results I've heard of over the years have come from unusual advertising approaches. For example:

1. The bank that used placards on the back of the local bus line to advertise its services. Since each ad consisted only of a clever headline and the bank's name, the entire cost of the campaign was the placement and the copywriting.
2. The retailer who told me he got more business from three bus bench ads than from any other source.
3. Businesses that put prominent advertising on the products they sell. Car dealers have been putting their name on the license plate holder for years. Some are so bold as to create a chrome name plate that is permanently attached to the car.

There's no reason you can't do the same. Take a look at every item you sell. Is there some way you can add your name and phone number without detracting from the value?

4. If you repair products, design an attractive decal with an easy-to-remove adhesive back that you can place on each item you repair. A chain of auto tune-up shops did this and wound up with hundreds of thousands of cars driving around their territory with the company logo in the rear window. It was soon clear to the rest of the population that lots of folks were using the services of this company.

5. If you're a service provider or sell an item where there is just no way to put your name on your product, consider gifts bearing your name. A close friend of mine has given away an executive date book with his name and phone number on the inside cover for years and years. One year he decided to stop this practice and save a little money. In no time at all he was besieged with phone calls wanting to know where this year's book was.

   Several years ago, we spent seventeen dollars apiece to purchase one hundred Cross pens with our corporate logo on the pocket clip. We made a big deal of handing these out one at a time to our best customers. If we had sent out a pen of lower value, we could not have made such a big deal of it. In addition, the customer would probably not have kept it as long. Moreover, we made a statement about the quality of our company.

6. Do you realize how inexpensive it is to send out door hangers? If I owned a restaurant, I'd pepper the local neighborhood with copies of my menu and some kind of special offer for my otherwise slowest night.

   Video rental shops can create a flier with the latest releases and a list of two-for-one specials. Even the local jewelry store could offer a special sale open only to those in the neighborhood. Movie theaters, dentists, bike shops, photo studios, and shoe stores should all be concentrating on their closest potential customers. It's amazing how many people within a mile of your business don't even know that you're there.

Part 4
Promotion

When you have more time than money, the best way to get more customers into your store is through the kissing cousin to advertising: promotion.

Here are a few very small business types with a suggested promotion for each:

A. Dress shop. Fashion show put on by local modeling school.

B. Camera shop. Free classes in improving home video production.

C. Computer store. Private showing of the latest breakthrough.

D. Dermatologist. Offer a demonstration in skin care and cosmetics.

E. Book retailer. Story time for kids.

F. Dry cleaner. Ten dollars per basket on Mondays.

G. Little theater. Prettiest baby contest.

H. Stationery store. Free quality pen to first one hundred customers purchasing any amount on Tuesday. (Of course, your name and phone number will be on those pens.)

I. Sports shoe store. Sponsor a tournament in any sport.

J. Music shop. Direct a small band and give free concerts.

K. Bank. Sponsor charity walkathon.

L. Church. Organize softball league with teams from other community groups.

M. Furniture store. Joint promotion with interior decorators. Free interior design consultation with no obligation to purchase.

N. Specialty grocery store. Wine tasting.

O. Restaurant. Sponsor a charity chili cook-off.

P. Travel agent. Joint promotion with hotel and airline. Free mystery weekend for top twenty clients.

Q. Wholesaler. Open house for dealers, with hot prices, free food, and a motivational speaker. Maybe fly in top dealers who are too far away to drive. Could also invite suppliers to show product in minishow.

R. Manufacturer. Contest where top five wholesalers receive a new DVD player.

S. Insurance agent. Bring in top speaker on retirement planning or some other financial topic. Make it a dinner function. You buy. See if one or more of the companies you represent will help to pay expenses.

T. Hair salon. Rent special video equipment that lets your customer see how they would look with various styles. Set up certain slow days to invite customers in.

U. Pet supply. Sponsor nonpedigree (anyone can enter) cat show. Let contestants and public vote on most beautiful, best groomed, prettiest longhair, etc.

V. Any retailer. Have moonlight madness sale from midnight to 6:00 a.m. Work with suppliers to create give-away prices on enough product to really pack 'em in.

W. Local inn or bed-and-breakfast. Invite business owners nearby to spend a free night (only on a weekend if that is your slow time) with their spouses in hopes of having them recommend you for their out-of-town guests.

X. Hardware store. Offer classes in home repairs and do-it-yourself projects.

Y. Miniature golf course. Work with local organizations to sponsor all-night charity golf tournaments.

Z. Ice cream parlor. Work with supplier to sponsor ice cream eating contest.

As you may have noted above, many such promotional events may be improved or made less expensive by the inclusion of other related companies, your suppliers, or local service organizations or charities. The keys to the success of these events are: careful planning, plenty of free publicity, and repetition. Each time you stage the event you'll do it better. People will begin to look forward to its coming. You'll build on your success.

Part 5
Trade Shows

The trade show is a method for businesses who have a common customer base to come together and share the expense of meeting those customers one-on-one in an environment controlled by the suppliers. These shows are produced by trade associations or private producers who charge businesses for space in the show.

Since this method of seeking sales is generally expensive and time consuming, it's important that your participation generate the maximum results possible. After participating in over one hundred trade shows, I have certain well-learned lessons I'd like to share.

1. You should start thinking about a trade show almost a year in advance. The best ones sell out prior to opening. The best locations are offered first to those who have been in the prior show. Thus, the sooner you sign up for a show, the more likely you are to get a good location.

2. If you've never attended the show you want to be in, try to do so at least once before your entry. Is it well attended? Find out what color badges your customers are wearing (badges are generally color coded by dealer, exhibitor, guest, manufacturer, and so forth). How many of those in attendance are wearing the color you'll be looking for when you're paying for space? This exercise will help you better determine whether attendance will be profitable.

You must evaluate the appearance of the booths. You'll certainly want to have a booth that is at least as good as the average booth. Appearance isn't everything at a trade show. But as with the look of your store, your stationery, or your personal dress, you don't want to start a new relationship by having to overcome a poor first impression.

3. Once you've made the decision to participate in a particular show, it's time to ask and answer that familiar question: "What do I want to accomplish at this show?"

Most writers on the subject feel that you should go into the show with the idea of writing enough business to pay for all the expenses. For some types of businesses and exhibits this is very true. It is certainly important to a retailer who participates in a consumer show. It will usually be a high priority for a wholesaler or manufacturer who sells dealer direct at a dealer convention. However, it may not be the primary motivation for a manufacturer who sells through wholesalers at a show primarily aimed at dealers. In this case, the interest is in supporting the downstream efforts of your customer, the wholesaler.

Another important reason for attending a show is to test. You can test prospective customers' reactions to new products or packaging. You can hone the sales pitch for a new or existing product. You can extract feedback from distributor salespeople, dealers, or even consumers with whom you may not generally have much contact.

Another opportunity offered by participation in such an exhibition is to create a certain image. It is possible that many of your customers have never been to your place of business and never will have an opportunity in the future to visit. Their image of you is based on your product, packaging, advertising, and people. Here is a chance to create a lasting impression that is considerably easier to stage than through advertising or promotion.

For many companies, prospecting is a far more important trade show function than finalizing the sale. It takes our sales reps almost half a day to fully present our line and consummate an order. It's impossible to allocate that kind of time to an individual customer at a show. However, there *are* companies to whom we currently sell one of our product lines that may have said no to another of our product lines for some reason. A clever presentation of this product at the show may get the company to reverse its decision.

Another possibility is that you have no knowledge of a particular customer or he has been unwilling to see your salesperson. You have tried everything you know, but alas, no appointment. The buyer will be passing your booth without even knowing that yours is the company he has so steadfastly refused to deal with. If you catch his eye with an interesting display, or he actually sees your product for the first time, you may have an opportunity to start a dialog.

Other reasons to attend a trade show would include: meeting new reps, learning of other product opportunities, participating in conversations with others to broaden your knowledge, gathering information about your competition, and taking the financial and emotional temperature of the industry.

Once you've determined what your goals for the show will be, you can begin the planning process in earnest. There are three things that can mean the difference in results:

1. You should make a statement with your booth. Don't buy a standard backdrop and decorate it with standard pictures and posters. Don't finish off your design with a little table draped with a red tablecloth sitting on red carpet all rented to you at outrageous prices by the show decorator.

Are you high-tech? Buy a black or gray carpet. Use lighting and mirrors on your backdrop to create a contemporary look. Create a three-dimensional display that captures your product in its best light. Dress your salespeople in futuristic clothing. Have a laser beam bouncing a laser light show off a mirror in your three-dimensional display and up onto the backdrop. Does this sound too crazy for you? Here are a few of the real-life things we've done over the years.

One year our plan for the show was to increase general interest in helmets. To bring attention to our helmets we built a cemetery. Each headstone had a limerick about some poor rider who didn't wear a helmet.

To create an image for my wholesale business, we constructed a four-hundred-square-foot bike shop on the floor of the show. It was complete with a brick facade exterior, shingle roof, display windows, and fully outfitted interior.

To draw attention in a show where the booths and product were becoming increasingly high-tech, we went against the trend. We built a four-booth island display to look like a circus. The product was displayed on a carousel. We had clowns handing out balloons with our name and phone number on them.

On another occasion, we wanted to take a large space, but the only place where that was possible was at the back of the show. To catch the attention of our customers as they entered the door we built a two-story booth. The top floor was set up with umbrella tables and a huge sign with the company name in aluminum foil letters. No one in the industry had ever done a double-decker display before, so we were a big hit.

2. You should create a carnival atmosphere. Give something away. Have a contest or a drawing. Hire a beautiful model. Create motion in your booth with display units that go round and round, side to side, or up and down. Produce a professional video or PowerPoint presentation telling about aspects of your product or service that are impossible to demonstrate in a booth.

The most successful booth we've ever created had nothing to do with the design or location. It was our first time in the show, and our product was totally unknown. Our goal: sell as many customers as possible a small opening order.

To accomplish this we decided to have a game. We handed out a key to every potential customer. This was done through the show producers, not at our booth. The key was attached to a brochure that explained how the game worked, including the fact that instant cash prizes would be awarded. It was also made clear that there were many potential winners.

When the attendees came to our booth, we showed them that there were two doors that could be opened with the key. The first door had a maximum prize of twenty dollars, the second a maximum prize of one hundred dollars. Those who placed a small order would get a shot at both doors. Those who did not place an order would get to try only door number one.

We then asked that they take just three minutes while we explained our product. No one said no. After we did our quick sales presentation, we handed out an easy order form and wrote up as many orders as we could. This idea worked so well the producers announced that we'd broken all records for orders taken at that show.

On another occasion our booths were split up over several locations. We wanted to be sure that our customers saw all of these booths. We accomplished this by wrapping up over one hundred gifts in colorful paper and piling them in our main booth. As each customer came to that booth, they were given a slip of paper that gave all the booth locations. They had to get stickers from each of the other booths on this slip of paper. Once they had done this, they would be eligible to pick a present.

We have used roulette wheels (made from a bicycle wheel, of course), bean bag throws (at our circus), and live-plant giveaways. One of our principals gave away yo-yos with his name on them. They were a very big hit.

3. Be prepared to execute your plan. If you are there to take orders, make certain that your salespeople are prepared to write orders. This means far more than having a pen and order form. (Yes, I've seen situations where companies have failed to bring order forms.)

Selling at a show is different from selling in the client's home, office, or store. You have only a few minutes to tell your story amid many potential distractions. Thus, you must develop a presentation that quickly qualifies the prospect as someone who can truly use your product. Shows are strange that way. You can talk yourself hoarse to someone who is merely a visitor, or another exhibitor's spouse who isn't active in the business.

When I'm in an aggressive mode at a show, I'll usually stand outside my booth. (Some folks are really shy about walking into a booth where an obvious salesperson is hovering.) I like to take the most unusual new item we're showing out in the aisle. I ask each passerby who is wearing the right-colored badge: "Have you ever seen the Acme handheld hedge trimmer before?" This is one of the few times in your sales career when you are hoping for a no.

Next, I provide a thirty-to-sixty-second pitch on the product. Most people in this situation are far too polite to say they aren't interested, so . . . without missing a beat, I next ask about their business. After qualifying them as an actual prospect, I then slow down the pace to provide them with a short presentation designed to get an opening order.

Are you too shy to play the barker? Then you'll need someone or something in your booth to bring the customer in. You can do this through the time-honored tradition of using a model to hand out literature. A professionally prepared video that reaches out and grabs attention (they must be loud and have lots of action to succeed) can help. Or you could offer some cute or appealing thing for free. For a while, it was those little warm fuzzies that stuck to your shoulder (with the company name on the tag, of course).

You might use one of the oldest carnival tricks in the world, the black-box-and-peephole gambit. Put something interesting inside a black box. Create a peephole so that the only way anyone will ever know what is in the box is to look in the hole. *Important!* Put a sign up that says: LOOK IN HERE! Most folks can't resist. While you have their attention, ask about their business. Then proceed on to your presentation.

A large part of preparation is training your salespeople how to sell in this environment, and letting them know what you want them to accomplish. You might be able to increase their effort by adding an incentive. This could range from a cash bonus to a promise of a big night out for the whole group if certain goals are met.

A second stage of preparation is making sure you schedule the important things you wish to accomplish. If you're hoping to take clients to breakfast, lunch, or dinner during the show days, you'll need to invite them well in advance. Everybody else has the same idea.

If it's critical that you see certain customers in the booth, make appointments for this as well. Not everyone will keep these appointments since show time is hectic, but you'll increase your chances of seeing someone if you try to schedule beforehand. Make sure you have plenty of brochures, price lists, and order forms. It's better to take some home than to run out. There are those who believe that handing out expensive brochures at shows is a waste of money. I tend to agree. Most attendees will take home their bag full of brochures, put it over in the corner, and never look at it again.

These same advisers claim you are better off taking names, passing out a simple, inexpensive brochure, and mailing your better stuff after the show with a well-written cover letter. Then follow up with a phone call or visit.

This is certainly a good approach for many kinds of companies. However, I prefer to get the customer home with something to remember me by. Samples, giveaways, mementos, even the imprinted bag to carry home all the brochures represent ways to keep your name in front of the customer.

The imprinted tote bag is an excellent way to advertise. Your customers and potential customers will be looking for some way to carry around all the brochures, samples, and other materials that they accumulate. When you hand out a bag for this purpose you accomplish at least two significant things. First, you meet a need; this can establish a pattern of meeting needs. Second, you create something that will be seen all over the exhibit hall, the headquarters hotel, and even in some of the restaurants in the area (thus, you want to make sure your name is in big letters).

There is one other aspect of show planning left to discuss: budgeting. The following list should cover every expenditure you're likely to endure.

1. Booth-space rental. This cost will normally range between six hundred dollars and two thousand dollars per booth, depending upon the location and popularity of the show. Most are around one thousand dollars. Generally a 25 percent deposit will hold your space until three or four months prior to the show.

2. Display purchase or rental. Most exhibitors who participate in more than one show per year purchase or build their own display booth. If you build it yourself, be certain to use lightweight components that are easy and inexpensive to ship and assemble. The surface should be durable, since shipping will exact a toll no matter how well you pack your crate. You should probably expect to spend at least two thousand dollars per space on a homemade exhibit when you figure in lighting, signage, and miscellaneous expenses. It could cost you much more depending on the quality image you want to project.

A second option is to purchase a ready-made display unit. New, these will range between five thousand dollars and ten thousand dollars per space. You'll still have the added expense of signage.

You could also consider having a booth designed and built by a specialist and customized to your needs. Don't be surprised if you spend well over one thousand dollars for design consultation alone. Custom exhibits usually start around ten thousand dollars.

The final option is to rent a ready-made unit from the show decorators or an outside vendor. The rental will generally range from five hundred dollars to two thousand dollars including the labor to assemble and disassemble it on the show floor.

3. Other decorating expenses. You'll need a carpet, some chairs, a coat rack in colder climates, and one or more tables. If you're crating up your own display and shipping it from show to show, it may make sense to purchase your own carpet, chairs, and what have you. The show decorators will charge you plenty for these per booth per show items. Plan to spend about five hundred to two thousand dollars if you rent all of the above.

4. Union labor. Most show producers have no choice but to use union crews to help exhibitors set up their booths. Unfortunately, this usually means that you'll be greatly restricted in what you can do to your booth without union help. A display you could set up unassisted in two hours may cost you sixty dollars an hour or more to have a union man do it. You'll be required to use this expensive labor whether you want to or not. At a union-controlled show, figure at least two hundred fifty dollars per space for setup.

5. Freight and material handling. When you send trade show material by truck, you pay the highest rate per pound they offer. If you can possibly justify it, call your "exhibit material" anything but that. Once the merchandise arrives at the hall, it will pass into drayage, where you'll generally be charged to store the booth until the show, to ship it from the storage location to the hall, and then get nicked again to bring it from the door to your booth. Figure about three dollars per pound for the total round trip of your crated display.

6. Other floor charges. You'll be charged if you use electricity. (Occasionally, a show will give you a couple hundred watts free.) You'll be charged to install any electrical systems. If your electrical doesn't meet local codes, you'll be charged to rewire. Would you like a sign or two? Be prepared to pay a major premium for not having that sign made at home. Figure at least another three hundred dollars per space for these charges. You can also rent phones, audiovisual equipment, flowers, or models.

Part 6
Using E-mail and the Web

MARKETING ON THE WEB

For most 21st-century small businesses the least expensive and commonly most effective method of reaching, selling, and transacting business with customers is through e-mail, a Web site, or both.

Starting from the most basic marketing of your new business, the gathering of information, research has become infinitely faster and cheaper. Here are a few of the things that you should research:

1. Put your product or service name in the search field. You will find Web sites for virtually every brand that you compete with along with their selling features. You may find sites that compare one brand against another. There will likely be places where complaints have been logged in chat rooms, blogs, or news articles. As you do the research you will see links that will suggest other ways to review the product category. These links will uncover new links.

In the course of this exercise you may also learn of trade shows, magazines, e-zines, books, and organizations related to this product or service. And you will find other ways to describe your own product. Keep notes of potential selling points, features, benefits, and sales approaches that you might want to use on your Web site. Then use some of the new key words you have picked up in a new search. You may be amazed at the different sites that show up with a small change in the key word used.

Of course, you may also find some discouraging information. More than once my brilliant new ideas have been shot down when I have done this type of research. Much to my surprise I have located similar or even better products already in existence. This doesn't necessarily mean that it is time to give up the idea. But it may mean that changes in product, packaging, pricing, or strategy are called for.

2. While doing the research above, you will likely begin to find some of your potential customers and suppliers. For instance, if you are selling commercial insurance to businesses, and you type "commercial insurance" into the search field, you will certainly find who the suppliers are. If you are selling lawn mowers to retailers, and you type "lawn mowers" in the search field, you will find thousands of dealers listed and virtually every manufacturer and distributor in the United States. You will also find quite a few from other countries.

To increase your chances of finding customers, use the type of customer you are seeking in the search field. Lawn mower dealers. Printers. Churches. Maybe you want to work in a specific geographic territory. Print services in Los Angeles will be a great place to start. But you may also want to try business card printers in LA, brochure printers in Los Angeles County, and other variations. It goes without saying that different search engines might have very different listings.

Next you may want to try the "Yellow Pages" and other such directories on the Web. From there, it is likely that you will find directories created by associations of that group. If you want to sell pet insurance through vets and animal hospitals, try veterinarian associations. In addition to these search methods you can also look on the Web sites of other suppliers to the same group. They will often offer listings by zip code or region of their customers. So, if you are looking for vets, you could look under flea prevention. Here you would find two or three brands of products used to eliminate fleas. The manufacturers will have a list of their customers that you can access, copy, and add to your own database. Sometimes these lists are even combined with map services to make it easy for you to construct a sales route.

3. So far in just a few hours you have done product re-search, found associations, trade shows, magazines, suppliers, and customers, and learned all kinds of words, phrases, and jargon used in the industry you are interested in selling. You have hope-fully copied and made notes, even bookmarked interesting sites that contain ideas you might use on your own Web site. If you're really serious, you have also collected phone, fax, and e-mail addresses of future contacts.

YOUR WEB SITE

There is probably some kind of business existing today that would not potentially benefit from a Web site, but it is hard to imagine what kind that would be. The first that comes to mind would be landscape service companies . . . the folks who mow your lawn and trim your trees. However, it would be so impressive to the homeowner to see picture examples of the company's work, an ad describing what it is that makes this landscape company better than the other guy, testimonials from satisfied customers, sug-gested schedules for trimming, fertilizing, spraying, and so forth, based on the specific neighborhood you are in. Of course, contact methods including cell phone, e-mail, and fax—potentially even a way to pay the bill by credit card at the site.

So, if the professional lawn service guy could benefit from a Web site, surely your company can as well. Like any advertisement, there is a process to undertaking the creation of such a marketing tool.

1. Determine what it is you wish to accomplish. There is a huge difference in the approach to a Web site depending on whether you are hoping to drive new customers to your company's offerings, provide working information to existing customers, or offer a place to consummate the sale. Sometimes you will want to do all three.

2. Next you need to decide how you will approach the customer. Will you use hard-hitting headlines, great storyboard openers, humor, news format, product photos, music, games, videos, animation, models, teasers? Do you want the site to come up quickly on even the slowest dial-up computer modem, or are you willing to risk losing a few customers in order to create a bandwidth-eating motion picture on your home page? Are you hoping to get the customer to stay and go deep into your site, or can you tell your whole story in ten to twenty inches of scrolling?

3. With those basic questions guiding you, the next decision is a big one. Will you do it yourself or get someone to do all or part of the work for you? My skill set does not include high-level computer capabilities or graphic competency in any medium.

However, many Web site hosts have made the basic setting up of a site so easy that I was able to do a pretty nice one 100 percent on my own. However, our company site, CaliforniaSprings.com, requires substantial work by professionals to keep it current and exciting.

A basic Web site that you can design yourself can cost as little as $100 per year. If you need a lot of content or bandwidth, or if you need shopping bag services and other more sophisticated elements, the cost can be much higher. However, for most small companies, the Web site is not a big expense. Spend your money on making the content as professional as possible.

4. You have now established your Web storefront, aka Web site. Just as is the case with a brick-and-mortar storefront, you have to let people know you are there. There are entire books written on this subject, and I won't pretend to be able to cover the possibilities. However, here are the basics.

A. Search engines. You must show up on the search engines. More than that you should be one of the first on the list. In 2005, you want to be at or near the top on Google for sure. You get to the top by having great headlines, creating clever and appropriate meta tags, and paying for placement. Many hosts will provide recommendations for creating the meta tags, and some will give you free applications to search engines periodically. There are also books, Web sites, and services specializing in getting you placement.

B. Links. Generally getting other sites to link to your site is free. Many organizations and even other companies use lists of links as a way to attract potential customers to their site. Do research to try and find good sites that might be willing to link to you. Example: You are an importer of specialty chocolates and have an exclusive to a particular brand. Check out the various sites that appeal to chocolate lovers and give advice on how to select them. They will undoubtedly want to link to you so the chocolate lovers who come to their site can learn more about your product.

C. Advertise on other sites. We've all seen the banner ad that asks us to bet a poker hand or answer some ridiculous question. These and other kinds of ads can attract people to your site. You can work out your own deal with specific sites that are in your industry, or you can use a service to place your ad at random throughout their locations. Most services today charge you by the number of times someone clicks on the banner and goes to your site.

D. Advertise and promote your site everywhere. Your Web address should be on your business card, letterhead, brochures, catalogs, e-mail signature, and invoices.

E. Have those downline in the distribution channels advertise your site. If you are a manufacturer, have your distributors and dealers show your product and your Web site on their site. If you are a distributor, see if your dealers will advertise your site. You may be carrying items that they don't have in stock, but by sending their customers to your site, it may result in sales your dealer would have missed.

F. If your Web site is very important to your business potential, use specialty products and promotions to encourage visits to your Web location. Offer an online contest or competition with prizes based on visits or activity during a visit to your site.

5. Review, measure, and change. There is a good chance that once you have completed all of the above, you will feel exhilarated and exhausted. You may also come to the conclusion that you can now move on to other things. Maybe you'll review the online project again in a year or two.

The job has really just begun. If this store was brick-and-mortar instead of virtual, you would be paying close attention to how many customers came in each day, what the traffic patterns were like inside the store, what items caught customers' interest, and what kinds of comments resulted from their visits. You want exactly the same kinds of answers about your virtual presence. Your hosting company will almost certainly provide ways for you to track both the amount of traffic, and quite a bit about the nature of each visit. If not, you can purchase software to do so. You can learn how many people come to the site. How many of those are unique as opposed to frequent visitors? How long do they stay? Where do they go after they arrive? If you sell product on the site, you will obviously monitor how many make a purchase per day, and what percentage of visitors are buyers.

You can further monitor all of this by how they came to your site. Did they click through from a paid advertisement, a free link, a search engine, or some other way?

Once you establish these patterns, you will be able to increase or decrease your advertising and promotional efforts based on what's working and what's not.

E-MAIL

There is no possible way to overstate the importance of e-mail. It is the opinion of this businessman that e-mail is the most important business advance of the last fifty years. Nothing else has impacted communication so dramatically. Cell phones have changed life for sales reps and others who travel or spend a lot of time out of the office. The Web has impacted sales, marketing, and purchasing. The computer has made cell phones, the Web, and e-mail possible, and completely changed bookkeeping and financial management. But e-mail is used by all of the above for both internal and external communication, mass sales efforts, and now even the transmission of all the documents of business.

Much of what is listed below may be obvious to some, but you may be surprised how few small businesses are using these capabilities.

1. Spend the few extra dollars per month to be live 100 percent of the time using DSL, cable, or a fractional T-1 telephone line. Generally the extra expense to have full-time access to your e-mail will be offset by a lower phone bill and virtually free 100 percent access to the Web at the fastest speeds and with the widest bandwidth. Your customers and vendors will appreciate fast responses to their communication by e-mail. It is very irritating to send e-mails that aren't answered the same day.

2. If you have your own Web site, take advantage of the free POP e-mail addresses. It looks far more professional to have the e-mail address YourName@YourBusiness.com instead of YourName3467843@aol.com. Remember the Web site can cost as little as $100 per year. My e-mail address is Randy_Kirk@ CaliforniaSprings.com. California Springs is one of our brands. We want to emphasize the brand rather than the corporate name. In other cases your corporate name may be more important. Most of my staff has changed to just their first name. I agree with that approach even though I haven't changed yet. The simpler the e-mail address to remember, the better.

Another advantage of using a totally personal e-mail address is that changing your e-mail address is more difficult on your communication than changing phones or physical address. When you are using an address like SBCGlobal.net or Yahoo.com, you will want to change e-mail address if you change service providers.

3. When sending e-mails, include a "signature" that includes your name, title, address, phone, fax, Web site address, and even a compelling message like your company slogan. It is so convenient for your customer, supplier, or associate to go back to your e-mail for that info when they need to call you or send something. It is better to make this signature text as opposed to a "preference attachment." Some spam filters don't like to see any kind of attachment, including such "signatures."

4. Include as much personality as possible in your e-mails. One disadvantage of e-mails is that it has had a huge impact on the amount of face-to-face and phone contact that we have with customers, fellow employees, and suppliers. Establish and distinguish yourself through the e-mail. Have fun. Use the smiley faces and shorthands that have become so popular in personal e-mail.

5. Keep the conversation going on one page. In other words, respond in a way that your correspondent can easily see what they have written and what you have answered. This encourages them to do the same. I have had e-mails that went back and forth ten or more times with the entire message on one page. It is so much easier to follow, and to go back to if you need to recall the conversation. If the conversation is complex, respond in a new color just below where the question was raised. This also improves the ease of following the subject matter.

6. Keep all e-mail. It makes a great history for proving a point, remembering a previous agreement, checking prices or old quotes to figure a new one, following up prospects, and much, much more. File the e-mails in some logical fashion so that you can easily find them in the future. Personally, I file received e-mails, but keep my sent e-mails in the sent folder. That gives me one file to look up by category, and one to look up by date, name, thread, etc.

7. Follow up phone calls and other conversations with a quick e-mail to list what was agreed upon. This would include interoffice conversations, too. I will commonly send an e-mail to an employee whom I can see from my desk, then ask her about it later.

8. Build your e-mail address book. You may have many address books. My most important address book is made out of paper and has been in my office for at least fifteen years. My second most important address book, however, is my e-mail list. If possible use a Palm or other PDA to keep the same list that you have in your computer. You may also want to keep a company database of e-mails that is much larger than your personal one. Our database has 9,000 names and we send out at least one advertisement to this list each week.

9. Advertise and promote through e-mail. It is almost free and so much more immediate than any other form of ad. In order to do this you need a list. You don't want your list to be spam. If you create your own list through asking customers for their address or addresses, scanning badges at trade shows, or buying lists that are "opt in," your customers should not be unhappy if you send them info. Make it reasonably easy for them to opt out. For $100 or so, you can buy very good programs for maintaining and managing your list, including automatic opt out methods. Put together a strategy for building the biggest list imaginable.

Like any advertisement, e-mail is more likely to be read and responded to if it is compelling. This might mean funny, outrageous, exciting, alluring, or even maddening. Contests, offers of free or discounted merchandise or services, and pictures of cute cuddly things work to capture the reader's attention in an e-mail just as they would in a mass snail mailing.

After your compelling opening, you need a great story including a reason why your customer should buy and buy *now!* Then you need to close. Tell them exactly how they can act now and how you will reward them for doing so. Make sure your phone number and contact person are clearly identified. Some folks still want the human touch, and will completely reject the offer because they can't find a way to contact you.

Part 7
Pursuing New Territories

Many companies find that after their first few years they hit a sales plateau. Up to a certain volume, business comes easy. Then there comes a time when it seems as if the next sales dollar is very elusive. Ironically, the sales ceiling usually hits just at the point where profits start.

A variation of this dilemma is the seasonal sales phenomenon. I know of one motorcycle parts distributor who made huge profits eight months out of the year, only to lose almost all of it in the winter months.

These are only two among many frustrating situations faced by the new enterprise struggling to create a stable sales level above break-even. See if any of the following sound familiar:

- Your business is dependent on certain types of weather.
- In a recession, you're the first to feel it, and the last to see it go.
- Foreign currency fluctuations can turn your black ink red.
- Your product line is greatly affected by cycles in popularity.
- Your company's success is closely tied to another's.

There is a common solution for most of these ills. Develop a new territory that will help provide balance in your business. In some cases this can be accomplished by specifically seeking a line of business that will have a cycle opposite that of your core activity. In others, you can create a more stable sales curve by moving into a territory that has limitless potential. A few ideas on how to accomplish this follow:

MASS MARKET

If you're currently a manufacturer, packager, wholesaler, or importer of consumer products, and you are selling only to independent retailers, you might consider offering your product to the major mass retailers. This would include department stores, discounters, warehouse stores, grocery and drug chains, convenience stores, and any other retailer that has a large number of locations.

The good news about selling mass marketers is the volume they move and the fact that they generally pay their bills well. The bad news can be pretty bad. Many of the top retailers will work you over real good for low prices, long terms to pay, freight allowances, advertising money, and every other discount imaginable.

Once you land a major account, you can become quite dependent on them if their volume becomes 25 percent or more of your total. Whether or not you let this happen, the buyer with such a big "pencil" (ability to write big orders) will likely exert pressure on you for a high level of service. You'll need to be prepared to ship on a dime, even if the account gives you no projections. Even if you are given projections, the first blip in the economy may cause them to reduce or even cancel purchase orders.

Here are some guidelines for working this territory:

1. Establish a solid base of business with independent retailers or wholesalers before you try the mass market.

2. Don't allow any one account to represent more than 20 percent of your business. The exception would be if you could sustain the loss of that business and still be profitable.

3. If you follow rules one and two, you won't be so desperate for this business that you fall into the trap of giving the product away or offering super-long terms. In most instances, you should be able to sell your product for the same price and terms to a major retailer's warehouse as you would to a wholesaler.

4. Change the product and the packaging from that which you sell through your dealer market. When possible, offer the dealer market a few more features so that your dealer will be able to combat the price advantage of the mass marketer.

5. To find excellent sales reps for the market, call the buyer for the customer you want to sell. Ask this buyer for his recommendation of a sales rep.

6. Watch all aspects of bookkeeping like a hawk. The volume you are doing will mean a large volume of bookkeeping. Invoices will be lost. There will be claims that shipments are short. Buyers may show terms on the purchase order that are better than those you offered in hopes that you will "cave in" and accept them without argument.

7. Collect from these accounts even more aggressively than the independents. When you call the accounting department of a major retailer, you're talking to a clerk, not the owner or buyer. You won't risk losing the business because you ask for your check when it is due.

8. Keep your eye on the newspaper regarding these customers. Call your rep frequently to inquire after the financial condition of these majors. You can afford to lose a few thousand dollars from the bankruptcy of one or two dealers. Can you recover from the loss of $150,000 when the next discount chain goes broke?

9. Maybe the best reason to stay away from mass merchants in the early going of your business is called "charge backs." Today all major accounts have a book of rules regarding everything from the way you have to receive the purchase order to the way you have to ship the product and how to send the bill. The book might be fifty to one hundred pages plus with details about package size and weight, pallet height and that the pallet must be certified bug-free, delivery windows, and instructions for placement of labels, UPC codes, and on and on.

If you fail to do any of the hundreds of things required in exactly the way you are instructed, you will be subject to a charge back. This can amount to $10, $100, $1,000, or even $100,000 for a single error. One distributor friend of ours has an $80,000-per-year vice president of charge backs to make sure that the company doesn't make any errors. His biggest job is to get reversals from the major mass market companies for charge backs that were charged when there was no violation.

It takes special skills to handle this type of business. If you and your staff are well suited to working out this type of detail, you can make a lot of money working with the majors. If not, you can lose a large amount of money even while selling huge amounts of merchandise.

GOVERNMENT

The United States government is the single largest user of product in the world. There are many different ways to sell this market.

A. The GSA (General Services Administration) buys most of the product for the various government offices. This is done primarily through a bidding process. Items that go out for bid have specifications associated with them that your product must meet to qualify. Many of these specifications must be laboratory tested for proof before your first shipment.

As you might expect, there are reps who specialize in selling to GSA. You can wade into the paperwork maze on your own if you wish, but be prepared to learn a whole new ball game.

B. Base exchanges (BXs) and commissaries serve our men and women in uniform. The BXs are one of the largest retailers in the United States. They, along with the commissaries, buy massive amounts of product. The largest of these is AAFES (Army, Air Force Exchange Service) located in Dallas, Texas.

It is very important to find a knowledgeable manufacturer's rep if you want to sell the BXs. Otherwise you're faced first with the job of unraveling the government system of doing things, and then selling the buyer.

C. Many agencies, including the military, have discretionary budgets that do not go through GSA or the major military buying offices. Sometimes they are required to put these requirements out to bid. Other times they can be sold without bid, as long as you're willing to meet the price of the primary supplier.

State, county, and city governments are also big users of many types of products and services. Write to the respective procurement offices to have your company name put on the bid list.

If you qualify as a small business or if you are minority owned you should be able to bid on items that are "set aside" for such enterprises. The agencies who do the purchasing can help you determine how to qualify.

INTERNATIONAL

You may be surprised at the opportunities your little three-person operation may find in the international arena. American products and know-how are in great demand around the world. (Many international consumers consider it high fashion to wear American clothes, watch American movies, and listen to American music.)

You may be able to attract a certain amount of export business just by putting up a sign in your booth at a trade show mentioning your interest in establishing international distributors. At the same time, keep your eyes peeled for individuals whose badges or accents give them away as potential overseas customers.

You can prospect for opportunities in other lands by checking with various federal, state, and city government branches. Many of these have programs designed to help small businesses gain access to foreign markets. Your local or national chamber of commerce also has helpful information.

Again, there are reps who can help you. Some are based here and travel abroad. Others are based in the country you want to sell.

A side benefit of developing your international business is that you'll be able to write off much of the travel you do.

PREMIUM

Would your product look good in or on a box of corn flakes? Would a major national fast-food chain give your item away with a cheeseburger, fries, and soft drink? Could other companies use your product or service as a prize for a sales contest? Is there any way to print a name on your merchandise so that it becomes a billboard?

There are many, many items that can be made to fit into the premium business. It may seem as if the industry is dominated by pens and calendars. However, in the bicycle industry we have seen seat bags, hats, helmets, water bottles, jerseys, pants, and number plates, to say nothing of the bicycle frame itself, used as sales media.

To pursue these opportunities, determine where your product fits, pick up the phone, and begin networking.

The two major shows in this industry are the PPAI show and the ASI show. Both are currently in Las Vegas. There are many other shows around the country. If you believe it would be profitable, take a booth. There are several magazines for this industry that also might suggest opportunities for you and your firm.

MAIL ORDER

You can take advantage of this huge and growing method of retailing by selling to the major catalogs and home shopping shows. I have personally had no success in finding representatives that work this territory. We have found our way into these catalogs through distributors who have good connections, by calling the buyers direct, and by meeting their representatives at trade shows.

OTHER DEALER NETWORKS

Can your item be sold in another, almost unrelated industry? If it won't work exactly the way it is presently configured, could it be changed in some minor way to work? For example, in the padlock business we sold the following industries. In each case the method of distribution is shown after the industry name.

Locksmiths	Through distributors
Hardware stores	Through distributors and co-ops
Home centers	Direct
Discounters	Direct and through feeders (wholesalers)
Automotive	Through warehouse distributors
Grocery	Direct, and through distributors and co-ops
Bicycle shops	Direct
Motorcycle shops	Through distributors
Marine hardware	Through distributors
Drug chains	Direct and through feeders
BXs	Direct
GSA	Direct
Vending machines	OEM and distributors
Fire extinguisher cases	OEM
Ministorage	Through distributors

Department stores	Direct
Convenience stores	Direct
Public schools	Direct and through distributors
Industrial hardware	Through distributors
Student unions	Direct

Any time is a great time to start considering expansion into other territories. It's generally less expensive to enter a new territory than it is to add new products to an existing territory.

A particularly good time to expand in this way is during a recession or other lean time for your business. If a recession would normally reduce your sales by 25 percent, you may be able to replace that and more by moving aggressively with one of the above approaches.

Managing Yourself and Others

1

The Managed Business

THERE COMES A TIME in the business cycle when survival is no longer the issue. Some of the signs will be: consistent monthly profits, three months or more of cash reserves, excellent banking and other credit relations, and an owner's income at least equal to what could be made for similar work if employed by someone else.

More than likely this will take place between the third and fifth year. While this would seem to be the perfect time to break out the bubbly and celebrate, it may actually prove to be a time of great stress. This is because a number of new challenges will emerge.

The first is that of making the transition from a "seat-of-the-pants" operation to a managed business. Most owners will recognize when this time has arrived, though they'll be hesitant to make the transition since it calls for a whole new set of skills. This is not the stuff of which most "entrepreneurs" are made.

IT'LL NEVER BE THE SAME

During the first three or so years, you are the chief cook and bottle washer, head salesperson, personnel department, bookkeeper, and, of course, janitor. But of all the hats you'll wear during this period, the one you'll wear the most is *firefighter*. The major difference between the start-up, survival-oriented business and the mature, "managed" company is that the first is *reactive* and the second is *proactive*. In the early years you're at the mercy of events. Only after traveling a lengthy learning curve will you be able to control most events.

(Note: The transition from a reactive "survival" phase to a proactive "managed" phase distinguishes the very small business from one that intends to grow well beyond ten employees. The owner who intends to have fifty, one hundred, or even thousands of employees will very likely go from the survival phase into a growth phase. While many sophisticated management tools may be in place during this growth period, there'll continue to be substantial amounts of reactive behavior and numerous learning curves.)

To illustrate the difference between these two phases, let's consider a doctor's office. We'll assume that Dr. Linda Smith is opening a new practice, and hasn't brought along any patients from her former employment.

During the first three years, she'll be in a constant fight to pay the rent and other bills since her gross income will be small. She may find herself offering special hours, making house calls, or working on call for other doctors at night or on weekends. She'll need a receptionist/bookkeeper, but won't be able to afford one. When it comes time to pay a major bill, she'll have to hustle even harder to try to get some cash in the door. Her few patients will benefit from this since they'll always be able to get a quick appointment.

Four years later the good doctor will have joined an HMO, worked the service-club circuit, tapped into the Medicare program, and built a thriving practice.

Survival will no longer be the issue. Managing two nurses, a receptionist, and a bookkeeper will represent constant drains on her time. She won't have to worry about income, but she'll now have to manage the patient load. She'll also have to fine-tune the appointment system so as not to unduly waste her patients' time in the waiting and examining rooms. And she may want to consider automating her record-keeping system.

The distinction between the two phases of small business development can best be seen in terms of planning. As the company becomes more oriented to management rather than survival, the planning is longer range. In the first few weeks of a new business, it's often hard to plan past the next weekend. In the five-year-old managed business, it would be common to have a fairly specific five-year plan.

The components of management (planning, investigation, evaluation, implementation, and oversight) require more reflection than survival. Managing is commonly more difficult and takes more discipline. Survival issues are constantly thrown in your lap and require immediate attention. You have to call on instinct, since there is no time to reflect. On the other hand, you have to *remember* to manage. If you forget, you'll fall back into a survival pattern when the result of your failure to manage comes home to haunt.

It is common business parlance to speak of the person in charge as putting out fires when he reacts to survival issues. Let's develop that comparison between an owner and a firefighter.

I'm no expert, but my instincts tell me that folks in that profession love the action in fighting a big fire. Such a situation most definitely puts them in a survival mode. To win this battle, carefully trained instincts must be brought to bear. The adrenaline is pumping and the feeling of satisfaction from success is quite exhilarating.

Contrast that portion of the firefighter's job with the long-range management of the fire district. Someone has to evaluate tract maps for the area covered by their station. The staff must analyze each different type of condition. Officers must be sent out for site inspections to ensure compliance with regulations. Citations must be issued and followed up. Given the choice, most firefighters would rather be out facing the fire. Unfortunately, no matter how good they are at putting out those blazes, some damage has already been done. The comparative drudgery of managing might have prevented its happening in the first place.

Many owners stay in the survival mode long after they should have moved into the management phase. They may have tried to make the switch and didn't have the skills. Maybe they didn't want to lose the adrenaline surge of a good firefight. Sometimes it's simply a case of not realizing that change is possible. The next several chapters cover specific areas where change should occur along with specific approaches to handling it.

CHAPTER

2

Managing Managers

Manager. An individual who directs and/or controls the activities of other individuals or of systems. Examples of systems would include bookkeeping, office, procurement, production, service, operations, and finance.

In the survival stage of your business you will undoubtedly hire some managers. If after a few years you have between five and ten people on the payroll, it is likely that someone will be functioning as an assistant. The title of this assistant may be vice president, executive secretary, or office manager. Call him what you will, this person is the one who takes over when you're gone, and who oversees that portion of the business that you don't.

You probably have also opted for a full-time bookkeeper. Most companies in this stage of development prefer to have someone on staff who can handle all issues related to accounts receivable, accounts payable, inventory, payroll, and general ledger. Frequently, this individual also handles the computer operations.

If you're not specifically in charge of sales, you likely have someone on staff who is. In a small company this individual may also have all or most of the marketing responsibilities as well.

Depending on the type of business, you might also have an

operations manager, purchasing manager, head cook, lead man, art director, or second shift supervisor.

Except in unusual situations, these employees were not hired for their managerial flair, but were added when the heat from a major flare-up caused you to scream for backup. For the first eighteen years I ran businesses, I would have suggested to anyone who listened that a company owner should add managers slowly and deliberately before the actual need. This is so they'd be trained and ready when the company's growth made their positions critical.

I would now maintain that during the survival period you shouldn't add the overhead until the need is so great that not to add the position might actually damage the company's profitability. Of course, this means that the hiring process will be done on a rush basis, and you may not always get great managers. That's acceptable. During this period, if they can handle the operations, you can take a little longer to train them for management. If they can't be trained, you'll eventually have to replace them.

What follows are the steps necessary for the proper management of managers. Their proper implementation takes a great deal of time. However, as with so many other aspects of leadership, the time devoted at the front end will pay big dividends later.

Part 1
Communicating the Vision

I recently read the most astonishing story about the concentration camps of Hitler's Germany. The story told of one facility where the workers were made to endure fourteen hours per day of the most horrible menial labor, seven days per week. This with poor rations and substandard living quarters. To make matters worse, they were making products that would be used to help the Germans prosecute the war. In the face of all these negatives, the workers remained relatively strong of mind and character.

There was a fire that destroyed the building where these hapless victims turned out the tools of war. The day following the fire, the workers were led out to the site and lined up at one end of the burned-out facility. Here, they were provided with the equipment necessary to pick up and haul away the debris. The wheelbarrows full of destruction were then hauled and dumped at the other end of the burned-out hulk. This activity was performed by the workers with the same relative equanimity with which they performed their usual tasks.

After having completed the clean-up, however, they were lined up at the end of the site where the trash had been dumped, and instructed to haul it back to the other end. As this process was repeated several times it became clear to those working that those in charge were merely creating useless work. It was only at this time that many began to crack emotionally and physically, resulting in numerous mental breakdowns and deaths.

The point here is that these individuals maintained their desire to live while enslaved to make material that would be used to destroy their brothers. But they cracked when given a meaningless task. The same intense frustration at seeming to perform a task that is of no consequence is often felt by managers.

If they feel that they are spending their eight or so hours per day just putting in time, if they're unable to figure out how their activity contributes to the whole, and if they're unable to determine exactly what the "whole" is, you'll have managers who are ineffective at best, and destructive at worst. On the other hand, if your managers believe their entire effort is designed merely to help the owners make money, they'll be more effective than if they have no purpose at all. Can you imagine how well things would go if all employees felt they had a stake in the company's goals?

Do you have a vision for your company? If you're not certain of your goal—one that you can communicate to your managers—it's important that you again go through the process of evaluating where *you* currently stand in your life's plan.

If you have a clear understanding of where you and the business are headed, then there remains the less difficult, but still substantial job of communicating this to your staff. Do this in a way that allows them to pass on this information to their subordinates, and to the company's vendors and customers.

As with most communication, you can express yourself in three ways. The first two are optional—the spoken or written word. The third is involuntary—your actions (and we all know what they speak louder than).

The most practical first step in establishing your overall objective for the company is to have a meeting with your managers, through which you involve them in the process of writing a mission statement. Through their participation, they'll become part owners of the statement, and as such will have a greater stake in seeing it fulfilled.

Possibly the most important step of all comes next. You can write it, and you can say it, but if you can't live it, nobody will believe it. Therefore, don't kid yourself, and don't try to kid your managers. You're unlikely to improve your company's management by changing your mission statement. You'll have to begin by changing yourself.

SET THE EXAMPLE

Your attitudes, priorities (or lack thereof), and business practices will have a way of trickling down. You shouldn't be surprised to learn that the negative ones will trickle down in torrents, while the positive ones will try to defy gravity.

If you feel that managers should not be clock watchers, then you can't work nine to four-thirty with a two-hour lunch and every other Wednesday off. If you're the first to arrive and the last to leave, it becomes embarrassing for a top manager to see your car in the lot when he comes and when he goes.

Do you want others to turn in reports on time? You'll need to do likewise. Do you want your people to answer the phone professionally and cheerfully? Make certain you do. Is quality or service important? Can those in your organization tell that by seeing your reactions to quality or service issues? Ask yourself these questions on an ongoing basis.

Part 2
Leadership

A manager's success is primarily dependent on whether or not she has the respect of her peers and her subordinates. That respect will come from three areas: (1) attitude about self, the company, and its products; (2) work ethic; and (3) ability to direct others with authority, empathy, and respect.

My partner says that having a manager in your organization with a bad attitude is "like a cancer." A person with an ax to grind will very likely talk to anyone who'll listen about how rotten things are. These bad cells will begin to infect the healthy ones, and soon your company morale will be in need of radical treatment.

If you have someone in a position of leadership who has an attitude problem, I'd heartily recommend a single warning to shape up. If there's no improvement, cut out this cancer before it spreads.

A common trap into which new managers fall is the idea that they can hand off all the distasteful jobs to their staff and keep the easy or fun stuff for themselves. Even the perception that this is happening can destroy the manager's credibility quickly.

When I first went to work for ABUS Security Locks, it was a five-person company. I was still in law school, which resulted in my having irregular hours. ABUS received shipments every ten days from the factory. These shipments consisted of wooden crates full of steel padlocks (they were heavy and unwieldy). Until I joined the operation, the shipping clerk and the president would usually wrestle these crates off the truck and into the warehouse.

I'd been there a few months when a shipment arrived on a day when neither the president nor the shipping clerk was around. To make matters worse, it was during a light rain. There was no choice but to go out there and unload that truck myself.

I'd noticed during my stay that the executive secretary and I weren't getting along that well. I concluded that she was just jealous of the salary I was earning, given my age.

I later learned that the executive secretary felt that I was manipulating my school schedule to ensure that I was never on the premises when a shipment came in. She'd noticed my wages, but it wasn't my youth she compared them to, but rather, my willingness to work hard . . . and dirty.

The day that I emptied the truck in the rain, the executive secretary decided I was okay!

Explain to your managers that they must be willing to wade in the muck, block the 350-pound lineman, and deal with an angry vendor if they hope to have their underlings' respect.

For those who direct others, the final link in the chain that determines how well they can manage their troops is the manner in which they issue orders. The three keys to success in that effort are authority, empathy, and respect.

You must make it clear that this individual has the necessary authority to hand out the orders he's giving. Once that's clear, the manager himself must be able to convey the attitude of authority. Others will not follow if directives are unclear, impossible, or issued without confidence.

Furthermore, those in authority must possess empathy. If you want a soldier to be the first to move into the line of fire, you'd better give him that order in a way that conveys appreciation, an understanding of the fear he must feel, and evidence that you believe everything will be okay.

Finally, there must be respect. If the supervisor conveys superiority or lack of civility, she will invite revolt. The fastest way to earn the respect of others is to show that you respect them.

GET OUT OF THE WAY

Once you've defined for your managers what their specific duties are, and encouraged them to get their hands dirty when the situation requires it, it's time to let them do their job. If you have any interest in their becoming something more than mindless robots, you'll want to provide them with an environment conducive to innovation and experimentation.

Don't hang over your manager's shoulder ready to attack each small detail that you might have done differently. If the work must be reviewed, do so after it's complete. Then evaluate only those aspects that might likely cause harm, and do so in a constructive way. Once a manager has shown that he can be trusted to do the work, let him do so without review. This will build his confidence and make him a better all-around producer.

Make it clear to your people that you encourage risk taking. Remind them frequently that you want them to try new ideas and approaches. You recognize that mistakes will be made, and that's all right. My feeling is that people who aren't making mistakes aren't making anything happen. Clearly, the mistakes should not be stupid or repetitive, but it's amazing how many fortunes have been made due to mistakes that opened the door to new possibilities.

Be careful not to discourage those who bring you new ideas. You may have tried it before and it didn't work, but maybe it will now under someone else's direction. If every idea that comes your way is met by, "That won't work, it's been done before," you can be sure that the supply of new ideas will soon dwindle.

Part 3
Compensation Concepts

Most honest individuals will put in a decent day's work with little more motivation than a reasonable wage. You'll probably want more than that from your people. I know nothing that tickles me more than to see an employee use her opportunity with our company to grow and prosper. However, to get these results, you must provide motivation.

The better you know your people the better you'll know how to motivate them. There are certain key things you can do, though, that will result in employees consistently going the extra mile.

1. Appreciation. Horticulturists believe that plants respond better to someone who really cares about them. If it's so for the flower, how much more important must this be for human beings?

My picture of the job of manager is one who helps and encourages employees to live up to their own expectations and beyond. For me, that starts with my walk around the building after arrival each morning. I make it a point to seek out each person and wish them a good morning. I address everyone by name. This greeting may result in a few moments of additional conversation on subjects ranging from aspects of the job to their childrens' success in the soccer play-offs.

The routine is repeated as the second shift arrives. And during the course of the day there are usually five more times that I walk throughout the facility. As I go, I try to find positive things to say about the work being performed. This is not to say that shoddy results are overlooked, but the emphasis is on encouraging good work.

Another aspect of these daily walks is to attempt to evaluate the overall performance of individuals. Are any of them showing leadership tendencies? Is someone ill suited to his current assignment who might do wonderfully at another position? Who are the troublemakers, the laggards, the undesirables? Who looks as if he could use cheering up?

2. Opportunities for growth and advancement. Most people are seeking to better themselves. They'd like to make more money and have more prestige. In motivating your employees you have a wonderful opportunity to discover talent and turn average workers into real assets.

Make it clear to your staff that you prefer to promote from within. I generally let new managers know that even my job is available if someone wants it bad enough to earn it. We're constantly cross-training everyone to do related jobs. As each individual's knowledge increases, so do her worth and feeling of self-esteem.

3. Spontaneous raises and bonuses. It's important to me that I give a raise or bonus to deserving employees before they ask for it. Many workers, when anticipating an annual wage increase, will put on a strong showing just before the review. Once they've received their increase they commonly drop down in performance. If your employees know they might get a raise or bonus when they've shown themselves to be superior workers, they'll likely show increased productivity all the time.

4. Piecework compensation. If you have positions in your company that lend themselves to piecework compensation, by all means use it. I've never had a bad experience with this approach when it was feasible.

In order for piecework compensation to be successful, the worker must be able to control the speed of production. At one point we were paying piecework rates for a task whose speed was controlled by the maximum output of the machinery. We were wasting money. On the other hand, I've had situations where we were paying $6.00 per hour to turn out three hundred pieces of work or $.02 per piece. No matter what we did to motivate these workers, we got three hundred per hour.

Then we went to piecework. We offered $.015 per piece. In no time at all we had several employees making six hundred per hour and taking home $9.00 per hour. Never once did I begrudge those $9.00-per-hour paychecks. I was saving 25 percent on my labor!

5. Performance bonus. A kissing cousin to piecework is a bonus tied to specific performance criteria. On several occasions, we've passed out a letter to each employee at the beginning of the month. In the letter we've indicated that we wanted to reach a certain sales level that month. We went on to explain that everyone in the company could contribute to our goal. Production needed to make enough; sales had to sell enough; bookkeeping had to keep up with the order writing, credit checking, invoicing, and collecting; purchasing had to stay on top of the vendors to ensure delivery of component parts; and everyone in the organization could be a bit of a nag with those who might be falling behind.

The final paragraph of the letter indicated the specific dollar amount of the bonus that this employee would earn if the team made the goal. We reached the goal 75 percent of the time. When we didn't, it was close enough to be a big help. On one occasion, we paid even though we were a few percentage points shy of the goal.

Put your imagination to work. Your specific type of business and workforce will respond best to ideas that fit their personalities.

CHAPTER
3

Personal Motivation Techniques

It can happen anytime. You get up in the morning and the prospect of going to the office doesn't stir your juices. Sometimes it occurs because of a specific issue or job that must be handled that day. Other times, it may be the weather, the business climate, or a simple matter of body chemistry being out of whack. These problems are generally short-lived and don't require much in the way of remedial action.

However, there are instances where the problems are more deep-seated. Possibly you don't feel like going to work almost all the time. You've concluded that your feelings aren't related to the type of work you've chosen. You've also ruled out other aspects of your life such as marital problems or a general emotional disorder.

You wonder, "How does that crazy five percent of the population do it? How do they jump out of bed every day with spring in their step, desire in their heart, and the willingness to do the things that have to be done without complaint or hesitation?"

1. *They believe that what they do will make a difference.* While they acknowledge that outside individuals and events can affect their plans, they know with certainty that they can, by their effort, make good things happen.

This idea goes beyond a belief in yourself. In fact, those who believe only in themselves are unlikely to be able to sustain this idea forever. Everyone will have a string of mistakes (slump, bad luck, bad timing) that can bring into question belief in self. However, belief in God as the personal sustainer of good for your life makes it possible to maintain a consistent attitude that your actions will have long-term rewards . . . even in the face of catastrophe.

The opposite approach can be seen in the individual who believes that no matter what they do, they are at the mercy of other persons, events, or beings from the spiritual world who are able to control their will (unlike the Judeo/Christian God who makes no attempt to control the will). These individuals will commonly use words such as "go with the flow." They will spend countless hours evaluating how their life has been shaped by their genetics, their parents, or their schools. These are the same folks who will look at the successful individuals around them and pronounce them "lucky."

The first step in personal motivation is to adopt a mind-set that says: "I am in control of my destiny. No one else can alter this without my permission. I can choose to fly with the eagles, swim with the sharks, or lie around with the sloths. **I make my own happiness.** It is a good idea for me to seek out others who can fill needs, but if I rely on them to make me happy, I can expect disappointment. I will refrain from offering excuses for those parts of my life that are not as I would like. I will replace that thinking with immediate movement to institute those actions that I believe will gain the ends I seek."

2. Keep making those lists. As mentioned repeatedly, you need to have long-term goals, short-term goals, and lists of tasks that need to be undertaken to get you to both. Don't forget to compile that to-do list on a daily basis. One of my associates once admitted to me that he got more satisfaction crossing out items on his to-do list than from almost any other aspect of his life. (My first response was "Get a life." On further reflection, though, I conceded that crossing things off that list did rank pretty high!)

3. Do you have daily, weekly, and monthly goals for each quantifiable aspect of your business: sales, collections, production, new customers, service levels, sales calls, whatever? The setting of these goals is very motivating as long as they're within reach. You'll want to be flexible about changing those goals in the face of surprises. It's not good for one's outlook to come up seriously short of plan.

Consider giving yourself a reward for meeting goals. Make certain, though, that the reward is something worth working for.

4. Read motivational books. Watch or listen to motivational tapes. Attend motivational seminars. While these usually wear off after a few days or weeks, they do boost the rockets for a while. Sometimes they provide enough boost to allow you to use your own power for a long time after.

5. Here's another golden nugget. Pay careful attention! *Find someone to be accountable to.*

One of the major reasons you started a business was probably that you didn't want to have to answer to someone else for your actions. But with no one looking over your shoulder, the opportunity for massive error is always just around the corner.

For years I would say to my accountant, a partner, or a friend: "I feel as though my company is sailing into uncharted waters. I've never run a company of this [pick one] size, type, complexity. I feel as though I need to sit down and talk to someone who has." I believe that if any one of those individuals had recommended such a person, it would have saved me more than a million dollars in the past five years alone.

What kind of person or group can fill this job? What are the characteristics to look for? What is their actual task? How do you work with them?

1. The person must have your respect. This doesn't mean that you never disagree. It does mean that his advice is at least as valuable as your own thinking.

2. The adviser must be tough as nails. She will be useless if she is unwilling to tell you things you don't want to hear. If she wants to be your friend first and adviser second, find someone else to be your adviser.

3. It's best if he has specific experience related to your type of enterprise. At the very least, you want someone who has excellent credentials and experience in the area of very small business management.

4. Lawyers and accountants are often used for this purpose. However, if you choose one of these, beware of two traps: They usually don't have actual experience or training in small business management, and they're generally naysayers. You'll do better with an adviser who has a balanced approach to new ideas.

5. You want someone with an inquiring mind. You shouldn't have to ask her for an opinion on everything. *She* should be asking *you* for specific information as to how certain aspects of the company are performing.

You may be able to find this person through your accountant, banker or lawyer, or by asking business associates and friends. The Small Business Administration offers a program whereby retired businesspeople offer services like this for free. It is called ACE/SCORE—Active Corps of Executives/Service Corps of Retired Executives. (See details about this group in the appendix.)

You could try to find your adviser through the Yellow Pages. Unfortunately, there are many folks claiming to be business consultants who are in that line of work only until they get a real job. When selecting your adviser, check references more thoroughly than you would for your highest-level employee.

If you bring in a stranger, evaluate his work very closely until you're certain he's providing value. Remember, you don't want a yes man. You won't be helped by someone whose sole job is to compliment your management techniques and laugh at your jokes. You want a tough-minded businessperson who'll let you know when you're headed the wrong way.

You'll know you have the right person if, when you're making a decision of consequence, you find yourself asking, "What will Jim say if I do this?" Sure, you're right back to having a boss, but this one is of your own choosing. If he's worth what you pay him, you'll improve profits, maintain higher cash balances, increase your service level, and feel better at the end of the day. And . . . you won't feel quite so lonely when you're making the really tough decisions.

The author is currently offering consulting services by phone or e-mail. Call 1-800-245-3737, ext. 223; or write to Randy_Kirk@CaliforniaSprings.com; or visit http://Help4SmallBusiness.blogspot.com for more information.

CHAPTER
4

If You Discover
"It's Just Not for Me"

IN 1983, I CAME TO REALIZE that I didn't care for the life of a distributor. Distributors have no control over their destiny. The manufacturer decides what products to offer and which distributors to sell through, and the retailer decides how to display the product and how much to charge.

As an individual with a need to control my destiny, it just wasn't working for me. For another personality type, a wholesale business is perfect. I considered building the company for a few more years and hiring a bright manager to run it for me. Instead, I decided to sell the business to a partner.

The key to this decision is to take your ego out of the equation. Of course, your brother, neighbor, or some other smart aleck is going to hang a failure sign around your neck. The fact that they haven't the slightest idea what is in your heart shouldn't change your mind one bit. A business may be the most successful one ever created, but if it isn't giving you personal satisfaction, why keep it?

What you do want to consider is whether you've truly determined that this business isn't what you want. I believe even the most contented company owner has days when she questions whether she can put up with all the nonsense for even another hour. The fact that an individual goes through a period of time when she isn't happy with her job doesn't necessarily mean it's time for a change.

A decision to exit a business that is still viable should be taken as deliberately as the original decision to enter the enterprise. Start from square one and evaluate yourself at this stage in your life. Move on to the next set of issues concerning what you really want and what you're willing to sacrifice to achieve. Factoring in the needs and wants of your family, ask yourself what the best decision is for you at this time.

After such a careful deliberation you may decide to keep on doing what you're doing. Case in point:

Years ago, my partner and I had seemingly hit or exceeded most of the goals we'd earlier established for the company. There was a chance that we could sell out for enough money to keep us well fed for the rest of our days.

We both went through a period of evaluation. I imagined that after six months to a year of goofing off, I'd want to pursue some kind of constructive activity. After extensive soul-searching, I determined that the most likely direction for me would be writing. I'd finally have the chance to indulge in my favorite pastime, full-time.

I thought about that for several more days and finally came to a conclusion. I really like to write. The twelve or so hours per week that I devote to writing is a great break from the constant interaction with family and employees that defines every other hour of my day. However, if putting pen to paper were to be my vocation, what had earlier been my avocation would become work. Worse, it would be drudgery. Why? I much prefer interaction with people to isolation with a machine. I love to be where there is a great deal of activity. Watching my fingers race across the keyboard isn't quite enough stimulation for me.

I also require variety in my daily activity. I'm never so happy as when I'm jumping from job to job throughout the day. Nor am I ever so bored as when I am forced to concentrate on a single effort for hours at a time.

It became obvious to me that if I were to retire, the only way I could be happy would be to own or manage another business. And since I totally enjoyed the associations in my current business, why change?

If you are seriously thinking of getting out, try this evaluation for yourself. If you still feel your best move is to leave your company, you should be able to do so without concern for the opinions of others. Section 5 provides you with a broad range of alternatives for the next step after you've made such a decision.

CHAPTER

5

Setting New Goals

ANOTHER IMPORTANT ASPECT OF THE CHANGE in your company from survival oriented to management oriented is the way in which you establish goals and monitor them. The following questions are designed to take you through a process of developing a new set of goals for your company:

1. What do you want the company to do for you in the next twenty years? Ten years? Five years? Twelve months? Are you primarily interested in the income stream that can be generated? Is wealth building, as opposed to income generation, your most important desire? Possibly you'd prefer a lighter work schedule, even if it means less income. Will you be happy if you aren't growing? Is it a high priority for you to broaden markets?

Once upon a time, not too many years ago, my partner and I were talking about our plan for the coming year. Before we got too far along in the conversation I mentioned that while we'd experienced 50 percent per year average growth for six straight years, it wouldn't bother me in the least if we had no growth at all in the next twelve months. I maintained that it would be a welcome breather and an opportunity to sharpen our skills in every area. I further predicted that we could expect substantial gains in profit through a planned year of no, or almost no, growth.

Just two years before we'd both opted for trying to triple our sales in five years. The lesson here is that goals should never be set with the idea that they exist in concrete. Circumstances change. Markets change. You'll change. Be prepared to rethink your long-term company (and personal) goals often.

2. What are your customers looking for from your company? Will they be satisfied to see you slow down? Are they more interested in your service level, your innovation, your prices, or your steadiness? If you change their perception of what your company is or does, will it leave the door open for another company to fill your niche?

An associate of mine was a photographer. He maintained a studio with a fairly prestigious address (and rent to match). For twenty years he'd offered a full range of services directed primarily at families. He became bored with doing weddings, family portraits, and the like, so he decided to try to develop a more commercially oriented clientele. He continued to do portraits, but stopped taking weddings.

Within three years of this decision, he was losing money and couldn't figure out why. He'd developed some commercial business, but his portrait business had totally dried up. In analyzing the situation with him, we determined that the portrait business was an outgrowth of the wedding trade. You have to have a photographer for your wedding. Therefore, unless you already know someone, you'll seek out a new supplier for this service. It's commonly your first encounter with a professional photographer as an adult.

If you're happy with the result, you'll likely return to this professional for your kids' pictures, your parents' twenty-fifth anniversary, a portrait of you and your wife for your parents, and so on. By altering his plan, it was as if his studio had become a new start-up business, not just a variation on the old theme.

As noted above, my partner and I might be willing to slow down. However, it's not uncommon for customer pressures to keep that from happening. Unless we just stop making presentations, it's likely that our existing customers will add items from us that they're not now carrying. Some of you may be saying: "Gee, I'd like to have some of that bad luck." Unfortunately, there are times when pressure for growth can indeed create substantial difficulties for a company.

3. What do your top managers expect from the company? Will a change in direction result in the loss of important employees? Worse yet, will such a change result in your management team losing enthusiasm while they stay on board and collect big paychecks?

Your employees can create even greater pressure on your direction than your customers. You may be excited about a new joint venture in a related field that you believe will add substantially to the power and financial strength of the company. No matter how you explain this to your employees, though, they may see this new move as a threat to their territory, an unwise use of corporate assets, or a breach of personal loyalty.

Another possibility is that you make the decision to rapidly increase the sales of the company. It's very likely that some of your staff who were very capable of handling their responsibilities when sales were at the $500,000 level may be quite over their head at $2 million. Some may be very comfortable in an office that has three or four employees, and feel quite lost and alone in one that has twelve.

4. Step outside the office environment for a moment. Let's talk about your home life. What have you been telling your wife, kids, and friends? Are you willing to explain your new direction to them? If you're thinking of shifting into high gear again, does this mean less time at home, and a similar upward shift in financial risk and strain? Are the rewards that you hope to gain worth the price that must be paid?

If you're thinking of slowing things down, will this affect the financial plans that others have been counting on? Will it mean the new house is out of the question? Will you now have time for the annual vacation, but no funds? Will it mean less help for your daughter's first year in college?

The last two paragraphs are not intended in any way to exert a moral pressure. The idea of this set of questions is to merely present the questions you may not be considering.

With these four sets of issues in mind, you should fully consider your long-term goals once again. In twenty years I would like to _____! It may take more prodding at this point in your career to get you to go through the evaluation process, since you'll have a fear of fiddling with success. This fear probably won't keep you from making adjustments in the company plans from year to year or month to month. But it will make it harder to think about possible fundamental changes in your *life*.

Take my advice: Go through the evaluation process. It's likely that you're already moving down the best road for you. However, your thoughtful trip into your deepest feelings *will* provide you with substantial extra enthusiasm, direction, and focus for your quest.

Managing Your Assets

CHAPTER

1

To Grow or Not to Grow

GEORGE HAS OWNED A SMALL MACHINE SHOP for about twenty years. He's very good at what he does. He delivers precision parts at good prices on time. He is so good that his customers are always pushing him to expand his capacity. You see, George has maintained his on-time delivery reputation by having the audacity (and the discipline) to turn down work he knows he can't deliver on time.

Five years ago George had eight employees. The business consisted of a bookkeeper, an estimator, a production supervisor, and five machine operators. George took home $90,000 a year and paid cash for each new machine. He owned the building free and clear. He had no bank debt.

The pressure for expansion mounted. Several of his most reliable customers indicated they might move all of their business elsewhere if George didn't give them more production time. What is a businessman to do?

You guessed it. He went for the pot of gold. In order to expand, he needed more space, more equipment, and more machine operators. With the additional people, he needed more supervisors. He then needed more clerical help to handle the paperwork. As he worked his way toward fifteen people, he felt he could no longer handle all the executive tasks in front of him and still do the selling. So he hired a salesman.

Five years later, he was making $90,000 a year, had $350,000 in bank debt, and was in the position of having to renegotiate the lease on the added space. His landlord wanted a 20 percent increase. To add insult to injury, his customers were still bugging him to expand.

His decision was to close the second facility, sell off the excess equipment to pay off the debt, and reduce his staff to the more controllable eight.

It is certainly possible that this situation could have turned out differently. He could have doubled his income. He might have taken the bait a second time and further increased his operation. Possibly the additional increase would have given him the additional income, wealth, and stability that would have made the extra headaches worth it. Maybe not.

Many small companies have opened second locations, expanded territories, added production capability, or torn out walls to increase their operations and have, in turn, been greatly rewarded for their effort. But my observation of small businesses leads me to believe that many successful owners who've tried to expand beyond ten employees have either failed at the larger size, or later downsized the company to a more manageable (and often more profitable) level.

Running a business with more than ten employees is really quite a different kettle of fish than running a firm employing fewer. There are skills required of the owner that aren't required at the smaller levels. Swings in the economy may take a heavier toll on the larger enterprise. Growth usually requires new capital. Unless the growth is deliberate enough that additional cash can always be internally generated, new capital has to come from outside sources. This will either reduce equity or result in interest expense.

One trap associated with increasing a company's size is that your attention will be further subdivided. For example, you may have been able to focus on the quality of the printing your print shop was producing when there were only five employees in one location. You may find you're no longer able to do so when you're jockeying back and forth between two locations. Your new focus may be to ensure that the managers aren't ripping you off when you are at the other location.

Each increase in volume generally brings with it an increase in leadership time required. This vacuum will have to be filled either by your giving additional time to your business or by hiring someone with the experience and expertise to fill the void. Such a person will come with a substantial income requirement.

Now that we have examined some of the negatives of expansion from a very small business to a medium-size small business, let's give equal time to the potential benefits.

One of the most important components of gross profit is the degree to which you're able to set your selling price. Your ability to set that price is largely a function of your control of the marketplace. At one extreme, you may have a patented product for which there is no substitute, and for which there is totally elastic demand (people will buy it at any cost). If that item costs you a dollar, you may be able to sell it for ten dollars, one hundred dollars, even one thousand dollars. At the other end of the spectrum, you may be selling wheat in Nebraska. In that case, it's unlikely that you'll be able to command one-tenth of one cent over the market price on the day you sell.

It's amazing how important control of the marketplace can be to a small company. Let's say there are five companies competing for your customers' business in your territory. If you open a second location, you'll go from representing 20 percent of the outlets in your area to 33 percent. If your aggressive action forces one competitor out of business, you'll have 40 percent of the locations. You'll clearly have a better chance of being the price leader (setting prices that will hold regardless of competitive action) with 40 percent than with 20.

The second advantage to expansion is in purchasing. Increased volume generally brings lowered costs from suppliers. The most sophisticated players use their leadership position to work for even lower prices.

Many suppliers are just as interested in market share as they are in customer base. As you square one vendor off against another, each may be willing to use an even sharper pencil to earn your business . . . just to create more awareness of their brand name in your market.

Price is not the only negotiable aspect of a purchase. Your additional market strength may allow you to demand terms, freight allowances, or merchandise set aside just for you in local warehousing to draw on as you need it.

The third opportunity afforded by growth is availability of lines. Certain products, franchises, and so forth, are considered to be premium. The suppliers of these items may wish only to deal with the largest operation in each area, or they may have a policy of servicing only a limited number of businesses. While you are still operating out of a four-hundred-square-foot ministorage unit, you may not be able to get their attention.

For many kinds of businesses there can be a substantial increase in income to the owner due to additions in volume. Although there are times when an increase in sales may actually result in a temporary decline in net profit, generally this will be more than offset as the company adds additional sales.

Many of the benefits of growth have nothing to do with money. Increased satisfaction may come from many directions. The challenge of learning new skills and dealing with new opportunities offered by a larger firm may be very appealing to some entrepreneurs. The appearance of success created by a large location, staff, or fleet of trucks is very appealing to others.

While this year's profit may not double from a doubling of sales, there will almost certainly be an increase in wealth. Since we'll be discussing the subject of wealth over the next several chapters, let's take a moment to differentiate between income and wealth.

Income is that amount you take home every week, month, or year. You generally use this money for current obligations, normal living expenses, and savings and investment. Unless you're a very unusual individual, you are probably using all of your "income" as you earn it. The average American puts less than 5 percent of his paycheck into investment.

Wealth is the ability of your net worth to earn income without any additional input from you. If you have a house that is increasing in value due to inflation, it is creating income just by virtue of the fact you own the house. This would also be true of stocks, bonds, savings certificates, rental property, and the like.

It's possible for a small business to be a mediocre income producer, but a fantastic wealth builder. This is because someone else is willing to pay you for your business based on a combination of asset value and the income stream your business produces.

Therefore, if you increase the size of your business, you may not take home much more current income. However, a purchaser will decide how much your business is worth based on various aspects that are generally related to size. Therefore, your growth may result in big increases in your "wealth."

CHAPTER

2

Buying Growth

THIS CHAPTER MAY SOMETIMES SEEM TO CONFLICT with a later chapter on how to sell your business. You see, in this chapter we'll provide suggestions on how to buy a business for nothing or next to nothing. Later, you'll read that you can sell your own business for a very handsome amount.

Both buying low and selling high are possible because owners know less about the value of their business than any other item in their portfolio. The market price of a house is usually known within a range of 5 percent or so. Check the current listings and the recent sales, and you can get a good idea of how much your home is worth.

If you own stocks, bonds, rare coins, or a car, there are exchanges, experts, or blue books that will give you an accurate picture of their worth. Even less liquid items such as art, collectibles, or raw desert land are rarely sold very far below some established market price.

This is not the case with very small businesses. It's common for owners to sell for inventory value only. I've personally seen businesses sold merely to escape debt. You can often purchase certain rights in a business for future royalties only.

In the meantime, individuals seeking to purchase a very small business are walking around with suitcases full of money ready to pay so-called book price, or multiples of earnings plus asset value. We'll discuss all of these ideas later.

Larger businesses are more likely to sell for full value. The very small business is the ideal candidate to be available for a song. Interestingly, some in this category merely fold their tent thinking that there's not even enough value to offer the business for sale.

The first step in any effort to buy a business for as little as possible is to have a clear, concise idea of which variables are critical and which are not. For instance, if you want to purchase a flower shop, and among your most important criteria is a minimum annual sales volume of $350,000, you probably won't be able to put a tight geographic limitation on your desire.

On the other hand, if geography is the nonnegotiable aspect, you'll either need to be willing to evaluate many different kinds of enterprises that are in that area, or select a business that can be operated anywhere.

Assuming this is a situation where you simply wish to expand your current business, your first step might be to buy a company that will allow you to do more of what you currently do. If you own an Italian restaurant, you buy another.

Your second approach might be to purchase a related company. The new business should piggyback as much as possible onto your existing operation. It's very easy to misjudge what appears to be a closely related business. Recently, my company was able to purchase a company doing seven hundred thousand dollars in sales in return for the paid, active consulting of the former owner. We believed that the match between our companies was quite good, since the customers and sales reps were essentially the same.

What we failed to consider was that the suppliers and the management style were not at all synergistic. Our basic business involves manufacturing and importing small plastic items. The new business required contracting for manufacture of garments, purchase of yard goods, elastic, thread, and other items from

150 vendors with whom we'd never done any other business. It was a disaster.

Contrast this with the decision we made many years earlier to purchase the "Snoopy" bicycle accessory division of a large automotive wholesaler. In this case the items could be sold to existing accounts through existing sales channels, and there was a single source for the entire product line. The items were purchased out of Hong Kong and delivered as finished goods to our warehouse. Every aspect of the acquisition fit with our experience, operations, and market.

Did we have to pay a lot more for this opportunity? No! We paid only for inventory at cost plus 13 percent, and were given very long terms to pay it off.

To add a related business to your current one, you should network everywhere possible within your industry and/or community. Talk to customers, suppliers, competitors, associates, and sales reps for companies that don't currently supply you, but who might if you were to purchase the kind of business you're seeking.

Make cold calls on every company that you think might be a purchase candidate. Tell them that you're interested in acquiring a company that would make a good fit with your existing operation. Indicate that at this point you're merely taking a survey to see who'd be interested in an exploratory meeting on the subject.

Are you looking to enter an industry that will allow you to use excess capacity on your equipment, but isn't necessarily related to your current marketing? In this situation, you'd start the same way you would if this were your first business venture. Call the major associations and magazines in that industry. Try to get a catalog or listing of companies that do the kind of business that you hope to acquire, or who sell to that type of business.

Industry trade journals sometimes have classified ads offering businesses for sale. These ads are more likely to produce a seller who doesn't know what her company is worth than ads in your local paper.

Many acquisitions are designed to increase market share. If this is the case for you, it may take months or years of planning. Begin by picking your first and second choice of competitors to acquire. Ask anyone you can think of what they believe the chances are of those two companies being available for sale.

If the climate seems right, make the exploratory phone call. Don't be surprised to find that the first reaction is rather cold . . . especially if your two companies have been tough competitors. If you get the cold shoulder, but believe it was a knee-jerk reaction, indicate that your quarry should think about his position for a few days. If there's still no interest when you call him back, try the other prospects.

If you're unable to get a deal going with either one, step up the competitive pressure. Spend the next several months producing one major sale, promotion, advertising campaign, or other marketing tactic designed to increase your marketing share at the expense of your target. Don't use giveaway pricing or ad campaigns aimed at the other store. You want this to appear as a positive effort to increase sales, as opposed to a program to take away business from him.

After this major effort has gone on for three months, call again and see if there's any softening in the position of either target. If not, and you are serious about expansion into that territory, you may need to open up a location nearby instead of buying out the competition.

To achieve expansion you may be better off looking for a product line to add rather than a company to buy. Try these ideas:

- Restaurant—open an attached grocery offering ethnic foods of the same type on your menu. Or begin a separate catering operation.
- Wholesaler—offer computer equipment and software specifically designed for your dealers.
- Movie theater—offer movie classics on Saturday mornings.
- Men's clothing store—import exclusive line of colognes and after-shave.

- Bookstore—create a large special section for children's books and offer readings on Saturdays.
- Manufacturer—seek new inventions in your trade that use your manufacturing expertise.
- Importer—use trademarks and copyrighted items to create special lines out of generic lines (for example, if you sell yo-yos, consider selling NFL yo-yos).

No matter what business you're in, there are ways to expand your operation incrementally and inexpensively by doing a thorough job of research.

CHAPTER

3

Selling Your Business

MANY SITUATIONS ARISE THAT MAY CAUSE YOU to seriously consider selling out. Among these are the obvious ones such as age, ill health, a decision to move your family to a new area, burnout, family pressure, or just the desire to move on to something new.

When selling becomes a serious option, you need at least nine months to find a buyer and consummate the sale. For even better results, plan to take two years. Here are the steps you should follow to obtain the highest price for your enterprise.

1. Change the way you do your bookkeeping one to two years before the sale. There are many different ways to prepare your income and financial statements that are legal and ethical. When selling the business is not a consideration, your priorities are probably determined by taxes or banks. You're either trying to limit your profits to reduce tax exposure or maximize profits to prove creditworthiness.

While this statement in no way condones any such practice, many businesses are also stretching the bounds of legality to the limit, or are outright "cooking the books." When preparing your business for sale, use straightforward accounting approaches that show your company in its best light. Any good accountant can help you do this. There are some sales agents and accountants who specialize in "recasting" your statements to facilitate a sale.

2. In the same way that you'd prepare a house for sale, you'll want your premises to sparkle in every possible way. Someone who is willing to part with top dollar will want a physical plant that he can be proud of. Do a thorough housecleaning. Paint the exterior. Make certain the bathrooms are clean and neat. Inventories and records should be neatly stored and arranged.

3. If the location is important to the sale, and the lease is anywhere close to the end, renegotiate with your landlord. Pay special attention to the transferability of the lease. It's common for a buyer to pay more for a good lease than for any other asset of a business.

4. In a similar vein, renegotiate any other contracts that are critical to the future of the enterprise. Do you have licenses, franchise agreements, exclusive territories, or special pricing arrangements? Make certain that each of these is transferable, and you'll look as solid as the Rock of Gibraltar to the prospective buyer.

5. Don't tell your employees of your plan. In fact, you'll want to use all types of subterfuge to keep your plan from them. It should go without saying that your workers will get very nervous if they know you intend to sell. They may worry that they'll be eased out after the sale, or they may be anxious about working for someone new. This could result in wholesale defections. Since most potential purchasers are going to want to retain most of your staff, it's critical that the staff does not learn of your plans until the timing is right.

6. Prepare a business plan. The outline was presented in section 2. There are numerous books that can provide other formats for such a business plan. You may wish to produce one that is more elaborate than what has been offered here. On the other hand, for your size business, the prospect may prefer a simple outline.

7. Marketing your business is the most complicated step. When you sell a home, it's usually advantageous to use a broker.

I've been told that this is because the realtor is not personally caught up in the sale. He can appear unbiased and makes a better presentation because of it. This logic applies to using business brokers.

Unfortunately, it's not as easy to secure the services of a good, reputable business broker as it is a real estate agent. There are many "brokers" who make most of their money *preparing* businesses for sale. While they do make a fee when a business closes escrow, if they never consummate a sale, they *still* make a profit. So there's a large incentive to get you to sign up, regardless of whether they think they can actually do something for you.

These "brokers" will help you through all the steps above. They'll prepare a great-looking set of documents, which could easily cost ten thousand dollars or more before the first ad is run. But, after charging you for all that fancy paperwork, there's no guarantee they'll be able to sell your business.

It's very likely that the thousands of dollars these companies will charge will result in a valuable set of selling aids, but not necessarily at a bargain price. Indeed, should you go this route, be certain to eliminate the steps above that would be redundant, such as the recasting of your financial statements. Ultimately, these types of brokers aren't very likely to sell your business.

There are other types of sales agents available. Their approach is more like that of a real estate broker, in that their primary effort goes into the search for potential purchasers. Both types of agents usually claim to have a ready list of potential buyers for companies such as yours. While it's true that many individuals who wish to purchase a business call these very same agents, there's only a slim chance that there will be an immediate match.

Whichever approach you use, attempt to find a business broker by networking with business acquaintances. Then check the broker's references thoroughly. Make certain that if you pay any advance fees or sign an exclusive contract, you are very clear on what you're contracting for.

8. Whether or not you use an agent, the next step in the process is to draw up a list of places to go looking for buyers. After creating a general list, you'd then try to flesh it out with real names.

A. The most likely place to find a candidate is right under your nose. One or more of your employees might be very excited about the prospect of taking over your firm. If they have the necessary cash or can borrow it, such a deal could be very uncomplicated. (You'll want to exercise caution here, though, since a discussion of this subject with employees may create the morale problem raised earlier.)

If they're not in position to come up with cash, you may want to look at a structured buy-out that might take five years or even longer. Here is another one of those areas where you'll want the help of an attorney to draft an agreement that protects your asset. Golden nugget: *Make certain that you're prepared to recover control in case the new team seems to be placing the operation in danger.*

Many employee buy-out agreements give the owner a totally inactive role from day one. The owner is happy to receive his monthly check, and hopes that all will go well. However, surveys indicate that the purchased business has the same failure rate as a start-up. Thus, a totally inactive role may put you in danger of seeing your payments stop far short of a full payoff. Your insurance against this is to maintain a position such as chairman of the board, make frequent visits to the office, and carefully review the monthly financial statements.

On the one hand, you'll want to let go so that the new management team can spread its wings. On the other hand, you'd be foolish not to stay close enough to the nest to rescue your fledglings, should they find themselves in grave danger.

Another alternative to the employee buy-out idea is an ESOP (employee stock ownership plan). In this arrangement, all of your employees buy you out, and they all end up owning stock in the new enterprise. You can either sell all of your interest or just part.

To raise the funds, the employees head down to a bank that is interested in funding ESOPs. The bank lends your staff the money based on the appraised value of the company and its ability to repay. To make this idea even more appealing, the government has established certain tax advantages to the seller and the bank.

There is great flexibility in an ESOP. You can continue to run the business or not. You can sell as much or as little of your ownership as you like. (However, the tax advantage to you doesn't click in unless you sell at least 30 percent.)

To be sure, there are also plenty of restrictions, red tape, and expense involved in the establishment of an ESOP. After all, it *is* a government program.

B. If one or more of your current employees is not a likely candidate for a buy-out, consider hiring your buyer. Begin an intensive search for an energetic, capable manager who could work toward ownership as part of his employment package. In this case, you could offer less pay than the individual might otherwise earn, but provide a certain percentage of ownership each year employed.

Another approach would be to find that talented individual who also has financial resources. The agreement might end up looking like a rent-to-buy. The manager would work her way toward running the entire operation over a two- or three-year period. When both parties were satisfied that the change in ownership and control could be smoothly transacted, the preset terms would be finalized.

In a variation of this idea, you could hire a partner. The future sole owner would initially purchase some amount up to, but not exceeding, 50 percent. When certain preconditions were satisfied the partner would have an option to purchase the balance.

C. Offer your business to a competitor or another company that could use your business as a line extension. This would be somewhat the reverse of the ideas discussed in the previous chapter. Of course, as mentioned there, you will be seeking top dollar for your operation.

It's significantly better that someone in the industry come looking for you, than that you let it be known you are available for purchase. You may be able to accomplish this by taking a very high profile. Hire a local public relations agency to prepare volumes of press releases about your company. Subtly include the type of financial information that might whet a purchaser's whistle. Start your own rumor among sales reps, trade magazines, and the known rumor mill about how successful your operation is. It may not normally be part of your personality to brag, but this is the time to do it.

If all this intrigue results in no progress toward a sale, and if you still believe your best chance of exacting a good price rests in finding an industry suitor, go to a broker. This situation, where you're specifically targeting another player in the industry, is where a broker can do you a great deal of good.

The broker can make confidential inquiries on your behalf. He'll usually begin by calling possible buyers and asking them in a very general way whether they have interest in an acquisition. Depending on their interest level, the agent will increasingly expose information about what and who. However, these discussions will be held only at the highest levels, and with confidentiality agreements signed by all who are "in the know."

If the situation gets serious enough to warrant a visit to your facilities, this too will be prepared in such a way that your employees will have no idea the people taking the tour are potentially their future bosses.

Having an advocate in this situation will generally result in a larger purchase price. The buyer will perceive the broker to be an expert in valuation, and he will provide them with backup to prove the worth of the deal to the buyer.

D. If you're unable to strike a deal using any of the above methods, you'll next want to compare the value of your business in an open market situation to its liquidation value. Only the rare very small business will have a large liquidation value. There is also the possibility of partial liquidation and partial sale.

Liquidation means selling off all the assets and paying all the liabilities. The net result is yours to take home (minus any taxes Uncle Sam may extract).

If you own a machine shop, you may do better in liquidation. Depending on the value of your equipment in the used market, you may be able to net more from selling it than you can from selling the going concern.

At the other extreme, a well-located trophy shop may have very little liquidation value, but the value of the ongoing business may be much higher than you think.

E. When all the above have been exhausted, and you clearly need to sell, find a broker through your lawyer, CPA, banker, or other trusted business acquaintance, and pursue the general population.

9. Concurrent with step eight, you'll want to arrive at a valuation for your business. What is your asking price? What are you willing to accept? What kind of terms are optimum from the standpoint of security and tax?

Your company is worth some combination of its asset value and its earning power. The following numbers will provide you with a good idea of what you should be able to ask.

BOOK VALUE

Each month or quarter you should be determining the company book value. This is the net worth figure on your financial statement. It's the difference between your total assets and total liabilities using all the rules of accounting and taxation. As you'll see, this has very little to do with the actual worth of your company.

LIQUIDATION VALUE

You would only rarely want to sell a successful business for less than liquidation value. You might do so to provide continued employment for loyal staffers, or some types of deals might include your continued employment or the receipt of certain royalties unrelated to the sale price. You arrive at the liquidation value by adjusting each asset to take into consideration its real value, as opposed to its book value. Next, you adjust liabilities to account for any amounts that aren't going to be realized. Finally, there's a cost of liquidation. Let's look at all three for some examples:

Assets

1. Inventory: You have product on your shelf that you could never sell for the amount it's currently valued on your books. Some should be discounted to zero. Some might be sold at half of cost. Therefore, the real value is less than the book value.

On the other hand, in a planned liquidation, you should be able to move the currently valuable items at something close to normal selling prices, minus selling costs. These items, then, may have a value greater than or equal to book. (Remember, however, that the minute your customers know you're going out of business, the value of even the best items on your shelf may decrease rapidly.)

2. Receivables: Call a factor (a company that buys receivables) and tell them you're thinking of liquidating. Have them give you the amount they'd be willing to pay for your outstanding receivables. Whether or not you decide to use the factor (the discount from face value of these invoices may be 7 percent or more, and they may not give you anything for items over sixty days), you'll have a good idea of the value of this asset.

3. Hard assets: To ascertain value of machinery and equipment, call an auctioneer. As in the above case, this professional will make you an offer for everything that isn't tied down. You may want to get more than one opinion. With this information, you'll know the least that your hard assets are worth. You may decide you're better off selling them yourself.

In determining liquidation value, its also a good idea to call in used equipment sales companies. You'll want one that specializes in each type of merchandise you have on your books.

It's in the area of hard assets that you're likely to make the best showing against book value. Many pieces of equipment, furniture, or vehicles may have been written off completely. Yet they do have a market value.

4. Intangibles: These are the hardest assets to determine the liquidation value of. Patents, trademarks, copyrights, and various contractual rights are more properly valued as part of the overall income stream. A minimum figure can be arrived at by dividing the cost of acquisition by the remaining life of the asset. In other words, if you spent seventeen thousand dollars to acquire a patent, and a patent runs for seventeen years, you'd value the patent at one thousand dollars for each year it still has to run. An argument could be made that the value should be higher than this, but you'd probably have to show that there was an interested buyer. The value may be much lower or worthless if the product of that patent is not currently on the market or is doing poorly.

5. Owned or leased real property: If you're selling property you own as part of the package, you can easily determine a value by having several appraisals done. If your liquidation decision hinges on this information you should also make sure to subtract the selling cost.

The liquidation value of a lease would be the difference between the market rent for your facility versus the actual rent you're paying for the remaining life of the lease, discounted to present value. You may be able to get a fast figure by contacting your landlord and asking what he'd pay to buy you out of the lease. If you're paying market rates for the lease, it probably has very little, if any, value.

Clearly, this is another area where you may pick up substantial increases in your net worth. You don't carry any type of value for a lease on your books. So, to the extent that there is a value in the lease, it's value that was not on your balance sheet. Similarly, if you own the property, you won't have previously realized the appreciation. (Neither the Internal Revenue Service, nor accepted accounting standards, allow a company to periodically appraise such items as real estate, which might have increased in value, in order to include any gain in the earnings of the company.)

6. You may have many other types of assets on your balance sheet, such as loans, deposits, contracts, and others. Using the basic principles described above, you should be able to come up with a valuation for each.

Liabilities

1. Payables: There are usually three possibilities for reducing the amount the company owes in accounts payable or notes payable. First, there may be items on your books that you still show as owing but are actually not (because creditors' invoices fail to record credits, charge backs, and discounts—or because you failed to record them yourself).

Second, you may be eligible for anticipation discounts that you wouldn't normally take. Possibly you have six months dating with 2 percent per month anticipation. If you were going to continue to run the business, you might not pay that item until the last due date. In liquidation, however, you use the cash to pay it immediately.

The third area for exploration is negotiated settlements. Do you have items in your inventory that you'd have to throw away or sell for less than cost? Do you currently owe that vendor money? Call him and see if you can return this inventory to reduce your bill.

You may also be able to settle disputes at this time. Tell the vendor that you're considering liquidation or selling, and you'd like to discuss the three-hundred-dollar credit you believe they should have allowed you. Offer a quick payment of all other cash owed if the supplier agrees to the credit.

2. Customer deposits: If you're holding large amounts of money for one or more customers as a result of advance payments or deposits, you may want to call them and suggest they use these up. Tell them this liability may be sold to the new owner. Explain that it would make more sense for them to take inventory now than hope to get a check later from the new owners.

Costs of Liquidation

If you were truly going to liquidate, you'd very likely see another 10 percent or more of your net worth taken up by other costs. You'll still be paying rent, salaries, and other overhead items until everything is disposed of. You may need to pay for truck rentals and equipment rentals to dismantle and ship some of the items. There will undoubtedly be some accounting costs.

All that is in addition to the expense of selling your receivables, auctioning your hard assets, or selling off your intangibles.

ASSET VALUE

For most companies the asset value should represent the lowest amount below which the owner might just as well liquidate. There are only two differences between asset value and liquidation value. In calculating asset value you don't have the costs of liquidation and you can be more generous in appraising certain assets than you might be if you had to liquidate.

INDUSTRY STANDARD VALUE

It's common in many industries to have a valuation method. Travel agencies are generally valued at ten times annual commission. Manufacturers' reps, on the other hand, are generally worth only one year's commission. Magazines use a certain number of dollars per subscriber. Manufacturers might expect to get between two and ten times annual earnings.

In some industries it would be very hard to get more than this standard valuation because everyone has used the rule for so long. This would be especially true if there are always several similar companies on the market at any given time.

On the other hand, some of these approaches are almost useless in assessing value. For most very small businesses, the real value is whatever the market will bear. The use of any type of industry standard, however, may help the seller convince the buyer that the offering is reasonable.

ENTERPRISE VALUE

The most logical and reasonable approach for both seller and buyer is to determine the enterprise value. Other than the esoteric aspects of ownership such as control, ego, and the like, the real value of the company to its owner is how much revenue and how much wealth it will produce. (And the seller can point out to the buyer that there would be certain costs to him if he were to attempt to build this enterprise from scratch. The buyer wouldn't want to pay much over what he could do it for himself.)

Revenue and wealth must always be weighed against risk. The seller must realize enough cash from the sale to produce the same amount of revenue adjusted for risk. (For example, a gift shop owner may be receiving $100,000 per year from her business, but admittedly incurring a certain amount of risk as well—a certain amount of sleepless nights. If she were receiving $75,000 a year from certificates of deposit or T-bills after the sale, the $25,000 difference would represent the amount the owner would be paying for the lower risk—the deeper sleep—associated with both the income and the principal in the CDs versus the gift shop.)

How does one arrive at enterprise value? A common method is to use five years of income plus ending liquidation value, discounted to present value. The next several pages will seek to explain that relatively complicated definition and describe the method for determining the dollar amount of enterprise value.

Begin by taking at least five years of previous income statements. If possible, recast these in the way the expenses would look if the company were (a) managed by an employee, rather than at the wage you pay yourself, and (b) fully capitalized. (There would be no interest expense.) You may also want to review some of the privilege-of-ownership expenses. For instance, would a totally profit-oriented company take the same trips, stay at the same hotels, and eat at the same restaurants? After these elements have been adjusted, there must also be an adjustment in taxation to account for the greater earnings.

Using this historic information, project the likely after-tax earnings for the next five years. Next, you'll want to calculate the liquidation value at the end of five years. This is the minimum amount that the new owner could realize from the sale of the business after taking the projected income for five years. You might use the current liquidation value. If you believe you can prove that the liquidation value would be higher at the end of the five-year period, back up such an assertion with solid arguments. You may find it easier to use the current liquidation value.

Determine the interest rate you'd need to offer someone to lend you enough money to run your enterprise at maximum efficiency, plus pay you back your initial investment and all loans you've made to the business. You can be relatively certain that it will be more than a few points above the best rate currently available for AAA bonds. Depending on how solid the buyer believes your enterprise is, you may end up with an interest rate between three and ten points over prime.

Whatever number you determine to be reasonable, you'll use this rate to discount each year's earnings and the liquidation amount to present value. This discounting is necessary because a buyer is not going to pay you, say, $100,000 today in the hopes of getting that $100,000 at the end of the year. (He could just stick that money in the bank and make more money.) He'll be willing to pay only whatever amount that, invested for that period, would give him the $100,000 later.

A graphic representation might look like this. We'll use 20 percent as the risk based return on investment. (The amount one could earn by investing in a high-yield growth stock, for example.) For instance, in the first year you project your business will earn $80,000. If I were to lend out $66,667 at 20 percent interest, it would yield $80,000 at the end of the year. I would have to loan $65,972 for two years to get $95,000 back at maturity, and so on.

The table below shows what the seller would have to pay, the "discounted" value, as an equivalent (with 20 percent interest figured in) to the projected earnings, including $241,127, which (with 20 percent interest figured in) equals the amount the company's assets would bring, "liquidation value," after five years. The yearly discounted earnings added to the discounted liquidation value equals the enterprise value of $556,862.

Year	Projected Earnings	Discounted
1	$ 80,000	$ 66,667
2	95,000	65,972
3	115,000	66,551
4	125,000	60,282
5	140,000	56,263
Liquidation	$600,000	$ 241,127
Enterprise Value		$556,862

In setting the price for your business, use any one of the above approaches, use them in combination, or use all of them. You may want to show the enterprise value method to a buyer who's already in the industry and will be using your company to expand, since she'll be able to realize the full enterprise value almost immediately and with a higher degree of certainty. You might find that the industry standard theory is the only one you can use for a savvy outside investor, since she'll recognize that there are plenty of opportunities to be had using that standard, and since she won't be limited to looking only within a specific industry.

CHAPTER
4

Selling Part of Your Business

THE NET WORTH OF MOST SMALL BUSINESS OWNERS is usually divided between the equity in their home and the net worth of their company. After selling a valuable business, it's usually best to assemble a diversified portfolio. Consider investing in an assortment of blue-chip stocks, tax-free municipal bonds, and treasury bills. These assets plus your house should provide excellent security into old age, and for your children as well.

But what is security if you no longer have any purpose in life? Common to most entrepreneurs is a love of what they do. Below, we'll explore a few options that will allow you to have it both ways.

You *could* sell just a portion of your business to raise cash for other investments. You'll want to make certain in so doing that you maintain control. As I heard stated recently, "One of the best parts of being your own boss is that you can't fire you." I've also heard many horror stories of owners who sold a controlling interest to supposedly benevolent investors, only to have these friends (or even family) kick them out of their own company.

Here are various ways to sell a portion of your business:

1. Private stock offering. This is generally the cleanest, easiest approach to raising cash without giving up control. Within certain limitations you can offer shares in your company to sophisticated investors or those who could be expected to know about your business. These could be close friends, vendors, customers, or employees. Or, being careful to follow the legal complexities, you could offer stock to sophisticated members of the public.

One word of caution. Limit this sale to the least number of people possible. If you want to raise $250,000, try to do so with five individuals putting up $50,000 each. You could have twenty-five at $10,000 each, but then you have the potential of twenty-five phone calls per month from partners "wondering how things are going."

2. Taking on one or more partners. Whether this is done as a formal partnership or as a stock offering, the difference is that you'll have active participation. This approach offers the advantage of reducing your personal commitment of time and energy. It brings with it the disadvantage of more mouths to feed. Working partners expect to get paid. Inactive stockholders may expect dividends, but can be made to see that retained earnings may be better than cash dividends. Another potential negative is that a partner represents one more person to get along with.

3. Going public. It's not common for companies with fewer than ten employees to go public. That doesn't mean it's impossible. There are two methods that can work for you.

The penny stock market can provide you with a vehicle for a public offering. The cost is high, but the reward can be great. Beware of the many shady individuals who inhabit this arena. Check with a broker/underwriter for more information.

The second approach is to purchase the shell of a public company, and merge your company into it. There are always plenty of companies that have ceased any active enterprise, but are maintained as corporate entities for just such a purpose. There are many major potential pitfalls to this approach, so you'd be well advised to use a lawyer with plenty of depth in this area. Find one who can provide you with a long list of personal recommendations.

4. Creating an ESOP. An ESOP can be used to sell your entire company. However, most folks use the ESOP as a method for selling just a part. You sell 30 percent of your company to your employees. You and they get a big tax benefit. They work harder because they own a piece of the pie. Everybody is a winner.

There are stories of owners who haven't had great experiences with ESOPs. In general, though, this approach is an attractive one for those wishing to get some cash out of their business.

5. Selling off a part of your business. Do you have three stores? Sell one! Is there an ethnic grocery store attached to your restaurant? Sell one or the other.

Conclusion

When I wrote these final words in 1993, everyone was complaining about the recession. People were being laid off, businesses were closing. The ozone layer was disappearing. Maybe that children's fairy tale was right after all. Maybe the sky was falling.

Then again, maybe it wasn't. It certainly wasn't for AC International. Our 1991 sales were 16 percent ahead of 1990's for continuing operations. We recorded a record profit. January of 1992 was running 44 percent better than January of 1991. Our plant was running twenty-four hours per day, seven days per week, and we still couldn't fill the demand. We refused to join the recession.

Did we know something that others didn't? I don't think so. Were we luckier than most businesses? Not at all. Is there a magic bullet that I can pass along? Not one, but several.

1. Always act as if your business is one month away from going under. Never rest on past success. Constantly scramble, scramble, scramble to retain current business and to find new sales.

2. Don't pay attention to the doomsayers. Recessions are a part of life. They'll always be with us. Prepare for them, but also prepare for the inevitable growth period that follows.

3. Do whatever is necessary to get rid of the following emotions: worry, discouragement, bitterness, and despair. Find ways to develop courage, confidence, hope, and a calm spirit.

4. Learn from others who've blazed these trails before. There is very little new under the sun. Read, listen to tapes, attend seminars, find a mentor or adviser. The more knowledge you have, the more choices you'll have.

5. Keep this book on top of your desk throughout your business career. You can't possibly absorb all of the information contained herein from just one reading. Use the information that is offered on each subject as a starting point to learn as much as you can about the situations you face.

It's my sincere hope that you'll find as much satisfaction from your career in business as I've found in mine. It's yours for the taking. Good luck and God bless.

Appendix: Additional Reading

SECTION ONE

Think and Grow Rich by Napoleon Hill

Think and Grow Rich is the basic textbook for salesmanship, for motivation, and for personal achievement. *Must read.* (Ralston, 1953.)

The Power of Positive Thinking by the Reverend Norman Vincent Peale

No one before or since has done a better job of laying out the techniques for driving negativism out of our lives and learning how to find the positive in everything. (Prentice-Hall, 1952.)

How I Raised Myself from Failure to Success in Selling by Frank Bettger

No other writer I've found deals more fundamentally than does author Frank Bettger with the subject of filling other people's needs. *Must read.* (Prentice-Hall, 1949.)

The Greatest Salesman in the World by Og Mandino

The basic tenets of professional selling in a succinct, memorable style. (F. Fell, 1968.)

What They Don't Teach You at the Harvard Business School by Mark McCormack

Street smarts to those of us in the business arena, rather than the highfalutin ideas being handed down by academia. (Bantam, 1984.)

Positioning by **Al Ries and Jack Trout**
> The definitive work on marketing for the late twentieth century. *Must read.* (McGraw-Hill, 1981.)

Magazines recommended for your monthly reading are: *Fortune, Inc.,* and *Boardroom Reports.* In addition to these general business publications, you'll want to try to get a subscription to trade journals that are published for the industry you think you may wish to enter. These will give you important insights into suppliers, business methods, the key players, and, most important, industry trends. Check with your librarian or search online.

SECTION TWO

How to Start, Run, and Stay in Business by **Gregory F. Kishel and Patricia Gunter Kishel**
> In chapter 12 Gregory F. Kishel and Patricia Gunter Kishel provide a good overview of business insurance. Chapter 13 offers a checklist to consider if you prefer to go the franchise route. Chapter 14 has lists and lists of places you can go for even more information. (John Wiley and Sons, 1981.)

Tough Times Never Last, but Tough People Do by **Robert Schuller**
> Robert Schuller has written a number of books, but this one is particularly effective at providing the reader with motivation regardless of circumstance. (Thomas Nelson, 1983.)

How to Stop Worrying and Start Living by **Dale Carnegie**
> This classic book should be read by anyone who has ever taken a Tums, chewed his nails, or had problems sleeping because of situations he faced that turned out to be far less of a problem than expected. (Simon & Schuster, 1948.)

The Small Business Administration maintains a program that could be of great help if you run into big problems in the very early going. ACE/SCORE is an organization of retired business-people who will come and give you advice on how to handle certain situations. This service is entirely free.

SECTION THREE

In Search of Excellence by **Thomas J. Peters and Robert H. Waterman**
Certainly this was the most important business book of the eighties. (Harper and Row, 1982.)

Marketing Warfare by **Al Ries and Jack Trout**
As suggested by the title, *Marketing Warfare* looks at the issues of sales, distribution, advertising, promotion, product development, and packaging through the eyes of a military man preparing for battle. (McGraw-Hill, 1986.)

Megatrends 2000 by **John Naisbitt**
Offers an approach to studying and predicting major shifts in society's thinking, habits, and preferences. (William Morrow, 1990.)

Age Wave by **Ken Dychtwald**
This book focuses on the graying of America and the amazing impact the population shift would have on our economy, social structure, and politics. (St. Martin's Press, 1989.)

See You at the Top by **Zig Ziglar**
Buy the book and the tape. You won't mind listening to this southern cracker over and over again. If he hadn't been so successful at selling, motivating, writing, and speaking, he could have easily had a career in comedy. (Pelican Publishing Company, 2000.)

Secrets of Closing the Sale by **Zig Ziglar**
If you liked *See You at the Top,* just keep reading. (Fleming H. Revell Company, 2003.)

How to Sell Anything to Anybody by Joe Girard

If you're in a business that depends on the sale of high-end merchandise such as automobiles, appliances, furniture, and the like, try to find a copy of this remarkable book. Girard's story also represents an excellent example of how unimportant your gifts are to success in business or selling. *Must read.* (Warner, 1977.)

You Can Negotiate Anything by Herb Cohen

In business, you'll find that almost everything is negotiable. Herb Cohen is a master of negotiation. He'll tell you where to sit, what time of day to plan the meeting, how to look for body language, and all kinds of techniques for getting the best deal. *Must read.* (Bantam, 1982)

How to Win Friends and Influence People by Dale Carnegie

Now in its umpteenth printing, *How to Win Friends and Influence People* has changed forever the lives of many who have read it. It is the foundation stone for almost every self-help and sales book written since. (Simon & Schuster, 1936.)

The Dale Carnegie Self-Improvement Course

One of the offshoots of the brilliant works of Dale Carnegie is a school that teaches the principles that he's written about. The most valuable of these is the basic self-improvement course. The focus of this program is teaching the individual how to get up in front of a group and deliver an interesting talk that will drive home its meaning.

Price Waterhouse Small Business Guides

Write to Small Business Services, 1801 K Street NW, Washington, DC 20006. Ask for a list of current titles.

Dun and Bradstreet's Challenges of Managing a Small Business

Call 1-800-367-7782 or write to Dun and Bradstreet Business Credit Services, 1 Diamond Hill Road, Murray Hill, NJ 07974.

For help in learning to export:

Write to the Office of the U.S. Trade Representative, Executive Office of the President, 600 17th Street NW, Washington, DC 20506. Or contact the Custom Services Public Information Division, 1501 Constitution Avenue, Washington, DC 20229.

SECTION FOUR

If you would like to get information about one or more business or professional associations that might apply to your business, you may be able to do so by contacting the American Society of Association Executives, 1101 Sixteenth Street NW, Washington, DC 20036.

Another approach would include a trip to your local library for one of the following:

Guerrilla Marketing by Jay Conrad Levinson (Houghton-Mifflin, 1984)

The Tipping Point by Malcolm Gladwell (Little, Brown, 2000)

1001 Ways to Motivate Yourself and Others by Sang Kim (Turtle Press, 1996)

National Trade and Professional Associations of the United States and Canada, Columbia Books

Encyclopedia of Associations, Gale Research Co.

SECTION FIVE

Wealth Without Risk by Charles J. Givens

I can't say enough about this intelligent, practical, easily understood guide to personal wealth. Mr. Givens walks his reader through every aspect of financial planning. He has excellent advice on subjects such as mortgages, insurance, taxation, wills, and investments. (Simon & Schuster, 1988)

Index

ABUS Security Locks, 329–30
accountability, 337–38
accounting, *see* bookkeeping, bookkeepers
accounts payable (A/P), 238–41, 325
  aging and, 187
  bookkeeping and, 222, 238–39
  business failure and, 211
  collection procedures and, 232–36
  creditworthiness and, 238–39
  and months two through six, 182–83, 187
  selling businesses and, 368–69
accounts receivable (A/R), 24–26, 325
  aging and, 186–87
  A/P and, 238–40
  balance and, 179–82
  bookkeeping concepts and, 222
  business failure and, 210
  collection procedures and, 227–38
  and months two through six, 179–83, 186–87
  selling businesses and, 367, 370
AC International, 95, 114, 124, 153, 377
  mission statement of, 90–91
  suppliers of, 99–100
advertising, advertising agencies, 26, 35, 55, 213, 232, 237, 361
  bookkeeping concepts and, 217–18, 221, 223–24
  budgeting and, 29–30
  business failure and, 206–7

business plans and, 87, 90–94, 107–16, 118–20, 125–26
business success and, 202–3
business types and, 39, 42–44
buying businesses and, 356–57
employees and, 244–46
fundamentals of, 282–84
grand openings and, 143–44, 162–65, 167
measuring effectiveness of, 284
media and, 282–83, 285–91
and months two through six, 178, 193
sales and, 255, 275, 281–91, 295, 299, 304, 306–7, 310, 312
advice, advisers, 17, 337–39
Amway, 258
appointment letters, 279–80
appreciation, managing and, 332–33
assets, asset value, 365–68, 370
audiences for advertisements, 282–84
authority, managing and, 330

banks, bankers, banking, 14, 202, 213, 321, 338
  A/P and, 240–41
  business failure and, 205–6
  collection procedures and, 229, 234, 236–37
  grand openings and, 143, 149–50, 155, 158
  growth and, 349–50
  legal requirements and, 130, 133–34, 139

banks, bankers, banking (*cont'd*)
  sales and, 289, 291
  selling businesses and, 359, 362,
    365, 372
base exchanges (BXs), 314–15, 317
bonds, 131, 137, 353–54, 372, 374
bonuses, 333–34
bookkeeping, bookkeepers, 10, 19, 21,
    24, 26, 49, 55, 237–39, 242–43,
    321–23, 337–38, 349
  A/P and, 222, 238–39
  budgeting and, 29–30, 213–15,
    217–20, 222–24, 227
  business failure and, 204, 206,
    208–11
  business plans and, 98, 105, 118,
    121, 222
  business success and, 200, 202–3
  business types and, 36–38, 42
  concepts of, 213–27
  first month and, 172–73
  grand openings and, 144, 147–48,
    155–56, 159, 162, 167
  legal requirements and, 132, 139
  managing and, 221, 322–23, 325, 334
  and months two through six, 184,
    186, 188
  sales and, 213–27, 308, 313
  selling businesses and, 359–60,
    365–66, 369
book value, 366–67
break-even analyses, 127–28
Brothers, Joyce, 50–51
budgeting, budgets, 26–31, 51, 246
  basic, 27–31
  bookkeeping and, 29–30, 213–15,
    217–20, 222–24, 227
  business plans and, 107, 109,
    115–17, 124–26
  for first six months, 29–30
  goal setting and, 70
  grand openings and, 143, 161
  and months two through six, 177,
    180, 182–83
  for opening the doors, 28–31
  sales and, 273, 300–302, 315

building trades, 40
business brokers, 361, 364–65
business plans, 143, 360
  advertising and, 87, 90–94, 107–16,
    118–20, 125–26
  bookkeeping and, 98, 105, 118, 121,
    222
  break-even analysis and, 127–28
  business purpose and, 84–91
  goal setting and, 78, 84, 91, 106,
    115
  incomes and, 104, 112, 116–26
  legal issues and, 98, 139
  locations and, 88, 91–99, 103–6,
    110–12, 114, 126
  mission statements in, 85–86, 90–91
  niches and, 85–91
  physical plant and, 105–7
  preparing of, 83–128
  suppliers and, 99–105, 110, 112–13,
    126

CaliforniaSprings.com, 305, 308
cash, 213–49, 321–22, 350, 352
  bookkeeping concepts and, 213–27
  business failure and, 204–5, 207,
    209–11
  collection procedures and, 227–38
  daily receipts and, 179
  employees and, 242–49, 251–53
  payables approaches and, 238–41
  selling businesses and, 362, 371
  see also loans
cash in advance (CIA), 149
cash on delivery (COD), 149
cash register tapes, 211
charge backs, 313–14, 369
checks, checking accounts, 211, 229
  balance and disbursements from,
    180–82
  bouncing of, 240–41
  grand openings and, 143, 155–56
  legal requirements and, 130, 135–36
  and months two through six,
    180–82, 189
closing, 268–74, 279, 287, 311

collection agencies, 237
collections, collection procedures,
    227–38, 334, 337
    and dealing with late payments,
    232–37
    determining creditworthiness and,
    228–31, 236
    invoices and, 227, 231–34, 236–37
    sales and, 227, 232, 313
commercial real estate brokers:
    locations and, 94, 96–97
    and months two through six, 193
compensation, 332–34, 337
    see also income, incomes; payrolls
competition, competitiveness, 14, 19,
    21, 38, 45, 206, 239, 243, 351
    bookkeeping concepts and, 219,
    221
    business plans and, 85–89, 94,
    99–100, 102, 104–5, 111
    buying businesses and, 356–57
    goal setting and, 60, 62, 82
    grand openings and, 145, 148, 150,
    154
    and months two through six, 188,
    191–92, 194, 196
    sales and, 266–67, 274, 276, 278,
    280, 283, 285, 288, 295
    selling businesses and, 364–65
complex businesses, profit analysis
    for, 124–26
computers, 21, 23, 26, 37, 177, 325
    business plans and, 101, 122
    collection procedures and, 227, 231
    goal setting and, 71, 81–82
    grand openings and, 143, 145, 147,
    155, 157, 159, 167
    sales and, 285–86, 291, 305, 308,
    310
    selecting businesses and, 33–35
concentration camps, 326–27
consignment, 152, 154
consumer shows, 113
contracts, 103
    grand openings and, 143, 156
    selling businesses and, 360–62, 368

corporations, 22–23, 228, 308
    C, 23, 135, 137–39
    legal requirements and, 132–39
    Sub S, 23, 135, 138–39
cost of goods, insurance, and freight
    (CIF), 152
cost of goods sold (or services
    rendered), 217, 221
    business plans and, 117–23, 126–27
credit applications, 228–31
credit cards, 225, 264, 304
    collection procedures and, 232, 236
    grand openings and, 158, 161
crises, dealing with, 188–96
customers, 25–26, 201, 251, 337, 375
    A/P and, 238–39
    bookkeeping concepts and, 216–17,
    219, 223–24, 227
    business failure and, 205–6, 210
    business plans and, 86–92, 94–95,
    99–100, 103, 108–16, 123, 126
    business types and, 36–40
    buying businesses and, 45, 47,
    355–56
    collection procedures and, 227–37
    creditworthiness of, 228–31, 236
    employees and, 243–44
    first month and, 172–74
    goal setting and, 79, 82, 344–45
    grand openings and, 143–54,
    157–59, 161–64, 166
    growth and, 349–52
    legal requirements and, 129–32
    managing and, 322–23, 328
    and months two through six,
    179–80, 186–91, 194
    partners and, 48–49
    proximity to, 94–95
    right stuff and, 13, 16, 18
    sales and, 257–78, 281–82, 284–88,
    290–300, 302–13, 315
    selling businesses and, 367, 369

daily cash receipts, 179
daily numbers, 176–83
dating and anticipation, 150–51

dentists, 9, 11, 24, 195–96, 291
desire, 200–201
direct mail advertising, 109, 112–13, 143, 285–87
disability, 195
discounts, discounting, 227
  A/P and, 238–39
  bookkeeping concepts and, 216–17, 220, 223–24
  business failure and, 206–7
  grand openings and, 145–48, 150–51, 153–54, 162, 164
  and months two through six, 178–79, 185, 189–90
  sales and, 265–66, 281, 310, 312–13, 317
  selling businesses and, 366–69, 372–73
doctors, 10–11, 19, 24, 39, 178, 237
  business failure and, 206, 209
  business plans and, 86, 88, 92–93
  grand openings and, 147, 160, 162–63, 165
  managing and, 322–23
  selling and, 258, 291
documents on presentation (DP), 150
dress rehearsals, 160–61

education, 10, 69, 79, 210
e-mail, 144, 191, 233
  advertising and, 110, 112
  sales and, 256, 287, 302, 304, 306, 308–11
empathy, managing and, 330
employee handbooks, 242, 251, 254
employee stock ownership plans (ESOPs), 363, 376
employment, employees, employers, 1–2, 207–13, 237, 321–22, 375
  A/P and, 239–41
  bookkeeping concepts and, 217, 220–21, 225
  business failure and, 207–12, 252
  business plans and, 93, 95–96, 100, 111, 117, 124, 126
  business types and, 36, 39–41
  buying businesses and, 45, 47
  conducting searches for, 242, 244–46
  evaluating need for, 242–43, 253
  first month and, 169–72
  goal setting and, 66, 68–69, 71, 78–79, 81–82, 345
  grand openings and, 143–44, 154, 156, 160, 163, 167
  growth and, 349–52
  hiring of, 35, 39, 171, 192–93, 210, 225, 242–48, 250, 252, 363
  keeping records on, 253–54
  legal issues and, 130, 132–33, 251
  management and, 242, 246–47, 249–51, 322, 325–30, 332–34
  and months two through six, 176–78, 186, 189–90, 192–93, 195
  partners and, 51–52
  part-time, 40–41, 54–56, 87, 208, 225
  payrolls and, 242–49, 251–53
  process for, 242–54
  retraining of, 169–70
  right stuff and, 13–17, 19
  sales and, 262, 276–78, 281, 284, 308–10, 313
  screening applicants for, 242, 246–48
  self-, 9–12, 20
  selling businesses and, 360, 362–66, 371
  termination of, 242, 250, 252–53
  training of, 35, 39, 169–70, 208–9, 242, 245, 248, 250–52
  work habits of, 16–17, 19
encyclopedia exercise, 66–67
enjoyment, 33–35, 336
enterprise value, 371–73
entertainment, see travel and entertainment
enthusiasm, 160
  goal setting and, 345–46
  sales and, 104, 256–60, 264, 279

equipment failure, 195–96
expenses, 13–14, 20–31, 38, 82, 201,
    322, 352–53
    bookkeeping concepts and, 214,
        216–18, 221–27
    budgeting and, 27–29
    business failure and, 204–5, 207–8,
        210, 252
    business plans and, 90, 98, 107,
        117–28
    definition of, 118
    employees and, 243, 245–46, 250,
        252–53
    fixed, 118–20, 127–28
    general and administrative, 124–27
    grand openings and, 144–46, 154,
        160–62, 165
    legal requirements and, 129, 133
    and months two through six,
        182–85, 192, 195
    sales and, 275, 277, 279–80, 287–88,
        294–95, 300–301, 305–6, 308,
        312–14, 318
    selling businesses and, 361, 369–70
    variable, 118–20, 127

families, 21, 26, 29, 41, 169, 179, 336,
    359, 374
    business failure and, 205, 211
    employees and, 244, 248–50
    and exiting from businesses, 340–41
    goal setting and, 60, 62, 66, 69–71,
        79–81, 344–46
    grand openings and, 165–66
    partnerships and, 50–53
    right stuff and, 13–17, 19
    sales and, 259, 263, 270
    selecting businesses and, 33, 35
    self-employment and, 10–11
    see also spouses
fear, grand openings and, 159
filing:
    grand openings and, 144, 156–57
    sales and, 309–10
financial statements, 229–30

first in, first out (FIFO), 184
fixtures, 23–24, 143, 193
    budgeting and, 29–30
    business failure and, 206–7
    business types and, 41–42
flooring, 152
franchises, 9, 208, 223, 352, 360
    business plans and, 89, 103
    general description of, 42–44
    part-time possibilities for, 55–56
freight terms, 152–53
frequency of advertisements, 283–84

General Services Administration
    (GSA), 314–15, 317
genie exercise, 65–67
goals, goal setting, 25, 169, 199, 250,
    341
    bookkeeping concepts and, 214–15,
        223
    business, 70–71, 78–81, 84
    business plans and, 78, 84, 91, 106,
        115
    establishing blueprint in, 78–81
    finalizing of, 77–82
    grand openings and, 148, 159–60,
        166–67
    managing and, 327, 334, 343, 345
    motivation and, 336–37
    new, 343–46
    personal, 67–70, 80–81, 84
    personal evaluation project for,
        58–67
    prioritizing, organizing, and
        internalizing of, 68–72
    sales and, 71, 78, 106, 214–15
    success and, 57–73
    three-track thinking and, 81–82
    trade shows and, 295, 297, 299
    writing down of, 67–68
government, 1, 23, 209, 363
    business plans and, 96, 108, 121
    business types and, 37, 39
    employees and, 249, 251
    grand openings and, 143, 156

government (*cont'd*)
  legal requirements and, 132, 134, 137–38
  sales and, 314–15, 317
grand openings, 142–68
  dress rehearsals and, 160–61
  first day and, 161–65
  last-minute attitude checks and, 158–60
  last-minute checklist for, 143–44
  operating procedures for, 144–58
  surviving first week and, 166–68
gross-profit margin method, 185–86
growth, growing, 349–58, 373
  buying businesses and, 354–58
  drawbacks of, 350–51
  goal setting and, 343, 345
  managing and, 322, 350–51
  potential benefits of, 351–52
guarantees:
  grand openings and, 144, 153–54
  sales and, 270, 274–75, 277

hard assets, 367, 370
hours of operation, 144–45
how I see myself exercise, 58–65, 67

income, incomes, 1, 33, 55, 144, 192, 199, 221, 321–22
  budgeting and, 27, 29
  business plans and, 104, 112, 116–26
  business types and, 38, 41, 44
  goal setting and, 69–70, 78–79, 343–45
  growth and, 349–51, 353
  legal requirements and, 129, 131–32, 137, 139
  managing and, 322, 330, 332–34
  projecting of, 116–26, 128
  right stuff and, 16–17
  sales and, 279–81
  self-employment and, 9–12
  selling businesses and, 359, 363, 367, 371–73
  terminology used and, 117–22

income statements (profit-and-loss statements):
  business plans and, 116–28
  and months two through six, 183
independent representatives:
  appointment letters and, 279–80
  hiring of, 276–77, 279–80
  sales and, 275–81
industry standard value, 370
intangibles, 367–68, 370
interest, interest rates, 30, 371–73
  bookkeeping concepts and, 218, 225–26
  business plans and, 125
  collection procedures and, 227
  growth and, 350
  legal requirements and, 138
  and months two through six, 190
  selling businesses and, 372–73
Internal Revenue Service (IRS), 135, 211, 368
international sales, 315–16
inventories, 24–26, 39, 46, 202, 222
  A/P and, 238
  budgeting and, 29–30
  business failure and, 205, 212
  business plans and, 86, 106, 121–22, 124
  buying businesses and, 354
  grand openings and, 143, 146, 162, 167
  managing and, 325
  and months two through six, 181, 183–86
  selling businesses and, 360, 366–67, 369
investing, investments, 15, 22, 353
  bookkeeping concepts and, 219
  budgeting and, 29–31
  business failure and, 205–6
  business plans and, 107, 116
  business success and, 199
  business types and, 38, 41, 43–44
  employees and, 242–43
  goal setting and, 69–70
  legal requirements and, 134–35, 138

and months two through six, 193
  partners and, 52
  sales and, 289
  selling businesses and, 372
  and selling part of businesses,
    374–75
invoicing, invoices, 241, 313, 334
  bookkeeping concepts and, 217, 222
  business failure and, 210–11
  collection procedures and, 227,
    231–34, 236–37
  grand openings and, 144–45,
    147–48, 151, 155, 157, 161,
    164–65
  and months two through six,
    179–80, 186
  selling businesses and, 367, 369

last in, first out (LIFO), 184
lawyers, 10–11, 19, 22–24, 39, 242
  advisers and, 338
  bookkeeping concepts and, 218
  business plans and, 92–93, 98
  collection procedures and, 237
  failure and, 208–9
  first month and, 172–73
  grand openings and, 147, 149,
    162–63, 165
  legal requirements and, 132, 139
  and months two through six, 188
  in partnerships, 50
  selling businesses and, 362, 365
leaders, leadership, 86, 250
  growth and, 351–52
  managing and, 326, 329–31
leases, see rent, rents, rentals
legal issues, legal requirements, 13,
  129–41, 359
  budgeting and, 29–30
  business licenses and, 139–40
  business plans and, 98, 139
  employees and, 130, 132–33, 251
  enterprise types and, 21–23, 129–39
  grand openings and, 143, 152, 157
  regulations and, 140–41
  sales and, 130–31, 136, 280

letters of credit (L/Cs), 149
liabilities, liquidation value and, 365,
  368–69
licenses, 23, 139–40, 143
limited partnerships, 22, 132, 134
liquidation, liquidation value, 365–73
listening, sales and, 267–68
loans, 202, 213
  bookkeeping concepts and, 220,
    225–26
  budgeting and, 29–31
  buying businesses and, 46–47
  legal requirements and, 133–34,
    136, 138
  and months two through six,
    181–82, 190
  right stuff and, 13–14
  selling businesses and, 363, 368, 372
locations, 143, 357, 360
  business failure and, 204, 206–7,
    209–10
  business plans and, 88, 91–99,
    103–6, 110–12, 114, 126
  business types and, 41–43
  growth and, 350–52
  legal requirements and, 139–41
  and months two through six,
    193–94
  parking and, 95–99
  and proximity to customers, 94–95
  sales and, 293, 296–97, 300–301,
    306–7
  traffic and, 92–94, 111
lottery exercise, 64–65, 67
luck, 336, 345, 377
  business failure and, 204, 209
  business success and, 200, 202, 209

magazine advertising, 109–11
mail order sales, 55, 317
managing, managers, management,
  17, 21, 29, 55, 136, 208, 213,
  321–40
  bookkeeping and, 221, 322–23, 325,
    334
  business plans and, 93, 104, 122

managing, managers, management
(*cont'd*)
  business types and, 37–39, 42–44
  buying businesses and, 46, 355
  communicating the vision to, 326–29
  compensation concepts for, 332–34
  components of, 323
  definition of, 325
  employees and, 242, 246–47,
    249–51, 322, 325–30, 332–34
  getting out of the way of, 331
  goals and, 327, 334, 343, 345
  grand openings and, 155, 163–64
  growth and, 322, 350–51
  hiring of, 326, 340
  leadership and, 326, 329–31
  of managers, 325–34
  and months two through six, 177,
    190
  motivation and, 332–39
  partners and, 48, 50, 329
  sales and, 255, 275–81, 325, 334
  selling businesses and, 362–63, 371
  setting example for, 328–29
  transition from reactive survival to,
    321–24, 343
manufacturers, manufacturing, 23,
  25–26, 55, 174, 209, 221, 252, 340
  business plans and, 85–88, 90, 93,
    95, 99–101, 107–9, 112–13, 117,
    122, 124–25
  buying businesses and, 355–56
  general description of, 36–37
  grand openings and, 147, 150, 158,
    162–63
  growth and, 358
  legal requirements and, 132, 135,
    140
  and months two through six, 178,
    195–96
  sales and, 275, 277–78, 281, 292–94,
    303, 306, 312
  valuation method of, 370
manufacturer's representatives, 140
  business plans and, 85–86
  general description of, 38–39

  grand openings and, 162
  sales and, 315
  valuation method of, 370
marketing, markets, 9, 18, 51, 194,
  219, 246, 325, 354
  business failure and, 206, 210
  business plans and, 88, 90, 111, 115
  business success and, 200–203
  business types and, 37, 40–42
  buying businesses and, 356–57
  goal setting and, 71, 343–44
  grand openings and, 148, 158
  growth and, 351–52
  mass, 55, 312–14
  sales and, 270, 276, 279, 302–4,
    308, 312–14, 316
  selling businesses and, 360–61, 365,
    368, 370
  on Web, 302–4, 308
  see also multilevel marketing
mass marketing, 55, 312–14
media, 282–83, 285–91
mission statements, 85–86, 90–91, 251
  grand openings and, 143
  managing and, 328
monthly statements, 183–88
motivation, motivations, 17–18, 210
  compensation and, 332–34, 337
  managing and, 332–39
  self-employment and, 9–12
  techniques for personal, 335–39
multilevel marketing, 55, 140
  general description of, 40–42

National Sales Headquarters, 286
needs, 326, 336, 341
  employees and, 242–43, 253
  establishing of, 263–64, 271–72
  openings and, 261–63, 271
  sales and, 260–64, 266–67, 271–72,
    274, 279, 300
negative emotions, 159–60, 163, 259
neighborhoods, 162, 206
  business plans and, 95, 102
  sales and, 290–91, 304
net terms, 150

net worth, 369, 374
    goal setting and, 79–80
newspapers, 111, 113, 130, 164
    buying businesses and, 356
    employees and, 244–45
    sales and, 313
niches, 206
    business plans and, 85–91
    goal setting and, 344

objections, sales and, 264–66, 268,
    270, 272–74
office equipment, office supplies, 23
    bookkeeping concepts and, 217–18
    budgeting and, 29–30
    business plans and, 118, 125
One Good Cop, 158–59
openings, sales and, 261–63, 271
optimism:
    bookkeeping concepts and, 214–15
    grand openings and, 159, 166
outdoor advertising, 111–12
overhead, see expenses

parking, 95–99, 210
partners, partnerships, 48–53, 188,
    211, 228, 252, 337
    comparisons between marriages
        and, 48–50
    and exiting from businesses, 340–41
    family members as, 50–53
    goal setting and, 70, 79, 343–44
    grand openings and, 156, 158
    legal requirements and, 132–36,
        138–39
    limited, 22, 132, 134
    managing and, 48, 50, 329
    right stuff and, 13, 17
    sales and, 256
    selling businesses and, 364
    and selling part of businesses, 375
partnership agreements, 22
patents:
    business plans and, 87, 90–91
    selling businesses and, 367–68
payrolls, 26, 30, 119, 213, 229, 234

bloated, 252–53
bookkeeping concepts and, 217,
    224–25
employees and, 242–49, 251–53
managing and, 325
and months two through six,
    180–82, 189–90
sales and, 277, 281
selling businesses and, 369
pensions, 133, 137–38
personal letters, 285–86
personal liability, 131–33, 135
physical plant, 105–7
piecework compensation, 333–34
plans, planning, 239, 292–93, 357
    bookkeeping concepts and, 214,
        222–23
    business failure and, 206
    business success and, 200, 203
    employees and, 246, 248–49
    goal setting and, 343–44, 346
    managing and, 323, 327
    motivation and, 335
    sales and, 278, 293, 295–302
    selling businesses and, 359–60, 367
    see also business plans
premiums, 114, 316
prices, pricing, 201, 340, 344, 354–55
    bookkeeping concepts and, 216,
        218–23
    business failure and, 204, 206–7
    business plans and, 84–87, 89,
        99–101, 105, 109, 117, 122
    buying businesses and, 355, 357
    grand openings and, 144–45, 147,
        151–53, 155, 165–67
    growth and, 349, 351–52
    and months two through six, 191
    sales and, 263–66, 272–73, 276,
        281, 287, 292, 299, 303, 309,
        312–13, 315
    selling businesses and, 359–61,
        364–67, 373
private stock offerings, 374–75
product liability insurance, 172–74,
    223

products, production, productivity,
  25, 34, 252, 337, 340, 355–58
  A/P and, 238, 240
  bookkeeping concepts and, 214,
    217–22, 227
  business failure and, 204–6, 211–12
  business plans and, 85–91, 94,
    99–106, 108–11, 113–27
  business success and, 201–2
  business types and, 37–38, 41–43
  buying businesses and, 45–46,
    355–57
  collection procedures and, 232,
    235–36
  first month and, 172–74
  goal setting and, 70–71
  grand openings and, 143, 145–55,
    160–61, 163–67
  growth and, 349–52, 357–58
  legal requirements and, 131–32
  managing and, 325–27, 329–30,
    333–34
  and months two through six, 178,
    181, 183–85, 188, 190–92, 196
  partners and, 48–50
  right stuff and, 18–19
  sales and, 257–58, 260–79, 281–84,
    286–87, 289–98, 302–7, 310–16,
    318
  selling businesses and, 366–68, 371
profit analyses, 123–26
  for complex businesses, 124–26
  for service businesses, 123
profit-and-loss statements, see income
    statements
profits, profitability, 15, 174, 209, 250,
    321, 326, 339, 377
  bookkeeping concepts and, 217–18,
    220–21, 224, 226
  business plans and, 89, 99–100,
    104–5, 118–28
  business success and, 201–2
  goal setting and, 71, 82, 343
  grand openings and, 144, 148, 159,
    163, 167
  gross, 118–27, 178, 185–86, 217,
    221, 351
  growth and, 350–52
  legal requirements and, 137–39
  and months two through six,
    177–78, 184–86, 188, 194
  net, 118–20, 125, 127, 218, 352
  sales and, 266, 294, 311–12
  selling businesses and, 359, 361,
    371
profit-sharing plans, 133, 137–38
promotions, 178, 203, 206, 357
  grand openings and, 142, 162, 165
  sales and, 256, 281–82, 291–93,
    295, 307, 310
public relations, 113–14
public stock offerings, 375
purchasing, 144–47

quality, 207, 222, 329, 351
  business plans and, 85–86, 100–101,
    116
  sales and, 265–66, 274, 276, 279,
    290

radio advertising, 113, 289
Radio Shack, 112
raises and bonuses, 333–34
references, 229–31, 247
regulations, 140–41, 153
rent, rents, rentals, 14, 24, 26, 49, 69,
    322, 350, 353
  bookkeeping concepts and, 217–18
  budgeting and, 28–30
  business failure and, 207–10
  business plans and, 92, 94–96,
    98–99, 101, 106–7, 117, 119–20,
    124, 126
  grand openings and, 155, 167
  and months two through six,
    192–96
  sales and, 255, 295, 300–302
  selling businesses and, 360, 363,
    368–69
respect, 330–31, 338

restaurants, restaurateurs, 140, 202,
206, 355, 357
business plans and, 92–95, 98, 107,
111, 122
grand openings and, 160, 163–65
and months two through six, 188,
195
sales and, 262, 289–90, 292, 300
retailers, retailing, 23–25, 37, 340
budgeting and, 27–31
business failure and, 206, 208–9,
212
business plans and, 85, 88, 90, 92,
98–99, 101, 106–9, 111, 122, 126
collection procedures and, 227, 232
first month and, 174
general description of, 39–40
grand openings and, 145, 147, 158,
160, 163
legal requirements and, 132, 140–41
and months two through six, 178,
190
part-time possibilities for, 55
sales and, 260, 267, 269, 277,
287–89, 291–92, 294, 303,
312–13, 317–18
selecting businesses and, 32, 34
retirement plans, 137–38, 292
returns, return policies:
grand openings and, 144, 154, 161
sales and, 274

salaries, see income, incomes; payrolls
savings, 54, 229, 353
budgeting and, 27–29
legal requirements and, 131–32
self-employment, 9–12, 20
self-evaluations, 58–67
selling, sales, salesmanship,
sales–people, 1, 11, 25–26, 55, 57,
174, 239, 253, 321, 337, 344–45,
350–77
advertising and, 255, 275, 281–91,
295, 299, 304, 306–7, 310, 312
analyses of, 187–88
attention-grabbing approaches for,
257–59
bookkeeping and, 213–27, 308, 313
building of, 255–318
of businesses, 199, 225–26, 340–41,
353–54, 359–73
business failure and, 205, 207–8,
210, 212
business plans and, 84–88, 90–91,
95, 98, 100–106, 108–10, 112–14,
116–28
business success and, 199–201, 203
business types and, 36–42
buying businesses and, 355–57
collections and, 227, 232, 313
drop-dead numbers for, 216
e-mail and, 256, 287, 302, 304, 306,
308–11
enthusiasm and, 104, 256–60, 264,
279
goal setting and, 71, 78, 106,
214–15
grand openings and, 143–53, 155,
159–62, 165–67
gross, 117–23, 127, 217
growth and, 350–52
independent representatives and,
275–81
legal issues and, 130–31, 136, 280
management and, 255, 275–81, 325,
334
and months two through six,
176–78, 180–90, 193–94
net, 217
of part of businesses, 374–76
personal, 255–74
pessimistic projections for, 215–16
principles of, 256–74
promotions and, 256, 281–82,
291–93, 295, 307, 310
realistic estimates for, 215
right stuff and, 16, 18–19
selecting businesses and, 32, 35
terms and conditions of, 144,
148–53

selling, sales, salesmanship (*cont'd*)
  territories and, 256, 278–80, 282,
    311–18
  trade shows and, 256, 275, 278,
    281–82, 293–302, 304, 310,
    315–17
  training of, 299
  in unrelated industries, 317–18
  Web and, 256, 287, 302–9
service, services, service businesses, 18,
  24, 26, 38–40, 46, 55, 178, 201,
  232, 337, 339, 352
  bookkeeping concepts and, 217,
    219–21, 224
  business failure and, 204, 206–9
  business plans and, 85–87, 89,
    92–93, 95, 97–101, 105, 107,
    109–11, 116–24, 126–27
  collection procedures and, 237
  employees and, 243–44
  general description of, 39–40
  goal setting and, 70, 78, 81–82, 344
  grand openings and, 143, 145, 147,
    149–50, 153, 158, 160, 163–65
  legal requirements and, 131, 140
  managing and, 325, 329
  profit analysis for, 123
  sales and, 257, 260, 262–63, 266–67,
    269, 272, 275, 278, 288, 290–93,
    296, 302–6, 309–10, 312, 315–16
  selecting businesses and, 34–35
sight drafts, 150
signage:
  legal requirements and, 141
  and months two through six, 193
  sales and, 300–301
small businesses:
  buying of, 32, 45–47, 142, 201, 208,
    354–58
  exiting from, 340–42
  failure of, 15, 45–46, 159, 200–201,
    204–12, 252, 362
  poor understanding of, 204, 210
  reasons for starting of, 9–12
  right stuff for running of, 13–19

  selecting of, 32–35, 70, 77–78, 81,
    139, 355
  sources of help for, 2
  statistics on, 1, 5
  success of, 15, 17, 79, 159, 199–205,
    209, 340, 346, 377
  types of, 21–23, 32–44, 77–78,
    129–39, 143
sole proprietorships, 22, 228
  legal requirements and, 129–33,
    135–36, 139
spirituality, 336
spouses, 11, 33, 161, 169, 211, 227
  employees and, 248, 250
  goal setting and, 60, 62, 64, 66–67,
    69–70, 72, 80, 344–45
  and months two through six, 193
  as partners, 50–53
  right stuff and, 13, 16–17
  sales and, 259, 274, 292
states, 211, 280, 315
  legal requirements and, 136–38
stocks, stockholders, 353–54, 372
  legal requirements and, 131–32,
    134–39
  selling businesses and, 363
  and selling part of businesses,
    374–76
suppliers, 14, 25, 213, 237–40, 344,
  352, 369, 375
  A/P and, 238–40
  bookkeeping concepts and, 220, 222
  business failure and, 205, 207, 211
  business plans and, 99–105, 110,
    112–13, 126
  buying businesses and, 355–56
  collection procedures and, 227–30
  first month and, 173–74
  grand openings and, 143, 146, 154,
    156–57, 161–63, 167
  legal requirements and, 129–30,
    132, 135
  managing and, 328, 330
  and months two through six, 180,
    186–87, 190–96

sales and, 292–93, 301, 303–4, 306, 308–9, 311, 313, 315, 317–18
supply/demand curve, 219

taxes, 13–15, 21, 23, 26–28, 39, 47, 98, 107, 143, 209, 211, 229, 277, 374, 376
  bookkeeping concepts and, 217–18, 227
  budgeting and, 27–28, 30
  business plans and, 121, 124–26
  legal requirements and, 129–40
  and months two through six, 180, 184
  selling businesses and, 359, 362, 365–66, 372
telephones, telephone bills, telephone calls, 49, 119, 229, 375
  A/P and, 239–41
  bookkeeping concepts and, 217–18
  budgeting and, 28–30
  business plans and, 86
  buying businesses and, 356–57
  collection procedures and, 232–35, 237
  employees and, 246
  grand openings and, 143–45, 161–62
  managing and, 329
  and months two through six, 189–91
  sales and, 261, 272, 277–78, 281, 284, 287–88, 290, 296, 299, 302, 308–11
television advertising, 113, 288–89
10th prox, 151–52
territories, 350, 357, 360
  sales and, 256, 278–80, 282, 311–18
theft, 222, 251
  business failure and, 204, 211–12
three-track thinking, 81–82, 176
time commitment, 204, 208
Trader Joe's, 88–89
trade shows, 113
  budgets for, 300–302
  opportunities offered by, 294–95
  planning for, 295–302

sales and, 256, 275, 278, 281–82, 293–302, 304, 310, 315–17
  well-learned lessons on, 293–94
traffic, 92–94, 111, 307
travel and entertainment, 28, 30
  and bookkeeping concepts, 218, 226–27
  and business plans, 107, 125
  and sales, 275, 277, 316
trial closes, 270–73

UPS, 152–53, 285
utilities, 49, 217
  budgeting and, 28–30
  business plans and, 106, 124–25
  sales and, 255, 301

valuations, 365–73
visibility of advertisements, 283
visualization, 71–72, 259

warranties, *see* guarantees
wealth, 78, 371
  growth and, 352–53
Web, Web sites, 23, 191
  business plans and, 86, 102, 104, 107, 109–10
  grand openings and, 144, 158
  marketing on, 302–4, 308
  sales and, 256, 287, 302–9
wholesalers, 23, 25, 55, 340, 356–57
  business plans and, 85, 88, 94–95, 99, 101, 106–9, 112–13, 122
  buying businesses and, 356
  collection procedures and, 227
  failure of, 205
  first month and, 174
  general description of, 37–38
  goal setting and, 78
  grand openings and, 145, 147, 150, 158, 160, 162–64, 167
  legal requirements and, 140
  sales and, 275, 292, 294, 296, 312–13

Yellow Pages, 287–88

About the Author

When folks ask me what I do for a living and I tell them I manufacture bicycle water bottles and Mr. Tuffy tire liners, they look at me in this quizzical way. I'm not sure whether it is what I manufacture or the fact that I manufacture anything in the USA in these times that causes such an unusual response. Anyway, that's what I do.

It wasn't necessarily planned that way. I took an undergraduate degree in psychology at UCLA, intending to save people one or two at a time. Then I took a law degree at the same institution with the goal of saving lots of people. I also love politics. Think of the potential for doing good (or evil) in that field.

Along the way, I fell in love with business—the bicycle business in particular. I tried retail and wholesale, but didn't like being at the mercy of my suppliers. Then I tried sales repping, marketing services, and insuring bikes against theft. But it was manufacturing that was the most satisfying, and that's what has paid the bills for the last twenty-five years.

Along the way, I wrote a few articles, delivered more than a few talks, and wrote four books for the bicycle industry. Some of the products we sold to the bike shops resulted in marketing efforts in almost thirty other industries. We also began to import and export. It was this background that resulted in the book you are now holding.

Finally, to round out the picture of your author, I am the proud dad of two grown daughters, who, depending on when you read this, have three or four little-bitty guys and gals for Poppy to play with;

and two sons still at home, who are keeping the old guy young. Running the home enterprise is the best wife in the world, Pam.

CONTACT THE AUTHOR

In addition to making those bottles and tire liners and writing on the side, I maintain a business blog. Please visit and check out the articles and comments of other owners who share their ideas in that forum. You can also e-mail me if you would like some individual consulting.

http://Help4SmallBusiness.blogspot.com
800-245-3737, ext. 223
Randy_Kirk@CaliforniaSprings.com